The Early Music Revival

A HISTORY

Harry Haskell

DOVER PUBLICATIONS, INC.
Mineola, New York

Copyright

Copyright © 1996 by Dover Publications, Inc.
All rights reserved under Pan American and International Copyright Conventions.

Published in Canada by General Publishing Company, Ltd., 30 Lesmill Road, Don Mills, Toronto, Ontario.
Published in the United Kingdom by Constable and Company, Ltd., 3 The Lanchesters, 162–164 Fulham Palace Road, London W6 9ER.

Bibliographical Note

This Dover edition, first published in 1996, is a corrected but basically unabridged republication of the work originally published by Thames and Hudson Ltd, London, 1988. The author has replaced his original Preface with an Introduction to the Dover Edition.

Library of Congress Cataloging-in-Publication Data

Haskell, Harry.
    The early music revival : a history / Harry Haskell.
        p.   cm.
    "A corrected but generally unabridged republication . . . The author has replaced his original Preface with an Introduction to the Dover Edition"—T.p. verso.
    Originally published: London : Thames and Hudson, 1988.
    Includes bibliographical references (p.   ) and index.
    ISBN 0-486-29162-6 (pbk.)
    1. Performance practice (Music)   2. Style, Musical.   3. Musical instruments.
ML457.H35   1996
781.4'3—dc20   96–16457
                                        CIP
                                        MN

Manufactured in the United States of America
Dover Publications, Inc., 31 East 2nd Street, Mineola, N.Y. 11501

CONTENTS

to the memory of
ROLAND GELATT,
in gratitude and admiration

INTRODUCTION TO
THE DOVER EDITION

W HAT is 'early music'? The concept has meant different things at different periods in history. In 1731, England's Academy of Ancient Music formally defined the ancients as composers 'such as lived before ye end of the Sixteenth Century'.[1] In the eyes of Brahms and his contemporaries, early music encompassed the High Renaissance and Baroque periods, from Isaac, Praetorius and Schütz up to Bach and Handel. Robert Donington ventures as far as the early nineteenth century in his classic *The Interpretation of Early Music*, while a prominent German musicologist describes early music more broadly as any music having 'an interrupted interpretative tradition'.[2]

The definition has gradually been expanded to the point where almost anything from an ancient Greek hymn to a modern Broadway musical can qualify as early music—that is, music for which a historically appropriate style of performance must be reconstructed on the basis of surviving instruments, treatises and other evidence. Whether this process constitutes a revival is open to question: much of the music to which the above definition applies—Gregorian chant, Palestrina, Bach, Handel and so forth—is in fact part of a *continuous* interpretative tradition, in some cases reaching back hundreds of years. The conclusion is inescapable that something other than chronological age is the determining factor here. Historical performance, as the musicologist Joseph Kerman has written, 'is essentially an attitude of mind rather than a set of techniques applied to an arbitrarily delimited body of early music'.[3]

Like most historical movements, the revival has no conveniently identifiable starting point. I chose to begin my account with Mendelssohn's 1829 *St Matthew Passion* because it was the first such performance to make an immediate and widespread impact on contemporary musical life. The great musicologist Friedrich Blume, in his book *Two Centuries of Bach*, argued that the entire early music movement stemmed from the Bach revival sparked by Mendelssohn's legendary performance.[4] In casting my book in the form of a continuous narrative, I do not wish to imply that today's historical performance movement is a lineal descendant of the nineteenth-century Bach revival or the aristocratic academies of the eighteenth century. History seldom moves in straight lines; the early music revival is as replete with detours and culs-de-sac as any movement. Yet certain themes recur, like strands in a tapestry, and precedents abound. In the late 1800s the violinist Ole Bull played with a rounded bow distantly related to the ones Baroque string players use today; Baroque-instrument chamber orchestras were active in France and Germany in the first decade of the twentieth century; eighteenth-century sets and costumes could be seen in productions of Handel's operas before the Second World War; Arnold Dolmetsch was experimenting with Middle Eastern performing techniques decades before other early musicians discovered them in the 1960s.

Apart from being absorbing in its own right, the story of the revival raises a number of profound questions concerning the nature of music and performance. To what extent is it possible or indeed desirable to present music of another era as its creators intended it to be heard? Is 'authenticity' a meaningful and legitimate criterion for evaluating a performance? Is musical revivalism—whether inspired by Albinoni or Alkan, Zelenka or Zemlinsky—a symptom of cultural decadence, as some would have it, or simply another manifestation of the yearning for roots that characterizes our deracinated society? Does the modern early music craze reflect genuine interest in the music itself, or merely a captivation with novel instruments and unfamiliar sounds? Is the concept of the 'standard' concert repertoire outmoded? And what does all of this tell us about the state of contemporary musical culture?

It is clearer to me now than it was in the mid-1980s, when I began work on this book, that the revival itself is fast becoming part of history. By this I mean not that it has run its course—far from it—but that the lessons it has to teach us have, by and large, been taken to heart by 'mainstream' performers and scholars. Early musicians are less and less inclined to see themselves as belonging to a distinct movement segregated from the dominant musical culture. They have, so to speak, rejoined the fold. They ask to be judged by the same criteria as everyone else. Their priorities and concerns are not after all so very different from those of their traditionally trained colleagues. The historically minded performer of, say, Schubert or Verdi is likely to have a good deal more in common with mainstream musicians than with specialists in Baroque or medieval music. As new alliances are forged, performers are at last moving away from 'instrumental fetishism' (Kerman's phrase) and addressing more fundamental issues of style, interpretation and expression—issues that concern (or ought to concern) musicians of every persuasion.

I have used the terms *subculture* and *counterculture* to describe the post-war early music movement because I believe the movement defined itself largely as an alternative to the prevailing musical culture. Yet a counterculture can exist only so long as it has something to react against. This is becoming less true at a time when many mainstream musicians are attuned to historical issues and when mainstream culture itself is increasingly pluralistic and fragmented. One can no longer speak of a normative style of performance which expresses the spirit of the age. The very concept of the canon, the body of musical works that defines Western culture, has come under attack in the era of multiculturalism. As a result, historical performance is rapidly becoming what many of its champions have long wished for: one among several 'authentic' modes of interpretation available to performers. It is this eclectic, post-modernist approach which embodies the true spirit of the late twentieth century.

A book of this nature rests on the work of many others, some of whose names are found in the endnotes and bibliography. I am further indebted to the musicians who consented to be interviewed, especially Christopher Hogwood, Anthony Rooley, Gustav Leonhardt, Ton Koopman, Frans Brüggen, Wieland Kuijken, August Wenzinger, Paul Sacher, Peter Reidemeister, Wulf Arlt, Michel Piguet, Carl Dolmetsch, Edgar Hunt, George Guest, Marco Pallis, Richard Nicholson, Richard Burnett, Melvyn Tan, Denise Restout, Suzanne Bloch, Gusta Goldschmidt, Josiane Bran-Ricci and Michel Sanvoisin. Yuske Arimura, Andres Mustonen, Fabian Dahlström, Peter Andreas Kjeldsberg and Markku Åberg kindly supplied information about early music activity in Japan and Scandinavia. Recent events in eastern Europe and the former Soviet Union have rendered my discussions of those areas somewhat out of date. But revising the text was impractical and would not, in any case, have altered the general picture in any essential way. I should like again to record my gratitude to Mirosław Perz, Jaromír Černý, Richard Taruskin, Karl-Heinz Viertel, Mirka Zemanová and Lukáš Matoušek.

John M. Thomson, Christopher Hogwood, Richard Taruskin, J. Bunker Clark and Daniel T. Politoske read all or part of the book at various stages and offered many valuable suggestions. Toni Greenberg and Carl Dolmetsch generously granted permission to quote from unpublished correspondence of Noah Greenberg and Arnold Dolmetsch. Thanks are also due to the many people who responded to my inquiries, clarified specific points and shared with me their observations, memories and enthusiasm. They include Karel Husa, Mauricio Kagel, the late Virgil Thomson, François Lesure, Suzanne Hess, Ille Strozza, Ros Morely, Nicholas Kenyon, the late Howard Mayer Brown, Laurence Dreyfus,

David Josephson, Howard Schott, Elliot Forbes, Waddy Thompson, Richard F. French, Fritz Muggler, Andrzej Szwalbe, V. Panchenko, David Hamilton, Rosemary Florrimell, David Hiley, Mark Deller, Margot Leigh Milner, Henri Vanhulst, Sophia Zachár, the late H. Earle Johnson, Jeannine Lambrechts-Douillez, Leslie Petteys, Delores Bruch, Robert P. Morgan, Michael Steinberg, Richard Sherr, Raymond Erickson, John Hsu, Sally Sanford, David Thomas, David Hill, Father M. Jorrot and Judith Ann Schiff.

HARRY HASKELL
Guilford, CT
1996

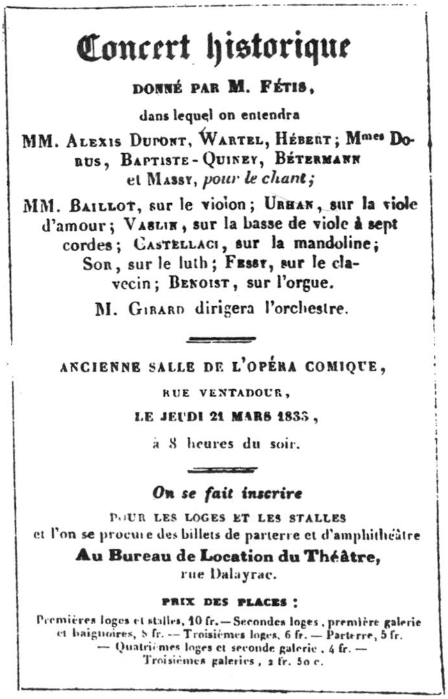

Concert historique

DONNÉ PAR M. FÉTIS,

dans lequel on entendra

MM. ALEXIS DUPONT, WARTEL, HÉBERT; Mmes DORUS, BAPTISTE-QUINEY, BÉTERMANN et MASSY, *pour le chant;*

MM. BAILLOT, sur le violon; URHAN, sur la viole d'amour; VASLIN, sur la basse de viole à sept cordes; CASTELLACI, sur la mandoline; SOR, sur le luth; FESSY, sur le clavecin; BENOIST, sur l'orgue.

M. GIRARD dirigera l'orchestre.

ANCIENNE SALLE DE L'OPÉRA COMIQUE,

RUE VENTADOUR,

LE JEUDI 21 MARS 1833,

à 8 heures du soir.

On se fait inscrire

POUR LES LOGES ET LES STALLES

et l'on se procure des billets de parterre et d'amphithéâtre

Au Bureau de Location du Théâtre,

rue Dalayrac.

PRIX DES PLACES :

Premières loges et stalles, 10 fr. — Secondes loges, première galerie et baignoires, 8 fr. — Troisièmes loges, 6 fr. — Parterre, 5 fr. — Quatrièmes loges et seconde galerie, 4 fr. — Troisièmes galeries, 2 fr. 50 c.

Fig. 1 Announcement of Fétis's third historical concert in Paris on 21 March 1833

1

'THE MUSICAL POMPEII'

Mendelssohn's St Matthew Passion *of 1829 · Bach and Other Pre-Classical Masters Rediscovered · Alexandre Choron's Institution Royale de Musique Religieuse · Church Music Reform and the Revival of Gregorian Chant · François-Joseph Fétis's Historical Concerts · The Rise of Historical Musicology · Brahms and the Nineteenth-Century Choral Movement · The Revival of Early Musical Instruments.*

BERLIN's stately Singakademie was filled to overflowing on 11 March 1829. Nearly a thousand people – among them the poet Heine, the philosopher Hegel and members of the Prussian royal family – had turned out on a balmy spring evening to hear Felix Mendelssohn conduct Bach's *St Matthew Passion*. The work had not been heard in public since the composer's death in 1750, and even at a top price of twenty silver groschen, tickets had sold out within hours. Thanks to a massive press campaign, the concert had been the talk of musical Berlin for weeks. Adolph Bernhard Marx, the influential editor of the *Allgemeine musikalische Zeitung*, set the tone for the occasion by proclaiming that the performance would 'open the gates of a long-closed temple', and that those who made the pilgrimage to the Singakademie would find themselves 'not in the sphere of a festival of art but of a religious high feast'.[1]

The Bach cult, of which Marx was a leading celebrant, was already firmly established by the time the twenty-year-old Mendelssohn conducted his epoch-making revival of the *St Matthew*. The publication of Johann Nikolaus Forkel's eulogistic biography in 1802 helped elevate the cantor of Leipzig, whom the late eighteenth century had dismissed as a fusty academic, to the status of a national hero. Mendelssohn, who hung a portrait of Bach over his piano, revered him as the father of German music, a view that struck a responsive chord among musicians and music-lovers gradually awakening to the rich legacy of the Renaissance and Baroque eras. It is no coincidence that the century which produced such notable archaeologists as Mariette and Schliemann should also have seen a concerted effort to resurrect the monuments of Western art music. The nineteenth century was an age of musical archaeology, and the *St Matthew Passion* was its first major find.

Mendelssohn was uniquely placed to preside over its exhumation. His mentor, Carl Friedrich Zelter, had long been a standard-bearer of the Bach revival. Shortly after taking charge of the Singakademie choir in 1800, Zelter began rehearsing Bach's vocal music in private, carefully editing the scores to purge them of the 'flimsy froth' which he attributed to French influence.[2] It was he who introduced young Felix to the St Matthew. Like most of his contemporaries, though, Zelter was convinced that Bach's oratorios and cantatas were impossibly difficult to perform and, in any case, unfit for public consumption. He scoffed at Mendelssohn's St Matthew project and only grudgingly gave his consent for the performers to use the Singakademie. Even Mendelssohn's partner, Eduard Devrient, who sang the role of Christ, confessed to having doubts. German audiences swallowed Bach's music in small doses willingly enough, he observed, 'but how would it be to have for an entire evening nothing but Sebastian Bach, whom the public conceived as unmelodious, dry, and unintelligible?'[3]

Such apprehensions were soon laid to rest. So enthusiastic was the reception for the St Matthew that it had to be repeated twice by popular demand, each time before a capacity crowd. Zelter graciously conceded defeat and agreed to fill in for Mendelssohn at the final performance on Good Friday. Devrient thought his conducting 'feeble' but, on the whole, pronounced the experiment an absolute success.[4] And so it was, judging by the sensation it provoked throughout Europe. The reasons are not hard to fathom. Bach's choral music was as yet practically unknown outside northern Germany; even his instrumental works, though widely studied and admired, were seldom played. Handel had long since been adopted as the patron saint of choral societies. Church choirs and organists more or less faithfully preserved the memories of Bach, Palestrina and a few other old masters. But, by and large, the pre-Classical repertoire was a closed book to Mendelssohn's contemporaries, who preferred to hear the latest works by the leading composers of the day. Is it any wonder, then, that the St Matthew struck many of its first-time listeners with the force of a revelation?

As a matter of fact, the early nineteenth century's rapturous rediscovery of Bach and other early composers was neither sudden nor entirely unprecedented. Attitudes toward music of the past had begun to shift even before Bach died, most conspicuously in Hanoverian England. John Pepusch's Academy of Ancient Music had been purveying Palestrina, Victoria, Byrd, Morley, Purcell and other 'ancients' with great success since the 1720s. The Madrigal Society, the Noblemen's and Gentlemen's Catch Club, and the Concert of Ancient Music (whose rules proscribed the performance of works less than twenty years old) followed suit in the ensuing decades.[5] England's Bach revival was spearheaded by the redoubtable Samuel Wesley, a man of burning convictions and extravagant rhetoric. Extolling Bach as 'the Jupiter of Harmonists', Wesley called for the creation of a 'Junto' dedicated to 'the overthrow of Ignorance, Prejudice, and Puppyism with regard to our Master', while denouncing the 'Pig Tails and Mountebanks' who obstinately held a brief for Handel.[6] Starting in 1808, Wesley and his self-appointed 'Sebastian Squad' regaled Londoners with a series of marathon Bach concerts up to four hours long, at one of which Wesley played all forty-eight Preludes and Fugues on the organ.

In Vienna, the home of the Austrian diplomat Baron van Swieten was a centre of musical revivalism in the late 1700s. It was there that Mozart fell under the spell of Bach and Handel, both essential influences on his music. The baron's compatriot, Raphael Georg Kiesewetter, championed the choral music of Bach, Palestrina, Marcello, Pergolesi, the Scarlattis and other early composers. His famous house concerts, which lasted from 1816 to 1842, became a Viennese institution and attracted a stream of distinguished visitors, including Beethoven, Schubert and Chopin.[7] Meanwhile, in Heidelberg, Anton Friedrich Justus Thibaut was whetting Mendelssohn's and Schumann's interest in pre-Classical music. A legal scholar by profession, Thibaut conducted an amateur choir which performed several times a year for invited audiences. Concerts were held in Thibaut's attic, 'a temple', as he called it, where 'Marcello furnishes the scriptural lesson for my edification, Handel delivers the sermon to me, with Palestrina I worship my God, and our religious language, the religion we practise, is music'.[8]

By the early nineteenth century, a taste for 'ancient' – that is, late Renaissance and Baroque – music had become fashionable among an élite circle of aristocratic amateurs and cognoscenti. To the average concert-goer, however, the early music revival amounted as yet to little more than an esoteric fringe movement. Mendelssohn changed all that by bringing Bach's music out of the salons and into the public domain once and for all. Marx was right: the revival of the St Matthew Passion did indeed 'open the gates' onto a new musical world. Fired by Berlin's example, cities all over Germany mounted performances of the oratorio in the 1830s and 1840s.[9] Bach fever proved contagious. By 1850, when the Bach Gesellschaft launched the first comprehensive edition of his works, a network of Bach societies was rapidly falling into place and performances of his music could be heard the length and breadth of Europe.

One can only imagine how these performances must have sounded. Contemporary reports and other evidence make it clear that little or no consideration was given to re-creating the performance practice of Bach's day. Mendelssohn engaged a choir of 158 singers and a full-sized modern orchestra, which he conducted from the piano, apparently from memory.

(This feat is only slightly less impressive when one considers that the performers had been rehearsing the work for more than a year.) He took it for granted that a complete *St Matthew* was out of the question. The version that Berlin audiences heard in 1829 was a far cry from today's scholarly *Urtext* editions. Procrustean cuts were made, reducing the performing time of the Passion by fully a third. Moreover, Mendelssohn substantially revised Bach's scoring and reassigned some of the solo parts in order to use singers from the Royal Opera. The tempo and dynamic markings that Mendelssohn neatly pencilled in his conducting score indicate that he placed a premium on dramatic contrasts and highly charged emotionalism – qualities that had more to do with the Romantic era than with eighteenth-century style.[10]

From a late-twentieth-century perspective, such interpretative liberties seem questionable at best, but no performer of Mendelssohn's day would have felt the slightest qualm about treating a piece of music so freely. While Mendelssohn's claim to have presented Bach's works 'absolutely as they were written'[11] has to be taken with a grain of salt, he was a paragon of fidelity and restraint compared with Zelter, not to mention such later editor/arrangers as Robert Franz and Heinrich Reimann. In any case, Mendelssohn would have been mystified by the modern concept of historical performance practice. He made his views on the matter abundantly clear in a letter to his sister Fanny in 1840. Describing his performance of Bach's Chromatic Fantasy and Fugue, the composer wrote: 'I take the liberty of playing [the arpeggios] with all possible crescendos, and pianos, and fortissimos, pedal of course, and doubling the octaves in the bass'.[12] Mendelssohn was no purist; he approached Bach's music as a practical musician eager to bring it to life for his contemporaries. If that meant Romanticizing it, so be it: no one was likely to complain that Bach was being misrepresented.

While the Bach revival was gathering momentum in Germany, a French educator and choral director was giving Parisians their first concentrated taste of Bach, Handel and Palestrina. Alexandre Choron's interest in early music stemmed from his activities as a music publisher at the beginning of the century. When Louis XVIII placed him in charge of the Paris Opéra in 1816, Choron seized the opportunity to tackle a problem that had concerned him for some time: the decline of the art of singing in France. But his reforms met with stiff resistance. Thwarted in his campaign to clear out the dead wood at the Opéra, he departed within a year and founded his own school of 'classical and religious music', a bold challenge to the all-powerful Conservatoire.

Contemporary chroniclers paint a vivid picture of Choron, a small, vivacious man with 'remarkably bright and penetrating eyes', scouring the French countryside on foot in search of gifted pupils. The school's fortnightly recitals of Renaissance and Baroque choral music in the 1820s delighted Parisians, who found the exotic delicacies of Monteverdi, Josquin, Marenzio and Marcello a welcome break from their customary musical diet. Choron, one commentator remarked, demonstrated to the powers-that-be 'that there is more to religious music than Pergolesi's *Stabat Mater* and the two or three other pieces that have been performed indifferently for twenty-five years with heroic consistency'.[13]

Such praise was by no means unanimous – one critic dismissed Choron's programmes as 'boring, badly organized and poorly directed'[14] – but no one could deny that he was giving the Conservatoire vigorous competition. Students flocked from all over France and abroad to his Institution Royale de Musique Religieuse. The inauguration in 1827 of the school's new auditorium on the rue Vaugirard, built to accommodate a choir of two hundred voices, was a gala affair, graced by the presence of royalty. But Choron's prosperity was pathetically short-lived: after Louis Philippe, the self-proclaimed 'citizen king', ascended the throne in 1830, his state subsidy was whittled down to a pittance, a crushing blow from which neither he nor the school ever recovered.

Despite this temporary setback, however, early music was quickly becoming a favourite pastime among the French upper classes, just as it was in England and Germany. Choron's work was carried on in the 1840s by the Société de Musique Vocale Classique, popularly known as the Société de la Moskova in honour of its aristocratic patron, the Prince of Moscow. The prince himself conducted the choir's concerts, which were devoted mainly to sixteenth- and seventeenth-century music, while his colleague, the Swiss composer Louis Niedermeyer, edited the scores for performance and publication. Both the society's membership and its audience consisted largely of well-heeled amateurs, a fact noted approvingly by the *Revue et gazette musicale*:

At a time when vapid music seems to hold sway unchallenged in all salons, when taste seems to be more depraved and incapable of appreciating serious classical music, the most eminent amateurs, women who by virtue of their social position are most susceptible to the caprices of fashion, are suddenly rebelling against this intolerable yoke, breaking all the chains that bind them to Rossini, Donizetti, Bellini and *tutti quanti*, to devote themselves exclusively to the cultivation of this grave, ancient, solemn music, devoid of passion, which engenders only sweet, calm and pious emotions.[15]

Piety, sweetness, solemnity: these were the virtues that the nineteenth century prized in pre-Classical music. Frivolity, bawdiness and irreverence

17

had no place in the Romantics' idealized conception of the Renaissance and Baroque periods. It was the perceived 'purity' of Palestrina's polyphonic style which appealed so strongly to conservative musicians like Thibaut, Kiesewetter and Choron, deploring as they did the decadent worldliness of modern religious music. This one-sided view inevitably coloured their performances of early choral works. Choron believed that Palestrina's music should be sung 'in legato and sustained sound, very softly, with precision, in a moderate, even way, very simply but with much sweetness and tenderness'.[16] Saint-Saëns testified that the Société de la Moskova performed the Pope Marcellus Mass so slowly and anaemically that Palestrina would hardly have recognized it as his work.[17] A few musicians spoke out against this genteel approach, arguing that pre-Classical music called for a more robust and varied style of performance, but their voices carried little weight so long as the leaders of the revival persisted in viewing the past through rose-tinted glasses.

This Romantic antiquarianism was especially deep-rooted within the Church. Religious reformists, such as those associated with the Oxford Movement in England, had begun to press for a return to the time-honoured rituals of the Anglican and Catholic faiths. High on their agenda was the reinstatement of unaccompanied plainchant, stripped of such meretricious accretions as anachronistic harmonies and instrumental accompaniments. Augustus Welby Pugin, a leader of the Gothic Revival in England, castigated his fellow architects in 1850 for designing churches 'whose appearance is something between a dancing-room and a mechanics' institute'. Church music was in a shambles and could only be salvaged by restoring 'the ancient Chaunt [sic] in all its purity'. Progressive clerics like the Rev. Thomas Helmore deflected such arguments with finely tuned sarcasm. To object to performing chants with modern resources, he protested, 'would be as absurd . . . as to object to traveling by railroad because it doesn't appear from records extant that these luxuries were enjoyed by the early fathers of the Church'.[18]

The tide, however, was inexorably turning in Pugin's favour. At the Benedictine abbey of Solesmes, in west-central France, Dom Prosper Guéranger had been conducting important research on Gregorian chant since the 1840s. Guéranger disapproved of the harmonized accompaniments and stiff, metrical style of chant-singing then in vogue, on the grounds that neither was conducive to religious meditation. In their place, he proposed that chant be sung in the flexible, speech-like manner that has since been adopted around the world. Guéranger and his successors, Dom Joseph Pothier and Dom André Mocquereau, revolutionized the study and performance of plainsong by basing their editions on a number of manuscripts instead of relying on a single source. Their goal, as set forth in one of the first volumes of the great Solesmes *Paléographie musicale* series, was 'to raise Gregorian chant from the abject state into which it has fallen' and to restore the 'full ancient beauty which made it so proper for divine worship'.[19]

Far from being a unified movement, then, the revival of pre-Classical music in the nineteenth century was actually a complex and multi-stranded phenomenon. The vanguard comprised an *ad hoc* coalition of musical and religious reformists, allied by virtue of their deep-seated dissatisfaction with the status quo, with a small brigade of historically minded amateurs bringing up the rear. But the revivalists were not simply aesthetic reactionaries bent on burying their heads in the sand. On the contrary, they considered themselves the true progressives of their time. They were convinced that the key to the future lay in the past, that modern music could only escape the cul-de-sac into which it had strayed by retracing the path mapped out by the old masters. Increasingly, they questioned the conventional nineteenth-century wisdom that modern music was inherently superior to music of earlier eras. One critic, upon hearing Choron's choir perform, ventured the opinion that while music had undoubtedly made significant strides since the days of Josquin, Palestrina and Handel, 'it has gained nothing in religious expressiveness and grandeur of scale'.[20]

The time was ripe for a radically new philosophy of music history, one that permitted early music to be appreciated on its own terms instead of filtering it through nineteenth-century preconceptions. One of the first to grasp the implications of this new historical awareness was the Belgian scholar François-Joseph Fétis. 'Art does not progress,' Fétis was fond of saying, 'it transforms itself.'[21] To illustrate his unorthodox thesis, he devised a series of 'historical concerts', each devoted to a specific period or genre of music. The first took place on 8 April 1832 at the Paris Conservatoire, where Fétis was serving as librarian. The lengthy programme surveyed the history of opera from Peri, Caccini and Monteverdi to Méhul, Rossini and Weber. Fétis filled the hall by astutely engaging an all-star cast, including the soprano Schröder-Devrient, the tenor Rubini and the bass Lablache. At the second concert in December, the audience was so enthused that it demanded five encores – after sitting through no less than four hours of sixteenth-century vocal and instrumental music interspersed with Fétis's learned discourses.

'I can't tell you how delighted I was by your concert the other day,' Victor Hugo wrote to Fétis. 'You are doing a great service to art by exhuming these marvels.'[22] Presumably the 'marvels' Hugo had in mind included not only the compositions but also the lute, viols, harpsichord and other antique instruments that Fétis used in his concerts. Whether the instruments in question had been preserved in anything like their original states is highly doubtful: the flautist Aristide Farrenc, for example, accused Fétis of deceptive advertising, alleging that what he called a 'violone' was nothing but a modern string bass.[23] Fétis also came under attack for arranging the music on his concerts heavily, a charge that seems plausible in the light of his well-known habit of passing off his own compositions as the work of old masters like Lassus and Stradella. Fétis's integrity was further tarnished by the scandal that erupted when he left Paris in 1833 to take charge of the new conservatory in Brussels, absconding with a valuable cache of books and manuscripts from his old library.[24]

An ebullient, Balzacian personality who thrived on controversy, Fétis shrugged off these peccadillos, protesting that he conscientiously strove to present early compositions 'with the instrumentation and the system of execution which their authors intended, so that a nineteenth-century listener would have the illusion of attending a sixteenth-century entertainment in the palace of a Florentine nobleman'.[25] Unfortunately, Fétis's powers as a conjuror were not sufficient to sustain the interest of the notoriously fickle Parisian public. When he returned to the city in 1835, announcing a pair of concerts outlining 'the progress of harmony and melody' in the sixteenth and seventeenth centuries, he received a frosty welcome. One critic pointedly observed that although Fétis had threatened to bring an assortment of old instruments from Brussels, 'he prudently left them at the frontier'.[26] So incensed was Fétis by these attacks that he cancelled the second programme and returned to Belgium forthwith, although he continued to present historical concerts intermittently in Paris and Brussels for more than twenty years.

The origins of these historical – or, as we might call them today, 'theme' – concerts can be traced back almost two centuries. In 1643, two musicians in Nuremberg presented a programme illustrating 'the practice and abuse of noble music' by means of selections ranging from Jewish temple songs to seventeenth-century motets.[27] Kiesewetter and his friend Simon Molitor were thus building on a long tradition when they introduced the custom to Vienna in the early 1800s. Kiesewetter devoted entire evenings to the choral music of Palestrina, Bach and Marcello, while Molitor's wider-ranging surveys bore imposing titles like 'Instrumental Music by Netherlands and German Masters from the Period 1500–1800'.[28] Nonetheless, Fétis deserves credit for popularizing this novel form of entertainment. Mendelssohn conducted historical concerts with the Leipzig Gewandhaus Orchestra in the 1830s and 1840s.[29] Around the same time, the pianist Ignaz Moscheles began playing historical recitals in London on an eighteenth-century harpsichord equipped with a 'Venetian swell', a device resembling a Venetian shade that modified the volume of sound like an organ swell. Fétis, who heard Moscheles in 1838, perceptively observed that 'there are only a very few pianists today who can perform the old music of Scarlatti and especially of

Bach, because the fingering habits it requires are almost incompatible with those developed in [modern] music'.[30]

Before long, historical concerts were all the rage in the musical capitals of Europe. Improbable as it sounds today, audiences paid good money to hear well-known singers and instrumentalists give long, didactic programmes, often accompanied by extensive commentaries, that seem better suited to a university lecture room than to a concert hall. The 'Six Historical Performances of Pianoforte Music in Strictly Chronological Order' which Ernst Pauer presented in London in 1863 may be taken as a typical specimen of the genre. The lavishly produced programme book distributed to concert-goers, containing detailed notes on each of the pieces to be played, reads like a syllabus for a music appreciation course. This penchant for historicism took many forms. Among the more remarkable is Louis Spohr's *Historical Symphony* of 1839, a kind of capsule survey of musical styles of the preceding 120 years. The first movement is based on a fugal theme from Bach's *Well-Tempered Clavier*; the second is a larghetto in the manner of Haydn and Mozart, followed by a Beethovenian scherzo and a finale ('The Period of the Newest of the New') satirizing the contemporary idiom that Spohr deplored.[31]

Ironically, despite the laudable intentions behind them, historical concerts ultimately reinforced the very prejudices they were designed to combat. Their schematic format, conjuring images of a Darwinian evolution of musical forms and techniques, equated only too readily with the increasingly dated concept of artistic progress. It did not help matters that performers generally treated the pre-Classical repertoire as an hors-d'oeuvre to whet the public's appetite for the main course of late-eighteenth- and nineteenth-century music. Even as enlightened a musician as Moscheles did not altogether avoid falling into this trap. Amidst preparations for his first series of historical recitals, the pianist recorded in his diary:

> I have burrowed again into the ash-covered treasures of the musical Pompeii, and brought many grand things to light. Beethoven is great – whom should I call greater? – but as the public is forever listening to his music, alternating with modern pieces written merely for display, I intend to introduce, first of all, those composers who gave the impetus to Beethoven's eagle flight. To have a proper appreciation of the art of our own day, we should not forget its past history; although I have begun with the old masters, I intend to lead my audience gradually up to our own time, and then they can compare and draw their own conclusions.[32]

Such a historical excursion would have been difficult to conceive, much less to execute, a few decades earlier. At the turn of the century, only a smattering of works by Handel, Bach, Palestrina, Pergolesi and other pre-Classical composers was readily available. More often than not, musicians like Moscheles who wanted to perform early music faced the laborious and costly task of copying it out from old scores and manuscripts. When Choron published an anthology of early choral music in the first decade of the century, it was quickly snapped up and circulated far and wide. In England, John Stafford Smith's pioneering *Musica Antiqua* paved the way for Vincent Novello's popularly priced editions of Purcell and the Renaissance composers, as well as the Musical Antiquarian Society's generous selection of early English music. Similar publishing ventures in other countries, such as those of Carl Proske in Germany and H. G. Nägeli in Switzerland, brought much of the pre-Classical repertoire within reach of amateur and professional musicians for the first time.

Scholarship and performance being two sides of the same coin, the course of the early music revival in the nineteenth century closely paralleled the rise of historical musicology. Performers could afford to ignore the historians and theorists as long as the concert repertoire was limited to music of recent vintage, but once they began to delve into the more distant past, they needed expert guidance. Friedrich Chrysander, who coined the German word for musicology, *Musikwissenschaft*, endeavoured to establish the principle 'that the music of past ages should be edited and performed in a scholarly spirit, without introducing additions or modifications to cater to the tastes of the present'.[33] A succession of brilliant scholars – men like Chrysander, Philipp Spitta and Otto Jahn – thrust Germany to the forefront of the field in the late 1800s.

Significantly, it was Bach who inspired the first great enterprise of modern German musicology: a complete scholarly edition of his music, published under the auspices of the Bach Gesellschaft, appeared in instalments between 1850 and 1900. Moritz Hauptmann, the first editor of the project, took a dim view of Bach's oratorio and cantata texts, which he considered far inferior to the music, but he was too scrupulous a scholar to tamper with Bach's work as Zelter and others had done.[34] The exacting editorial standards that Hauptmann and his successors established for the Bach edition set the pattern for a long line of monumental editions produced in Germany and elsewhere. By the end of the century, music by Handel, Rameau, Palestrina, Buxtehude, Corelli, Schütz, Purcell, Sweelinck and dozens of other pre-Classical composers had been published in up-to-date scholarly editions.

The steady expansion of scholarship and publishing made the vast repertoire of early music increasingly accessible to composers as well as performers. One has only to think of Schumann's piano fugues, Brahms's choruses, the organ music of Franck and Reger, Grieg's *Holberg* Suite or the oratorios of Mendelssohn, Liszt, Saint-Saëns and Bruckner – to cite just a few outstanding examples – to realize how far-reaching an impact the revival of Baroque and Renaissance music had on composition in the late nineteenth century. Having resuscitated the pre-Classical repertoire for their edification and enjoyment, many Romantic composers proceeded to incorporate it into their own musical idioms, or to bring it up to date as Wagner did in his arrangement of the Palestrina *Stabat Mater*.

Brahms is a special case. For him, early music was not only a spur to creativity but also a practical vocation. In addition to collecting and studying old scores and treatises throughout his life, Brahms took an active part in the revival as a performer, particularly in the middle of his career. From 1857, when he became choral director in Detmold, up to and including his tenure with the Vienna Singverein in the mid-seventies, Brahms conducted a huge amount of music by Isaac, Schütz, Byrd, Handel, Gabrieli, Bach, Palestrina and others.[35] Like Mendelssohn, Brahms edited without compunction, making cuts, adjusting the instrumentation and even altering notes wherever he thought it necessary. Even by nineteenth-century standards, his programmes must have seemed fairly weighty, but he compensated by avoiding the bloated, heavy-handed approach that most conductors of the time considered appropriate for early choral music.

The proliferation of amateur and professional singing societies in the late 1800s was a crucial factor in sustaining the growth of the revival and enlarging its following. Every European country had a *Caecilienverein* or some such organization dedicated to raising the standard of vocal performance and composition, usually by cultivating the *a cappella* choral works of the sixteenth and seventeenth centuries. A movement was initiated to improve the singing of church choirs, and schools of religious music, such as the famous one that Louis Niedermeyer founded in Paris in 1853, made choral singing the focus of their curriculum. The choral movement offered something for virtually everyone, from small madrigal ensembles to huge community choruses, from women's choirs to the male *orphéons* in France, from the humble village *Singverein* to venerable institutions like the Sistine Chapel Choir in Rome.

As more and more people discovered the pleasures of choral singing, pre-Classical music ceased to be the preserve of a small, privileged minority. At long last the revival was turning into a genuinely broad-based (though still far from 'popular') movement. The repertoire it encompassed, on the other hand, remained remarkably constant for the better part of the century. Bach, Handel and Palestrina formed the central trinity, towering above a crowd of lesser figures. Early music, in the minds of most musicians in the nineteenth century, extended from the late Renaissance to the Baroque. Gregorian chant excepted, the medieval period was virtually unexplored, although the odd piece by Dufay or Adam de la Halle occasionally turned up on the programmes of adventurous choral directors like Emil Bohn in Breslau and Karl Riedel in Leipzig.[36] Unlike Gothic art and architecture, the music of the Middle Ages languished in near-oblivion, its beauties glimpsed only by a select few.

Yet European musicians were energetically broadening their horizons in other areas, notably those of non-Western and vernacular music. The worlds of 'ethnomusicology' and early music overlapped to a considerable extent: both offered the tempting prospect of escape from the increasingly hackneyed standard repertoire of Western art music. Kiesewetter's concerts of Renaissance polyphony thus shared a common impulse with his studies of Greek and Arab music. The French composer Louis Bourgault-Ducoudray, whose choir won renown for its performances of early music in the 1860s and 1870s, predicted that European classical music would be 'rejuvenated' by an infusion of exotic resources. 'No element of expression existing in a tune of any kind, however remote in origin, must be banished from our musical idiom', he declared. Chrysander, the greatest Handelian of his day, wrote an article about ancient Indian Vedic sacrifices in which he argued that *all* music should be studied in the context of the society that produced it – a plea that both ethnomusicologists and students of early music have taken to heart.[37]

Sooner or later, the cultivation of non-traditional music was bound to stimulate an interest in the instruments it had been played on. The last decades of the nineteenth century saw the formation of many important instrument collections by men like Victor-Charles Mahillon in Belgium, Alessandro Kraus in Italy, Daniel Scheurleer in Holland, Paul de Wit in Germany, Auguste Tolbecque in France, Morris Steinert in the United States and Thomas Taphouse, Carl Engel and A. J. Hipkins in England. There were even isolated attempts to reconstruct the old instruments, either as museum pieces or, in the case of harpsichords, as functional instruments. The successful forgeries by unscrupulous instrument-makers like Leopoldo Franciolini and J.-B. Vuillaume attest to the growing market for such commodities. If all this did not quite add up to a fully-fledged revival of early instrumental music, it was at any rate an important step in that direction. More and more old instruments were being taken out of their cases and played. De Wit, for example, was widely known as a gambist; his repertoire extended from Baroque dances to Liszt's fourth *Consolation*, arranged for the improbable combination of gamba and organ. On the whole, early instruments were still viewed as antiquarians' playthings, but the fact that they were being revived at all shows how rapidly nineteenth-century attitudes were changing.

'The philological, historical view that suffuses the culture of our time', wrote Otto Jahn, 'demands that the enjoyment of a work of art be founded on historical insight and evaluation, and that the work of art be presented exactly as the artist created it.'[38] An understanding of the issues underpinning the early music movement was clearly spreading, even among musicians who were not closely associated with the revival. It is rather startling to find Anton Rubinstein, one of the giants of Romantic pianism, arguing that early keyboard music could be properly executed only on period instruments. The harpsichord and clavichord, he surmised, 'must have had tone-colouring and effects that we cannot reproduce on the Pianoforte of today'.[39] When the violinist Joseph Joachim was invited to direct a Bach festival at Eisenach in 1884, he decided to perform the B minor Mass using a modern replica of an oboe d'amore and a so-called 'Bach trumpet' (which actually bore little resemblance to the valveless trumpet of Bach's day). The novel sonorities produced by these instruments prompted at least one critic to revise his estimation of Bach. A report published in the Monthly Musical Record contains the arresting observation that 'the deficiencies in Bach's music, as we commonly hear it, are due, in fact, not to the author, but to the imperfection, in several remarkable respects, of our vaunted modern orchestra'.[40]

Thanks largely to Fétis, Brussels had become a centre for the revival of early instrumental music by the late 1800s. Upon becoming director of the Conservatoire in 1871, François Gevaert abandoned the tradition of historical concerts that Fétis had cultivated over the years. 'When one isn't certain about imposing an old piece that one is taking from oblivion, the best proof of respect one can give it is to leave it alone', he remarked.[41] Yet it was Gevaert who appointed Mahillon curator of the splendid instrument collection that Fétis had bequeathed to the school, and he continued his predecessor's policy of featuring the old instruments in public concerts from time to time.

One of these concerts, on 23 December 1879, is of particular interest. It was devoted to the customary cross-section of Renaissance and Baroque music, played on viols, harpsichord, virginal, positive organ and regal.[42] Both music and instruments made a deep impression on a young French violinist who had come to the Conservatoire to study with Henri Vieuxtemps. His name was Arnold Dolmetsch.

2

'THE APOSTLE OF RETROGRESSION'

Arnold Dolmetsch as Instrument-Maker, Performer, Scholar and Teacher ·
His Predecessors and Contemporaries in England · The 1885
International Inventions Exhibition in South Kensington · Early Music and
the Arts and Crafts Movement · Richard Terry, Edmund Fellowes and
'Elizabethan Fever' · The Haslemere Festival · Dolmetsch's Inconsistency
and Eccentricity · Other Members of His Family.

VICTORIAN society, forward-looking in many respects, was conspicuously conservative in musical matters. English musicians and audiences clung tenaciously to the bulwark of tradition, wary of the waves of innovation lapping at their shores from abroad. Tradition, so far as early music was concerned, was epitomized by the gargantuan Handel festivals at which more than three thousand performers set the glass panels of the Crystal Palace vibrating to the strains of *Messiah*, *Judas Maccabeus* and *Israel in Egypt*. As late as the 1920s, the choir director Richard Terry complained that the British passion for Handel was inspired by a very sketchy knowledge of his music:

> A triennial orgy at the Crystal Palace, when an impossible collection of impossible people meet together and try to perform him under impossible conditions; a more or less moribund 'Handel Society', whose attachment to 'the Master', until Goossens took them in hand, was but lukewarm – to judge by the number of other composers to whom they devote themselves at their infrequent public performances; a regiment of tenors who bleat 'Kormafort ayee' on every possible occasion, and bellow 'Evoree varley' in and out of season; a battalion of basses who bawl 'Ho roddyer tharn the cherry' and persistently inquire 'Whoy doo thor nations so furiously rage togethor?'; two or three songs which now and then stray into the programmes of a vocal recital. And that is all.[1]

Such was the state of affairs that greeted Arnold Dolmetsch when he arrived in London in 1883. No one, not even Dolmetsch himself, could have foreseen at that juncture how swiftly he would set the British musical establishment on its collective ear. In retrospect, though, it is clear that the country was ready for just such a shaking-up. Samuel Arnold had initiated a complete Handel edition in the late eighteenth century. The old Handel Society (a predecessor of the one that incurred Terry's scorn) had published several of the composer's works in the 1840s, well in advance of Chrysander's monumental Handel edition, while scholars like William Chappell and Edward Rimbault explored less familiar byways of the pre-Classical repertoire. Samuel Sebastian Wesley (the illegitimate son of the Bach enthusiast), F. A. G. Ouseley, John Hullah and other reformist choral directors joined their Continental counterparts in promoting early music as a salutary model to contemporary composers and educators. The Purcell Club's semi-annual observances at Westminster Abbey and other venues added fuel to the revival in mid-century. Renaissance and Baroque music later featured prominently in the programmes of London's Bach Choir and the Henry Leslie Choir, to say nothing of the sundry madrigal societies, whose repertoire ranged from Tudor works to modern madrigals by Robert Lucas Pearsall and Arthur Sullivan.

Despite this crescendo of activity, though, England's early music movement was still mired in the bookish, antiquarian attitudes that J. A. Fuller Maitland encountered as a student at Cambridge in the seventies: 'The professorial lectures which often admitted the existence of madrigals, virginal music, and such things, nearly always took it for granted that there was no beauty such as could appeal to modern ears, so that the respect with which we were encouraged to approach them was purely due to their antiquity.'[2] This prejudice was bolstered by the popular institution of the keyboard lecture-recital. These historical surveys typically included one or two illustrations on an antique harpsichord, a well-intentioned gesture that frequently proved counterproductive, as the instruments rarely seem to have been kept in satisfactory playing condition. George Bernard Shaw fled one such exhibition by the pianist J. H. Bonawitz, grumbling that 'the harpsichord jingled like a million bellwires'.[3] Carl Engel and A. J. Hipkins apparently took better care of their instruments. Engel put one of his clavichords on display in 1879 and invited music-lovers to come and hear for themselves how Bach's music was meant to sound. Hipkins mastered both the clavichord and the harpsichord, and his frequent appearances before the Musical Association and other learned societies did much to foster an appreciation of old instruments.

In 1858, nine years after the British founded their own Bach Society, the composer William Sterndale Bennett treated Londoners to a substantially complete *St Matthew Passion* at St Martin's Hall. He modelled his performance closely on that of his friend Mendelssohn, though he was evidently more reluctant to go beyond the letter of the score. At a preliminary rehearsal, Bennett was asked if the singers might be allowed to inject some expressive nuances in Bach's chorales. 'Oh! Yes, by all means', he replied. 'There are none in the original, but I see no objection to some being introduced.'[4] In due course, Bach took his place beside Handel as a mainstay of the choral repertoire. The Bach Choir celebrated the composer's bicentenary in 1885 with a performance of the B minor Mass at the Albert Hall. It was conducted by Otto Goldschmidt, whose celebrated wife, Jenny Lind, led the sopranos. Although the Musical Times found only 'antiquarian interest' in the solos, the reviewer reported that 'the marvelously intricate and florid choruses, for a long period regarded as all but impossible of proper execution, were given with clockwork precision' – no mean feat for a group of some six hundred singers. Furthermore, 'some of the obsolete instruments in the score were remanufactured, including the oboi d'amore and the peculiar high-pitched trumpet, for which a player was fetched from Berlin.'[5] (He was, in fact, the same Julius Kosleck who had taken part in Joachim's performance in Germany the year before.)

Several months after this landmark performance, Londoners had an opportunity to see and hear more 'obsolete instruments' at the huge International Inventions Exhibition in South Kensington. Hipkins organized a series of historical concerts to supplement the displays of instruments, manuscripts, printed books, pictures and other musical artifacts in the Albert Hall galleries. Victor-Charles Mahillon brought a group from Brussels to play three programmes of early music featuring instruments from the Conservatoire museum. 'Some of the effects were beautiful as well as curious, while others were only curious', the Musical Times opined cautiously.[6] The Bristol Madrigal Society sang Tudor and Victorian music, a chamber choir conducted by the eminent musicologist W. S. Rockstro performed sacred works by old English and Italian composers, and Daniël de Lange's small Amsterdam A Capella Choir gave three concerts devoted largely to Dufay, Josquin, Ockeghem and other early Netherlandish masters. Fuller Maitland, a noted critic, harpsichordist and editor of early music, recalled that the choir's concerts 'first fired my antiquarian zeal, for the singers revealed the underlying beauty of these things quite apart from their historical interest'. Shaw later reckoned that the Dutch ensemble 'was worth ten Handel Festival choirs placed one on top of the other'.[7]

Dolmetsch in all probability attended the exhibition, for he was then teaching violin to schoolchildren at Dulwich College in southeast London. He had enrolled at the newly opened Royal College of Music in 1883, but soon realized that he was cut out to be neither a violin virtuoso nor an academic musicologist. He might well have made his name as an organ-builder, a trade he had learned at his father's workshop in Le Mans, but his vocation lay elsewhere. At Dulwich he earned a reputation as a gifted, if unconventional, teacher who encouraged his students to play unusual music by the likes of Handel, Purcell and Corelli. The interest in old instruments that he had developed in Brussels was rapidly blossoming into an obsession. One day in 1889 he bought a viola d'amore at auction, mistaking it for a modern viola. His curiosity piqued, Dolmetsch restored the instrument to its original state and began practising on it. From that point his fate was sealed. He promptly acquired a set of viols, then a spinet, then a lute, and so forth, until he had assembled a sizeable collection of historical instruments.

A mercurial, quick-tempered man, standing barely five feet tall, Dolmetsch never doubted his mission in life. He came to early music in an entirely different spirit from that of the scholars and collectors whose knowledge of performance was largely second-hand. Not for him the myopic pedanticism of Rimbault, who prefaced his 1843 edition of Gibbons's viol fantasies by noting 'the infantine state of instrumental music at the period in which they were composed, and the limited powers of the instruments upon which they were performed'.[8] As a resident foreigner who never lost his French accent (and who waited until 1931 to take out British citizenship), Dolmetsch remained something of an outsider in London's tightly knit musical community – a fact that neither his admirers nor his detractors seemed to tire of pointing out. Captivated by his eccentric, bohemian lifestyle, the Bloomsbury set adopted him as one of their own. In the words of his biographer Margaret Campbell, Dolmetsch's velvet suit, complete with knee britches, lace ruffles and shiny shoe-buckles, made him look 'more pre-Raphaelite than the pre-Raphaelites themselves'.[9] The illusion carried over into his house in West Dulwich, which he furnished in an Elizabethan mode and christened 'Dowland' in honour of the composer.

William Morris, the patriarch of England's Arts and Crafts Movement, was one of Dolmetsch's earliest admirers. Though hardly a connoisseur of music, Morris spied in the young musician an ally in his quest to rekindle the spirit of medieval and Renaissance culture. Just as Dolmetsch sought to revive the music of the past in its authentic form, Morris took pains to achieve historical verisimilitude in works like 'Sigurd the Volsung'. The painter Edward Burne-Jones brought Morris to one of Dolmetsch's concerts in 1894. 'He understood the music at once,' Dolmetsch recalled years later, 'and his emotion was so strong that he was moved to tears! He had found the lost art!'[10] Thereafter Morris was a regular visitor to 'Dowland', and it was he who persuaded Dolmetsch to build his first harpsichord for the Arts and Crafts Exhibition Society show in 1896. Shortly before his death that year,

Morris asked Dolmetsch to bring his virginal to Kelmscott House and play some of his favourite Elizabethan music.

Shaw, sensing the natural affinity between the two men, wrote of Dolmetsch's first clavichord that it was 'likely to begin such a revolution in domestic musical instruments as William Morris's work made in domestic furniture and decoration, or Philip Webb's in domestic architecture'.[11] Like Morris's followers, Dolmetsch turned his back on the Industrial Revolution and the grandiloquence that characterized so much Victorian art, music and architecture. Instead of factories for mass-production, they dreamed of re-creating the cottage industry society of the past, with small teams of artisans working harmoniously to produce refined handiwork. This 'small-is-beautiful' aesthetic was permeated with nostalgia – what Arthur Symons, in a poem dedicated to Dolmetsch, called 'a melancholy desire of ancient things'.[12] The intimacy of Dolmetsch's 'house concerts' and the mellow voices of the old instruments appealed to listeners sated with late-nineteenth-century bombast. 'How much pleasanter', Shaw exclaimed in one of his less Wagnerian moods, 'it would be to live next to Mr Arnold Dolmetsch, with his lutes, love viols, and leg viols, than to an ordinary string quartet!'[13]

Dolmetsch's 'revolution' started modestly enough with the reproduction of viols of various sizes in his small home workshop. At Hipkins's behest, he tried his hand at restoring antique keyboard instruments – spinets, harpsichords, clavichords and virginals. Soon he began manufacturing them from scratch, gradually refining his designs by 'a patient process of experimentation and artistic trial and retrial'.[14] Orders came in, slowly at first, then in ever-increasing numbers, until Dolmetsch was hard pressed to cope with the demand. Owning a Dolmetsch instrument became a status symbol in smart society. Mrs Patrick Campbell ordered a set of psalteries to use in a performance of *Das Rheingold*, and Yeats purchased one for his friend Florence Farr to play while reciting his poetry. James Joyce inquired about buying a lute, planning to 'coast the South of England from Falmouth to Margate singing old English songs', but Dolmetsch tactfully put him off.[15] In 1897 Hans Richter engaged Dolmetsch to play the recitatives on his harpsichord in *Don Giovanni* at Covent Garden. Over the years, Dolmetsch expanded his line to include not only harpsichords, clavichords, lutes and viols but also spinets, fortepianos, harps, rebecs, Baroque violins and vihuelas. To the world at large, however, his name is invariably associated with the high-quality recorders that he began to manufacture in the 1920s. The instrument caught on immediately and has been the mainstay of the family business ever since.

In reconstructing old instruments, Dolmetsch had little to go by besides practical experience, intuition and the antiques preserved in museums and private collections. Only Mahillon, Tolbecque and a few other craftsmen had seriously attempted to reproduce early instruments before, and then only as a sideline. Pleyel and Erard, the major French piano firms, began building harpsichords commercially in the 1880s, but with their thick frames, heavy construction and robust sound, they bore little resemblance to the delicate, sweet-toned instruments of the seventeenth and eighteenth centuries. Dolmetsch took a different tack and returned to historical principles of construction, while at the same time experimenting with such innovations as a sustaining pedal, an 'improved' action (which proved hopelessly temperamental) and even a vibrato-producing device. If Dolmetsch kept at it long enough, the saying went, he would end up reinventing the piano. Dolmetsch himself insisted that he was merely doing what the old harpsichord-makers would have done sooner or later if the piano had not put them out of business in the early nineteenth century. Shaw's tongue may not have been entirely in his cheek when he suggested that Dolmetsch design an automatic player mechanism for his clavichords, along the lines of a pianola, to help boost his sales.[16]

As a businessman, Dolmetsch foresaw that the early music revival would eventually generate a brisk demand for reproductions of old instruments. He did his utmost to prime the market, not only by building fine instruments and selling them at remarkably reasonable prices (often less than what it cost to make them), but by performing and lecturing with seemingly boundless energy. On 27 April 1891, he hired Prince's Hall in Piccadilly to present 'A Concert of Ancient Music of the XVI and XVII Centuries', featuring the work of Morley, Locke, Simpson, Tomkins and other English composers. This was the first of many concerts that Dolmetsch gave with members of his family and friends in small concert halls and private homes, chiefly in the fashionable Bloomsbury district. His wife Mabel has left us an evocative description of a house concert at 'Dowland' in the mid-nineties:

> The concert room, tinted a soft diaphanous green, was entirely illuminated by wax candles, set round the walls in hand-beaten brass sconces, and interspersed with rare lutes and viols, suspended from hooks. ... There was a pleasantly informal atmosphere at these concerts; and the interludes, during which excellent coffee and *petits fours* were handed round, enabled one to appreciate the unusual nature of the audience.[17]

Artists, painters, poets, playwrights, actors – the cream of London's artistic society – turned out in force to sample Dolmetsch's musical novelties. Arriving late and leaving early were frowned upon, and applause was firmly discouraged. Otherwise the concerts were relaxed affairs, with the performers dressed in period costumes and Dolmetsch bantering amiably with the audience between selections. If a performance displeased him, he thought nothing of stopping in the middle of a piece and starting afresh, in defiance of conventional concert etiquette. The calm, otherworldly atmosphere of 'Dowland', so different from that of London's bustling concert halls, enchanted Arthur Symons. 'It is a house of peace,' the poet wrote, 'where music is still that refreshment which it was before it took fever, and became accomplice and not minister to the nerves, and brought the clamour of the world into its seclusion.'[18]

Critics, in the main, found Dolmetsch's unorthodox style as refreshing as did the public. Shaw, the arch-iconoclast, and the equally irreverent John Runciman of the *Saturday Review* declared themselves his staunch champions from the outset of his career. 'We cannot do without Mr Dolmetsch', Runciman wrote in 1898. 'A knowledge of the old music is as essential to a musical man as a knowledge of the poetry before Shelley and Keats is to a literary man. .... By reconstructing the old instruments and playing the old music as it was intended to be played Mr Dolmetsch has shown us to what an astounding extent our musical history is compact of fibs begotten in ignorance; and if only in the interests of truth he should be supported by those whose business it is to educate the young.'[19]

The reservations voiced by other critics centred on the peculiar sounds of the old instruments and the deliberately anti-Romantic style of playing cultivated in the Dolmetsch circle. 'On what authority', one writer demanded to know, 'is it to be assumed that the performances of our forefathers on stringed instruments were absolutely devoid of musical expression and dynamic light and shade? Certainly our modern classic virtuosos do not adopt that view.'[20] To compare Dolmetsch to a late-nineteenth-century virtuoso betrayed a fundamental misconception of his art, and such reactions undoubtedly spurred him on to redouble his efforts. It was harder to placate otherwise sympathetic critics who complained that Dolmetsch should be more discriminating in his choice of repertoire. There is no question that much of the music he exhumed was hardly worth the effort, and it did no harm to remind him that age was no guarantee of quality. As Shaw remarked, 'Once my bare historical curiosity has been satisfied, I do not value the commonplaces of *circa* 1600 a bit more than the commonplaces of *circa* 1900.'[21]

That Dolmetsch frequently let his enthusiasm get the better of his critical judgment is understandable, for the revival was still at the stage of winnowing the grain from the chaff. In the 1890s only a handful of amateurs gave any thought to playing early English instrumental music. Francis William Galpin, the vicar of a small country church in Hatfield Regis from 1891 to 1915, organized concerts and rustic fêtes of the 'Ye Olde Englyshe Pastymes' variety, using recorders, cornets, serpents, lutes and other instruments from his noted collection.[22] One of the few academics who took an active interest in the revival was Frederick Niecks of the University of Edinburgh. 'To read of old musical works is something,' Niecks wrote, 'to see them in print or manuscript is more, but to hear them adequately performed – to come, as it were, in contact with the living things themselves, not with the dead presentments – is the only satisfactory mode of making their acquaintance.' Dolmetsch, who often took part in the historical concerts that Niecks presented in Edinburgh, would certainly have subscribed to his maxim that 'ancient compositions should be performed exactly as they were written – by the same voices and instruments, and without any changes in harmony, &c.'[23]

As Dolmetsch soon discovered, however, it was one thing to pay lip-service to such an ideal and another to put it into practice. Despite his conservatory training, Dolmetsch was not a musicologist in the formal sense, and the scholarly world regarded him with a mixture of bewilderment, condescension and scepticism. George Grove, the first director of the Royal College of Music, supported Dolmetsch publicly while privately admitting that he had little sympathy for his pupil's work. 'People now go in droves to hear Dolmetsch play J. S. Bach and other ancients on the original instruments', he wrote to a friend in 1895. 'I confess I don't care more for it than I do for the poetry of that period. Pope and Dryden are to me dead except historically, and so are the composers. Their choruses are an exception – but the mass of instrumental works – no!'[24] Grove's prejudice was widely shared, a fact that may account for the snub Dolmetsch received in 1904, when the Worshipful Company of Musicians mounted a large exhibit of instruments in London. As Margaret Campbell points out, the list of participants included virtually every British authority on early music and instruments *except* Dolmetsch.[25] Edward Dannreuther, the musicologist and Wagner expert, declined invitations to attend Dolmetsch's concerts. 'No one', he wrote in the preface to his book on musical ornamentation, 'will care to advocate the revival of a host of obsolete curlicues and twirligigs, or the resuscitation of a habit of improvising facile *variantes* or running into division. Divisions and graces have had their day and have served their purpose.'[26] Despite such seemingly deliberate slights, Dolmetsch enjoyed the friendship and esteem of eminent musicians like Hipkins, Chrysander, F. T. Arnold, Ernest Newman and Percy Scholes, who genuinely understood and appreciated the work he was doing.

Dolmetsch, for his part, harboured a lifelong mistrust of the musicological profession, a mistrust amounting at times to paranoia. Acutely aware of his lack of academic credentials, he was quick to detect and resent any criticism of his scholarship, no matter how innocuous. Like many self-educated men, he was scornful of academicism and book-learning. When Niecks politely hinted that he should keep his spoken commentary to a minimum at a concert in Edinburgh, Dolmetsch flew into a rage. 'I have something to say, and I assure you it is not anything like what has been said in the [i.e. Niecks's] lectures.'[27] This defensiveness became more pronounced as Dolmetsch grew older. In the 1930s Anselm Hughes noted that 'the old man appears to despise all musicology'.[28] When Hughes remarked that his transcription of a medieval piece would not pass muster with certain musicologists, Dolmetsch roared: 'Les musicologues? BAH! I know how it goes. It is here, in my head.'[29] Dolmetsch was not mollified by the respectful reception that greeted his major scholarly work, *The Interpretation of the Music of the XVIIth and XVIIIth Centuries*, in 1915. In it, he left no doubt as to his views on the priorities of the musicological fraternity:

> Is it worth while to devote years of labour to compile an exhaustive list of all the operas and other compositions that were performed at some German Court during two or three centuries, with the names and particulars of all the composers, musicians, dancers, copyists, &c, employed there, and the dates of their entering and leaving the service, and their salaries, &c, when not a single phrase of any of that music can be correctly heard? What avails it to know when the grandfather's uncle of a certain lutenist was baptized, or how many wives he had, if neither the lutenist's music nor a lute is procurable? We crave to hear the music itself in its original form, and this is what the 'musicologue' hardly ever thinks about.[30]

Under the circumstances, it is scarcely surprising that Dolmetsch was not offered, nor did he seek, the prominent teaching post that his admirers felt he deserved. 'In Germany', Runciman wrote, 'Mr Dolmetsch would long ere now have been appointed as a professor or lecturer in one of the big music schools and directed to tell all that he knew about the facts of musical history. Our English schools, wishing to preserve a simple faith in Burney, Macfarren, Hullah and all the old gang, offer him no appointment, though it is possible that one would quickly be offered if he would give an undertaking not to discredit the gods of English music.'[31] Had he allowed himself to be roped into the academic fold, Dolmetsch's career might well have taken a different course, but it is difficult to imagine such a prickly individualist ever feeling at home in the structured environment of a university. To the end of his life, he refused to run a formal school and only occasionally accepted private pupils. As 'a skilled craftsman, a performing musician, a bit of a composer, a scholar, and an impatient enthusiast all rolled into one person',[32] Dolmetsch, for better or worse, simply fell between the cracks.

Yet if he remained an odd man out in the musical world, Dolmetsch found a comfortable niche among the literary and artistic avant-garde. George Moore's *Evelyn Inness* was inspired by his work – Moore sought Dolmetsch's advice in writing the lengthy musical passages in the novel – and the portrait of old Mr Inness, the 'dreamer and propagandist of old-time music and its instruments', is clearly drawn from life. Dolmetsch makes cameo appearances in Joyce's *Ulysses* and in the *Cantos* of Ezra Pound, who, together with Yeats, heard echoes of his own poetical theories in Dolmetsch's music.[33] William Rothenstein, 'in spite of an unmusical soul', was drawn to Dolmetsch's concerts and sketched him playing virginal, lute and viola d'amore.[34] Isadora Duncan and Loie Fuller danced to his accompaniments. Gabriele d'Annunzio asked Dolmetsch to write and perform incidental music for his play 'La Pisanelle', in which one of the characters plays the viol,[35] and for several years he collaborated with William Poel on period-style productions of Elizabethan and Restoration dramas.

In time, however, Dolmetsch came to feel that he deserved more of the limelight. Impatient with British resistance to change, he yearned for more congenial surroundings. Opportunity came knocking in 1905, when the American piano firm Chickering invited him to open a department of early keyboard instruments, lutes and viols at their headquarters in Boston. This was an offer Dolmetsch could scarcely refuse, especially when Chickering sweetened the bait by promising him the pick of their craftsmen and freedom to travel and give concerts. Dolmetsch built a house in Cambridge to his own designs and lived on a scale he had never been able to afford in England, lionized by Boston society and even summoned to the White House to give a command performance on his clavichord for President Theodore Roosevelt. Frequent tours took him all the way from New York, where W. J. Henderson of the *Sun* dubbed him 'the apostle of retrogression', to the West Coast.[36]

Once the exhilaration of his new-found fame and prosperity wore off, however, Dolmetsch began to feel cut off in America. Chickering's decision to close their early instrument department as a result of a financial downturn in 1911 prompted him to uproot himself again. All three of the leading French piano firms had expressed interest in his work. In the end, Gaveau made the best offer and Dolmetsch soon found himself back in Europe, supervising the production of historical keyboard instruments at their factory near Paris. A few months later he returned to England. No doubt he was tired of working for other people, even on terms as generous as Chickering and Gaveau had provided, and he must have seen that he was in a much stronger position to realize his ambitions than he had been when he went abroad. And so, as the clouds of war gathered over the Continent, Dolmetsch quietly moved back to London and picked up where he had left off a decade earlier.

Many changes had occurred during his absence. English music, long subservient to Continental influences, was at last coming into its own. The musical 'renaissance' embodied by Elgar and Vaughan Williams was fuelled by a new appreciation of the nation's cultural patrimony. Thanks to such scholarly publications as Godfrey Arkwright's *Old English Edition* and the *Fitzwilliam Virginal Book* (edited by Fuller Maitland and his brother-in-law, William Barclay Squire), more attention than ever was being directed to early English composers, from Dunstable to Purcell. The latter's bicentenary in 1895 had been marked by a cluster of performances, including a service at Westminster Abbey and a production of *Dido and Aeneas* by students of the Royal College of Music. Early vocal music, a field in which Dolmetsch was only marginally involved,[37] was blossoming. Barclay Squire's anthology of English madrigals, like the *Fitzwilliam Virginal Book*, had been published in Germany by Breitkopf & Härtel, there being, as Fuller Maitland drily observed, 'no firm of English music-publishers with the requisite foresight'.[38] England's madrigal tradition was kept alive by ensembles like the Oriana Madrigal Society, which Charles Kennedy Scott and Thomas Beecham founded in 1904.[39]

Performances of early vocal music still left much to be desired. Old habits died hard and few singers or choral directors saw any point in studying vocal styles of the pre-Classical period. Edmund Fellowes complained that it 'became more and more irksome to hear the services of Byrd, Gibbons, Farrant and the rest drawled out at a low pitch, with false verbal accentuation; and the same was true of the performance of the anthems and the madrigals. The stately way in which it was thought right to sing Morley's "Now is the month of maying" seems now incredible.'[40] Fellowes worked assiduously to overcome these problems, through his useful editions of early vocal music (in particular the enormously influential *English Madrigal School* series), his many performances as choral director and lutenist, and the popular lectures he gave throughout the United Kingdom and North America.

Richard Terry, Dolmetsch's counterpart in the choral field, took the lead in systematically reviving the liturgical music of the Tudor composers. Like Dolmetsch, Terry started his career as a schoolteacher. In 1896 he joined the faculty of the school attached to Downside Abbey, a Benedictine establishment in Somerset. He spent most of his holidays doing research on Renaissance polyphony and plainchant at the British Museum and in Oxford. The Benedictines were sympathetic employers. The monks of

Solesmes had already established close ties with British churchmen and musicians, a bond that was cemented during the monks' exile on the Isle of Wight between 1901 and 1922.[41] The Plainsong and Mediaeval Music Society was founded in 1888 by H. B. Briggs, a British civil servant who had visited Solesmes. The society's annual report for 1892 announced the formation of a male choir to sing 'in accordance with the method of the Abbey of Solesmes', but it was not until Anselm Hughes became secretary, in 1926, that the society undertook an extensive programme of performance, broadcasting and recording.[42]

Terry made his mark in London with a performance of Byrd's Five-part Mass at the dedication of a Catholic church in Ealing in 1899. Among the critics in the audience was Terry's cousin, John Runciman, who informed readers of the *Saturday Review* that the Downside Abbey choir 'sang in tune and generally with the greatest possible expression'.[43] Terry's rising reputation in the Church and the musical world made him the logical choice to become the first choir director at the newly opened Westminster Cathedral in 1901. Terry turned the cathedral into a musical showplace, accomplishing for early English vocal music what Dolmetsch was doing for the instrumental repertoire. His choir of some forty boys and men sang music by most of the great Renaissance masters – Palestrina, Victoria, Lassus, Hassler, Gabrieli, Sweelinck, Byrd, Tallis, Taverner, Tye, Shepherd, Willaert, Morales and dozens more. Many of these works appeared in the *Tudor Church Music* series, which Terry edited for a short time. He also delved into the medieval repertoire, performing works by Dunstable, Fayrfax, Power and others, and championed modern music by the likes of Howells, Holst, Vaughan Williams and Elgar. Terry expected his choristers to be able to read any music at sight, and the consistently high calibre of their performances made Westminster Cathedral a landmark on any musical tour of London.

Between them, Terry and Fellowes were largely responsible for the 'Elizabethan fever' that swept across the country in the wake of the First World War. Holst, who had performed a fair amount of early English music before the war at Morley College and St Paul's School for Girls, was pleasantly surprised to hear British soldiers singing part of a Byrd mass after a concert in Constantinople in 1918. 'England – for the first time – is really learning her own music', he declared.[44] Fellowes's madrigal editions were taken up in the twenties by the English Singers, the most popular and widely travelled madrigal group of the day,[45] and later by T. B. Lawrence's Fleet Street Choir. The fever reached epidemic proportions in the great Byrd Festival of 1923. The *Musical Times* apologized to its readers that the sheer number of events made it impossible to note, let alone review, all of them.[46] Hundreds of amateur and professional choirs participated in the nationwide competitive festivals held from 1923 to 1926, the test pieces for which were drawn exclusively from the Elizabethan repertoire.[47]

As for Bach, Londoners could choose between Vaughan Williams's traditionally large-scale performances with the Bach Choir[48] and the more historically correct, chamber-sized renditions of Charles Kennedy Scott's Bach Cantata Club. The latter's performance of *Jesu, meine Freude* prompted one reviewer to comment: 'It would be absurd to forbid Bach's Motets to big choirs, but this performance left no doubt that the listener gets the truth of the music from voices few and picked.'[49] The revival was even starting to spill over into the realm of Baroque stage works, which were produced with increasing frequency at Cambridge and Oxford in the twenties and thirties. All in all, it was a heady time to be involved with early music. 'The rediscovery of old composers goes on steadily', the *Musical Times* observed in 1929. 'From a Scottish newspaper report of a musical service at a church near Berwick we learn that the programme included examples "from the works of Descant, Faux, and Bourdon." We hope the choir will now turn its attention to those neglected masters Gymel, Organum, and Diaphony. We think, too, that the time is ripe for a performance of the best works of Hocket.'[50]

The revival of early instruments had stalled during Dolmetsch's absence. None of the leading English piano makers, for example, had followed the French lead in manufacturing harpsichords. Hipkins's death in 1903 had deprived Dolmetsch of a kindred spirit and valued ally. Indeed, it had become increasingly clear since his return to England that Dolmetsch belonged not in the hurly-burly of London but some place apart where he could work at his own pace. In 1917, he and his family moved into a modest house in the picturesque Surrey town of Haslemere, less than an hour by train from central London. Marco Pallis, a young viol player from Liverpool who was one of Dolmetsch's most devoted protégés, financed the long-overdue expansion of his workshop. In this idyllic environment, he set about realizing his dream of creating an enclave dedicated to the study and performance of early music.

Now in his sixties, Dolmetsch was no longer willing or physically able to be a travelling salesman for early music. He reasoned that people could come to him for a change. And come they did, to buy instruments, to solicit Dolmetsch's advice, and to attend the annual chamber music festivals that started in 1925. The first Haslemere Festival comprised a dozen concerts spread over two weeks – a greater concentration of pre-Classical music than any major city could boast – and served as the prototype for the early music festivals that have since proliferated around the world.[51] Musicians, scholars and craftsmen descended on Haslemere from all quarters. Ernest Ansermet questioned Dolmetsch about the fine points of Baroque style, Andrés Segovia listened to him discoursing on the lute, and Yeats wrote to introduce 'a young man called Harry Partch' who 'wants an organ made on certain principles of his own'.[52] Through it all, Dolmetsch maintained his habitually gruelling routine of writing, lecturing, performing and, increasingly, recording.

Despite these trappings of prosperity, the chronically impecunious Dolmetsch was often forced to borrow from friends to make ends meet. The pressures eased somewhat with the creation of the Dolmetsch Foundation in 1928 and the announcement, several years later, that he had been awarded a modest but welcome state pension of £110 a year. Both initiatives were endorsed by an impressive array of artists, politicians and sundry public figures. Dolmetsch accepted this belated recognition as no more than his due. When Hubert Foss invited him to help compile an anthology of early English instrumental music for Oxford University Press, he declined on the grounds that he required complete editorial control. 'It is gratifying', he added petulantly, 'to see that my discovery of the English Instrumental music 1500–1700, and 50 years of hard work on my part have not been entirely wasted.'[53]

This was an exaggeration, of course. The value of Dolmetsch's work had been acknowledged almost immediately by an important segment of the musical community, and by the 1930s he was beginning to have a demonstrable impact on the way music was performed, studied and taught in England. Few pioneers have lived to see their ideas so resoundingly vindicated. Temperamentally, though, Dolmetsch was not a team player. He insisted on calling the shots; if others joined him, they did so on his terms, whether they were highly experienced professionals or rank novices. As a result, many musicians who might otherwise have been his natural collabora-tors gave Dolmetsch a wide berth.

In many ways, Dolmetsch inflicted this isolation upon himself. He was never an easy person to work or live with. Domineering, brusque and monumentally self-assured, he neither suffered fools gladly nor readily admitted his own shortcomings. After meeting Dolmetsch in 1932, the young harpsichordist Ralph Kirkpatrick reported to his family in America: 'He is in some respects decidedly warped, to the point of craziness, and said many foolish things, but he does know a great deal and admits it to be only a small fraction of potential knowledge, although he is conceited to the utmost and will tolerate no disagreement.' Percy Grainger, the Australian pianist and composer, more sympathetically described Dolmetsch as 'intimate, natural, affectionate, inconsistent, wilful and tyrannical – as we like truly great and sincere beings to be'.[54]

Dolmetsch's achievement might indeed have been greater if he had been more diplomatic, more willing to collaborate with and learn from his peers. Yet his stubborn resolve to forge ahead, heedless of what others thought, was perhaps his greatest source of strength. If his judgments were often blinkered, his vision was consistently clear. No one knew better than he how many pitfalls lay in his path. The discoveries of other scholars and performers were of little use to Dolmetsch; they were likely to contain too many half-truths and misleading inferences. He insisted on drawing his own conclusions from the old treatises, manuscripts and instruments. This independence of mind cost him dearly, for inevitably he came to be regarded with that bemused tolerance that the English reserve for men and women of genius who do not quite fit in. Writing after Dolmetsch's death in 1940, the critic Ernest Newman observed that 'the current British notion of him is that of an amiable old gentleman who made, and encouraged others to make, queer sounds on queer old instruments, and showed a regrettable preference for the music of the past over that of the present'.[55] Basil Maine put it this way:

> There are some, I know, who look upon Dolmetsch as a picturesque fanatic. They betray a superficial knowledge of the man. It is impossible to talk with him (or rather, to hear him propound) for more than a few minutes without becoming conscious of the unusual force of his faith. Of course, it seems fanatical for a man to stand up and declare to this idolatrous and professional generation that applause at a concert is heretical – that, indeed, the whole idea of concert-giving is antithetical to the true spirit of music – that music-making in the home is the ultimate ideal. But the fanaticism begins to reflect the colours of good sound sense when we find that the man who is so vehement in his speech is also zealous in his works.[56]

Listening to the recordings that Dolmetsch made in the twenties and thirties, one can easily understand why he elicited such strong and often contradictory reactions. The quality of his performances is maddeningly erratic, even allowing for the fact that he was in his seventies when most of the recordings were made. Grainger admired the 'wayward *rubati*, sparkling high speeds and vivid contrasts of *staccato* and *legato*' that characterized Dolmetsch's keyboard playing,[57] but he could also be just plain sloppy. Technique was never his strong suit – as one of his pupils remarked, 'Study is problematical with a man who prides himself on never practicing'[58] – and Dolmetsch spread himself too thin to keep his fingers in top condition. On the other hand, nearly everybody who heard him play talked about the extraordinary sounds that Dolmetsch drew from an instrument, be it clavichord, lute, or Baroque violin. Elizabeth Goble recalled that 'his rather clinging touch on the harpsichord coaxed a very full and beautiful tone from the instrument, more telling than that produced by others. His playing was full of imagination and a kind of magic.'[59] Dolmetsch was not oblivious or indifferent to the demands of performance, as some have implied, but he rejected virtuosic display and treated recordings and concerts as demonstrations of work in progress rather than polished performances. Reviewers seemed to sense this and wrote more about the unusual music Dolmetsch and his family played than about their often inadequate performances. All the same, even partisans like Shaw, Runciman and Scholes felt obliged from time to time to register vehement objections to the amateurish standards that prevailed at Haslemere.

No matter how gently or tactfully phrased, such criticisms invariably stung Dolmetsch to the quick. So did insinuations, more frequently voiced in later years, that his scholarship was less rigorous than it ought to have been. As he grew older, Dolmetsch placed more faith in intuition and less in solid historical evidence. He once adapted some fragments of fourteenth-century polyphony for a mellifluous but historically implausible ensemble of voice, recorders and viols. 'I do not doubt', remarked the musicologist Thurston Dart, 'that the same technique of removing most of the accidentals would work wonders even in Schönberg, especially if his music was re-scored for recorders and viols, but I do not know that the composer would have been very gratified with the results.' Dart seldom passed up a chance to go out on a limb himself, but he took strong exception to Dolmetsch's 'slap-happy . . . approach to the complex problems of medieval music'.[60] Not everyone was willing to take Dolmetsch's hunches on faith, as Grainger did when he wrote: 'Such conceptions as yours convince without proofs – the proofs merely confirm the basic impression of rightness, but are not needed to establish it.'[61]

After visiting the Haslemere Festival in 1931, Grainger took up Dolmetsch's cause with the fervour of a disciple, deluging him with letters signed 'Yours ever worshipfully'. In an article for the *Musical Quarterly* entitled 'Arnold Dolmetsch: Musical Confucius', Grainger urged 'all forward-looking musicians' to skip the summer festivals at Bayreuth and Salzburg and go instead to Haslemere, where they would glean the knowledge of early music 'that so soon will become a necessity to any self-respecting musician'. Grainger was deeply impressed by Dolmetsch's 'breadth and universality of vision', as reflected in his interest in ethnic music (a field also close to Grainger's heart).[62] Dolmetsch once improvised an accompaniment on his viola d'amore to an elaborate Indian raga, much to the surprise of the Indian singer, who confessed 'that he would never have believed that a

European musician would have been capable of such a feat'.[63] Dolmetsch's interest in historical dances paralleled the revival of folk dance in England by Cecil Sharp and others in the early 1900s. He collected dance treatises and showed them to friends and acquaintances, hoping to interest them in reconstructing the old steps and patterns. His third wife, Mabel, eventually took up the challenge and became an acknowledged authority on historical dance.[64]

That Dolmetsch's children and grandchildren should have gravitated toward early music seems almost preordained. Rudolph, by all accounts the most gifted of the younger generation, had just embarked on a promising career as a harpsichordist, gambist and conductor (of modern music) when he was lost at sea during the Second World War. His younger brother Carl, a well-known recorder player who co-founded the Society of Recorder Players in 1937, assumed control of the family business upon their father's death. Their sister Nathalie founded the English Viola da Gamba Society in 1948. Dolmetsch's work was carried on by dozens of pupils and protégés, among them the instrument-makers John Challis and Günther Hellwig, the performers Jean Buchanan and Suzanne Bloch, and the scholars Robert Donington, Gerald Hayes and Diana Poulton. Many who were too young to know him personally acknowledged their debt to Dolmetsch. Frank Hubbard formulated his revolutionary ideas about harpsichord design as an apprentice at Haslemere in the late 1940s, and Thurston Dart's book *The Interpretation of Music* paid more than nominal tribute to Dolmetsch's pioneering study.

All of which would seem to have ensured that Dolmetsch's accomplishments would be recognized by later generations of early music specialists. But the disruption of musical life brought about by the Second World War threw up a barrier between him and his successors. Musicians and scholars who picked up the thread in the late forties and fifties found it easy to believe they were starting afresh, when in fact they were building on a foundation laid by Dolmetsch, Terry, Fellowes and others. There is, it must be admitted, more than a grain of truth in the complaint of Dolmetsch's descendants that his work has never been sufficiently appreciated. Newman wrote that Dolmetsch 'combined the ardour of the artist with the self-discipline of the true scholar', adding: 'that he should have had practically no influence on the English concert world is only what might have been expected. Scholars, as a rule, do not perform; while not one performer in a thousand has any pretensions to scholarship.'[65] Even Dart, while sharply critical of Dolmetsch's scholarly methods, admired his 'obstinacy' and willingness to make 'wild guesses', without which 'no musician and no musical scholar will ever get anywhere'.[66]

As a young man, Dolmetsch doubtless realized he would have to be a jack-of-all-trades in order to fulfil his ambition of bringing early music back to life.

Scholars had covered much of the ground before him; inquisitive musicians had dusted off the old scores and performed them from time to time; instrument-makers had reproduced the decaying relics in museums with varying degrees of fidelity. But no one before Dolmetsch had put all the pieces together and grasped the all-important link between the theoretical and practical aspects of reviving a lost performing tradition. And in an age of increasing specialization in all walks of musical life, it seems doubtful that any one person will have the ability or the mettle to attempt such a feat again.

However one assesses Dolmetsch's strengths and weaknesses, it would be short-sighted indeed to deny that he was the seminal figure in the modern early music movement. It was he who set the agenda for and defined the issues addressed by the revival. He anticipated and articulated the preoccupations of latter-day early musicians, notably their concern for 'authenticity'. He demonstrated convincingly that a piece of music could not be fully understood without reference to the sonorities of the instruments on which it was originally played and the performance practice of the period in which it was written. His lifelong bias toward early instruments and instrumental music helped determine the course that the revival would take for decades to come. Last but not least, he showed that music centuries old could speak to modern ears without being translated into a modern idiom. The final sentence of his book concisely sums up the late twentieth century's dominant musical outlook: 'We can no longer allow anyone to stand between us and the composer.'[67]

3

FROM SCHOLA TO SCHOLA

The Schola Cantorum of Paris · Charles Bordes and the Chanteurs de St Gervais · Two Sociétés d'Instruments Anciens · Wanda Landowska and the Harpsichord Revival on the Continent · The Deutsche Vereinigung für alte Musik · Collegium Musicum Groups · The Organ Revival, Youth Movement and Singing Movement · Safford Cape's Pro Musica Antiqua of Brussels · The Schola Cantorum Basiliensis.

THE 1889 Exposition Universelle in Paris, like the London event four years earlier, featured a wide array of musical exotica, from a Javanese gamelan ensemble to an exhibition of historical instruments, which the musicologist Julien Tiersot described as 'a veritable museum of musical archaeology'. Alongside the antiques lent by various museums and private collectors were displayed reconstructions of medieval instruments made by Léon Pillaut, the curator of the Paris Conservatoire collection. Among them were a rebec, a lute and a thirteenth-century harp 'constructed by the Erard firm after a bas-relief at Chartres Cathedral'. Tiersot thought it a shame that the old instruments could not be played and hoped that 'some artist enamoured of the old-time art' would one day reanimate them with the spirit of Bach, Rameau, Couperin and Mozart.[1]

The organizers of the exposition had not left everything to the visitor's imagination, however. They engaged the distinguished pianist Louis Diémer to play a pair of recitals on an eighteenth-century harpsichord in a specially built auditorium in the Trocadéro. Poorly attended as they were, the concerts attracted widespread interest in musical circles. Tiersot singled out the concerted pieces of Marais and Rameau, in which Diémer was joined by the cellist Jules Delsart on the viola da gamba, the violinist Louis van Waefelghem on viola d'amore, and the flautist Paul Taffanel. Tiersot praised the 'charm', 'sweetness' and 'fullness' of van Waefelghem's viola d'amore and observed that the gamba, though less powerful than the cello, had a clearer and sharper sound. He noted that Taffanel modified the piercing sound of his Boehm flute 'to give the impression of the old recorders'.

Diémer, Delsart and Taffanel, all renowned as soloists and as teachers at the Conservatoire, had been giving concerts for several years with notable success. 'The illusion could not have been more perfect if MM Diémer, Delsart and Taffanel had worn powdered wigs, clock stockings, knee-breeches and long-tailed coats', wrote a reviewer in 1888.[2] Delsart made a speciality of the gamba, which he had 'fitted with sympathetic strings like the viola d'amore', according to the English gambist Edmund van der Straeten.[3] Around 1895, Delsart and Diémer formed a quartet with van Waefelghem, who had been one of Dolmetsch's fellow students in Brussels, and Laurent Grillet, who played the hurdy-gurdy. Calling themselves the Société des Instruments Anciens, the ensemble toured France, Belgium, England and Switzerland in the late nineties. As the first regularly constituted early music group, they made news wherever they played. The novelty of their programmes invariably attracted attention, not all of it favourable. Auguste Tolbecque disparagingly referred to a certain 'fameuse pièce pseudo-ancienne' popularized by Diémer and his colleagues. 'Eh bien,' he wrote to Dolmetsch, 'no one protests and these four humbugs must have a good laugh when they go backstage.'[4]

Diémer was no charlatan, however. He had been playing the harpsichord in public since the 1860s, and it was his instrument – a two-manual Pascal Taskin dating from 1769 – that French piano-makers chose to copy in the eighties. (He later switched to a modern Erard harpsichord, which was more practical for touring.) But neither Diémer's concerts nor the historical organ recitals that Alexandre Guilmant had been giving at the Trocadéro since 1878 caused anything like the éclat that Fétis's historical concerts had sparked. Parisians were less blasé about vocal music. When Charles Bordes, then the young choirmaster of St Gervais, performed Palestrina's Stabat Mater and Allegri's Miserere during Holy Week in 1891, the large church was so overrun with worshippers and curiosity-seekers that visiting music critics were obliged to squeeze themselves into confessional booths.[5]

Bordes's contribution to the choral revival in France was as great as Terry's in England. Keenly interested in folksong, chant and early polyphony, he sought out the handful of Parisian churches and choir schools where the old sacred music could still be heard. With the blessing of his ecclesiastical superiors, he set out to re-establish the tradition of musical excellence that generations of Couperins had maintained as organists of St Gervais. In January 1892 the parishioners heard works by Victoria, Josquin, Bach and Palestrina sung by a choir of eighty voices. Since women were forbidden to sing in church, Bordes had recruited boy sopranos and altos, but he quietly slipped in a few women as last-minute reinforcements. Holy Week that year was devoted entirely to plainchant and early a cappella music, an event of such distinction that Le Figaro gave it front-page coverage. In view of the difficulty of the music, Bordes and his colleague, Vincent d'Indy, insisted on holding no fewer than 103 rehearsals. Their labours were amply rewarded: the composer Paul Dukas, one of the more discerning French critics of the day, reported that the choir sang 'with a most remarkable rectitude of style and a vocal perfection worthy of all praise'.[6]

Bordes, whose youthful appearance earned him the sobriquet 'the choirboy', was an intensely charismatic man. 'He had only to ask to get what he wanted', said one of his friends. 'The professionals gave their time, know-how and talents; the rich and famous gave their money; the press gave publicity.'[7] Among those who succumbed to his charm was d'Indy, then in his early forties and regarded as one of the most promising composers of his generation. Assured of his support, Bordes picked two dozen singers to form the nucleus of a permanent ensemble called the Chanteurs de St Gervais. Membership was open to men, women and children (the latter being admitted 'in case of choral performances of religious masterpieces in churches') and the repertoire was to consist of sacred and secular works from the fifteenth to the nineteenth centuries.

Bordes's plans grew ever more ambitious. In their first year, the Chanteurs de St Gervais performed major works by Josquin, Victoria, Palestrina, Lassus, Ockeghem and Janequin. In June 1893 Guilmant invited them to perform Bach's *Trauer Ode* at the Trocadéro. The following year they took part in several historical concerts organized by the Swiss conductor Gustave Doret, as well as inaugurating an annual Bach cantata series at the Salle d'Harcourt. Bordes himself edited most of the music the choir sang. The first volumes of his *Anthologie des maîtres religieux primitifs* appeared in 1892 under the imprint of the Chanteurs. The same year saw the publication of the first of Guilmant's landmark editions of early organ music. Clearly the revival was poised to take off in France as it was in England.

By early 1894 Bordes, d'Indy and Guilmant (at fifty-seven, the senior member of the triumvirate) felt sufficiently in accord to found a school to spread their ideas. They contemplated calling it the Société de Propagande pour la Divulgation des Chefs-d'Oeuvres Religieux (the Propaganda Society for the Dissemination of Religious Masterworks), but eventually settled on a simpler and more historically evocative name: the Schola Cantorum. D'Indy took the lead in formulating the school's curriculum, which was to be based on a study of plainchant (according to the Solesmes principles) and sacred polyphony of the Palestrina school. Not for nothing had Bordes and d'Indy studied with César Franck, that stalwart champion of Bach and other pre-Classical masters. Franck's influence on the Schola was so pronounced that d'Indy affectionately referred to him as the 'grandfather' of the institution.[8]

Like Choron and Niedermeyer before them, the Schola's founders believed that contemporary composers would benefit from immersing themselves in the well-springs of their art. But a sense of history was equally useful to performers, d'Indy wrote, 'for it is as profitable for them to know how to sing a liturgic monody properly, or to be able to play a Corelli sonata in a suitable style, as it is for composers to study the structure of a motet or a suite'.[9] When the Schola opened its doors in the autumn of 1896, ten students and almost as many faculty members shared rented rooms in the rue Stanislas. Mushrooming enrolment soon dictated a move to larger quarters. A former Benedictine monastery in the rue St Jacques was duly acquired and the chapel converted into a serviceable concert hall. D'Indy, in recognition of his outstanding skills as an educator, was appointed sole director of the Schola, freeing Bordes to do what he did best: raising money, publicizing the school's activities and conducting the Chanteurs de St Gervais.

The choir's connection with its eponymous church had grown increasingly tenuous. Since 1894 the Chanteurs had travelled the length and breadth of France on numerous tours and ventured as far afield as Vienna, Turin and London. During the 1900 Paris Exposition, some sixty thousand visitors passed through the replica of a fourteenth-century church erected on the banks of the Seine, where the Chanteurs gave short performances every day for six months. Bordes had a genius for publicity. The Chanteurs were featured on the Concerts Lamoureux, at the Folies Bergères and with Yvette Guilbert, the famous chanteuse.[10] An admirer dubbed Bordes the 'Pasdeloup of Palestrinian music', alluding to the conductor of a popular concert series. Bordes's worldly acclaim apparently displeased the church authorities. They began to have second thoughts about their enterprising choir director, and in 1902 he was effectively forced to resign. The incident flared into a *cause célèbre*. Various reasons were advanced for Bordes's fall from grace, including his persistent use of female singers at St Gervais, but the critic Pierre Lalo probably hit the mark when he accused France's religious establishment of being incorrigibly anti-musical:

A spirit of hostility toward the Christian musicians of the Renaissance prevails throughout the world of choirs, choir schools and vestries. This hostility is easy to explain. All, or nearly all, choirmasters are trained composers who furnish their parish and editors with musical material. Every one of them has written some syrupy, sickly-sweet *Libera* or *Pie Jesu*, dripping with false unction and steeped in mawkish, theatrical tears. These are nothing but hypocritical operatic arias which have neither true passion nor sincere piety; they banish all beauty and truthfulness and dishonour both music and religion at the same time. ...

The day when the Chanteurs de St Gervais revealed this nobler and more sacred art to the masses, the choirmasters sensed that their privileges and rights were in danger. Lassus and Palestrina seemed to them intruders and usurpers, and the resurrection of their music a treacherous plot. Since Palestrina and Lassus are out of reach, the choirmasters jealously attack the musicians who champion them. When the *Douce mémoire* or Pope Marcellus masses have been chased from the temple, the syrups of the *Libera* and *Pie Jesu* settings can once again flow in peace.[11]

Predictably, the controversy surrounding the Chanteurs' expulsion from St Gervais damaged neither Bordes's career nor the fortunes of the fledgling Schola. Both secured the allegiance of independent-minded musicians who resented the Conservatoire's stranglehold on French musical life. The Schola, in the words of one observer, stood for 'a return of natural classicism against academicism'.[12] Bordes's call for *discours libre*[13] – literally, free speech – in music was eagerly answered by composers like Debussy who wanted to cast off the fetters of tradition and lead music down new paths. 'M. Charles Bordes is universally known, and for the best reasons in the world', Debussy wrote in 1903. 'He is an accomplished musician in the fullest sense of the word, and his personality could be compared with that of one of those old musicians whose courage grew the more they were faced with danger. Certainly, it is less dangerous teaching the masses the catechism of Palestrina than teaching savages that of the Gospel. But in both cases there is a similar hostility, only reaction is different: in one case they yawn, in the other they have your scalp!'[14]

The heterogeneous mixture of Schola audiences appealed to Debussy as strongly as their rapt concentration. 'It's a strange thing, but at the Schola, side by side, you will find the aristocracy, the most left wing of the bourgeoisie, refined artists, and coarse artisans. But there is little of that empty space too often found at the more famous establishments. One feels they understand. . . . I don't know if it is because of the smallness of the room [the Schola's concert hall seated about 500], or because of some mysterious influence of the divine, but there is a real communion between those who play and those who listen.'

Although religious music formed the core of the Schola's curriculum, the secular repertoire was by no means neglected. Bordes and d'Indy took a lively interest in the early French opera and song composers, whose works were beginning to resurface at the turn of the century. French musicians, rebounding from their infatuation with Wagner, turned inward and drew sustenance from indigenous traditions. Debussy bitterly resented the 'Wagnerian hypnosis' that held many of his contemporaries (d'Indy included) in thrall. His intemperance extended even to Gluck, whose operas could still be seen occasionally in Paris. '*Vive Rameau! À bas Gluck!*' he cried when the Schola revived the former's pastoral opera *La Guirlande* in 1903. Constant Zakone, reviewing the performance in the *Revue musicale*, reserved his fire for the Italians, another favourite target of France's cultural chauvinists: 'How much closer this is to us than the heavy-handed platitudes, the trivial foolishness and the impoverished harmonies to which we were later condemned by a theatre corrupted by contact with a degraded Italy.'[15]

Played against a simple rustic set in the Schola's open-air courtyard, *La Guirlande* anticipated the more elaborate performances (chiefly in concert form) of Lully's *Armide*, Monteverdi's *Orfeo* and *L'Incoronazione di Poppea*, and Rameau's *Hippolyte et Aricie*, *Zoroastre* and *Dardanus* that the Schola presented in later years. This ambitious series of revivals culminated in 1908 in a fully-staged production of Rameau's *Castor et Pollux* in Montpellier, where Bordes had retired on account of poor health three years earlier. From his Mediterranean retreat, Bordes used the Schola's house organ, the *Tribune de St Gervais*, to advocate the formation of a society devoted exclusively to reviving early operas, an idea that came to fruition only after his death.[16] Bordes was not alone in his conviction that modern singers had much to learn about Baroque and Renaissance style. Romain Rolland complained that the Chanteurs de St Gervais 'sing sometimes (too often) incorrectly, constantly with negligence, almost always heavily. They haven't the slightest grasp of the style of the sixteenth-century French *chansons de cour*. They take away all of the music's spirit and light grace.'[17] Few critics, however, objected to d'Indy's heavily Romanticized and abridged performing editions of Baroque operas, which remained in circulation for many years.

Bordes's Bach cantata performances in the mid-nineties had been lavishly praised by no less an authority than the Bach expert André Pirro. 'At his behest,' Pirro wrote, 'the orchestra more often than not became precise and colourful, and choruses sprang to life. Several of the soloists, amenable to his guidance, became not only sound interpreters of the notes but moving translators of Bach's thought. The cantatas were resuscitated by his breath, and if they sometimes lacked perfection, they never lacked soul.'[18] Pirro was not an impartial witness, having served on the original Schola faculty, but his esteem for Bordes was widely shared and it was generally agreed that standards slipped after Bordes's departure. 'Glance around the concert hall after the first moments of interest are over and you will see wandering eyes and long, drawn faces', Jules Ecorcheville wrote in a review of Bach performances at the Schola in 1907. 'Everyone struggles in vain to focus his flagging attention and to discover beauties that remain hidden.'[19] Ecorcheville concluded that 'purely historical interest has got the better of artistic feeling', a statement that could hardly have been made while Bordes was in charge.

Nevertheless, the Schola's influence continued to spread, in part through the branches of the school that were established in Montpellier, Lyons, Marseilles, Bordeaux, Avignon, Nancy and other provincial cities. Bordes enjoyed an international reputation and his many musical editions, published by the Schola in a cheap and practical format, were welcomed by choral directors around the world. D'Indy's *Cours de composition musicale*, charting the development of musical forms from early chant to the twentieth century, became a standard conservatory text. Though the Schola produced a number of distinguished scholars and performers, it was chiefly known for the outstanding composers who passed through its doors, among them Albert Roussel, Erik Satie, Isaac Albéniz, Joaquín Turina, Edgard Varèse, Bohuslav Martinů, Georges Auric, Arthur Honegger and Quincy Porter. Bordes died in 1909, Guilmant in 1911, leaving d'Indy to carry on alone until his death in 1931, an event that effectively marked the end of the Schola's contribution to the revival.

In the first decade of the century, the Schola had served as a catalyst for an unprecedented early music 'boom' in France. Schola pupils and faculty founded both a Bach Society and a Handel Society in Paris.[20] Henry Expert, who had studied with Franck at the Niedermeyer School, conducted the Chanterie de la Renaissance and gave popular lecture-concerts on early music at the Ecole des Hautes Etudes Sociales. Eugène de Bricqueville, an amateur scholar and instrument collector in Versailles, assembled a Baroque chamber orchestra called 'La Couperin' whose players used authentic old instruments.[21] Concert series devoted to the history of the string quartet, the lyric drama and the violin repertoire drew large crowds. Pianists like Joaquín Nin, Ricardo Viñes, Blanche Selva and Diémer regularly featured early music on their recitals. The Parisian public was becoming increasingly venturesome and sophisticated in its tastes. 'To pass, from one day to the next, from Rameau to d'Indy, from Mondonville to Ravel, from Weber to Palestrina, demands a certain aplomb', Ecorcheville noted approvingly.[22]

One early music ensemble, the Société des Instruments Anciens Casadesus, achieved commercial as well as artistic success. Founded in 1901 by Henri Casadesus, with Saint-Saëns as honorary president, the society toured extensively throughout Western and Eastern Europe, North America, the Middle East and even Russia. Tolstoy described their concert in Moscow in 1910 as 'one of the greatest musical pleasures I have ever experienced'.[23] Like the Diémer quartet, the Casadesus society consisted of harpsichord and historical string instruments. Besides Henri, who played the viola d'amore, the personnel included (at one time or another) his brothers Marcel and Marius on gamba and pardessus de viole, and his sister Régina Patorni-Casadesus on harpsichord. Another brother, Francis, occasionally conducted the ensemble in larger works. Their repertoire centred around minor Baroque and early Classical composers like Francoeur, Borghi, Bruni, Mouret and Nicolini, whose music pleased the public but not always the critics. Henri's attitude toward historical propriety was cavalier at best. The composer Alfredo Casella, who played harpsichord with the group for a short time, quit 'because almost all of the music played was either apocryphal or had at least been cleverly "retouched" by that talented and sympathetic rascal of a Casadesus'.[24] Although financial pressures obliged Henri to sell the bulk of his instrument collection – 144 pieces – to the Boston Symphony Orchestra in 1926, the society remained active until the eve of the Second World War.

The most celebrated early musician in Paris was not a member of any ensemble and studied at neither the Schola Cantorum nor the Conservatoire. Wanda Landowska arrived in the French capital in 1900. Like most Polish pianists, she had been weaned on a diet of Chopin and the Romantics, but under the influence of Bordes and his circle she soon branched out into the pre-Classical repertoire. Borrowing a Pleyel harpsichord, she cautiously tested the waters by inserting a sample clavecin piece in her piano recitals. In 1905 she played Bach's G minor Concerto on the harpsichord at the inaugural concert of Gustave Bret's Bach Society. Bordes disapproved, complaining that the harpsichord 'reduces superb and often large-scale works to the size of its tiny, spindly legs'.[25] But Landowska's personal magnetism and the missionary zeal with which she proselytized for her chosen instrument gradually won over many sceptics. Albert Schweitzer, the Bach scholar and organist, was an early convert. 'Anyone who has heard Wanda Landowska play the *Italian* Concerto on her wonderful Pleyel harpsichord finds it hard to understand how it could ever again be played on a modern piano', he wrote in 1905.[26]

Most other harpsichordists of the time either considered themselves pianists first, like Diémer, or subordinated their study of the instrument to other pursuits, like Dolmetsch. Landowska was a specialist and a professional to the core. She combined a virtuoso keyboard technique with the flair and temperament of a born prima donna. In the beginning, her only serious rival was the English harpsichordist Violet Gordon Woodhouse, Dolmetsch's star pupil. Moreover, Landowska played not only the trifling miniatures of the French clavecinist composers but also the big works – Bach's concertos and partitas, Scarlatti's sonatas, the suites of Handel, Couperin and Rameau – which pianists had hitherto treated as their private property.[27] Her performances ignited a heated debate over the relative merits of the two instruments. Musicologists like Karl Nef and Richard Buchmeyer exchanged arguments in learned journals, while Landowska and Joaquín Nin squared off in the performers' ring.[28] At the 1911 Bach Festival in Eisenach, Landowska took part in a 'match' at which the Chromatic Fantasy and Fugue and the *Capriccio sopra la lontananza del suo fratello dilettissimo* were played on both harpsichord and piano. The contest resulted in a draw as far as the press and public were concerned,[29] but Landowska had scored her point: no longer could the harpsichord be regarded as a mere antiquarian curio.

In her eagerness to haul the harpsichord into the twentieth century, Landowska worked closely with Gustave Lyon of the Pleyel firm to design a more resonant instrument suitable for modern concert halls. Unveiled at the 1912 Bach Festival in Breslau, the 'Landowska model' was distinguished by its sturdy wooden frame (later cast in iron), high-tension strings and a powerful sixteen-foot register. Landowska sought, without copying them exactly, to emulate the harpsichords of the mid-eighteenth century, 'when they had reached the height of their glory for richness of registers and beauty of sonority'.[30] Her Pleyel was a very different kind of instrument from the more historically faithful harpsichords that Dolmetsch was building, and it is not surprising that Landowska nowhere mentions him in her widely-read polemic *Musique ancienne* of 1909. Landowska disdained historicism for its own sake and cared little for Dolmetsch's beloved clavichord. 'Authenticity', in her mind, was not a matter of literally re-creating the past but of honouring its spirit. 'I am aware that the disposition of the registers in the harpsichord of Bach's time differed somewhat from those of my Pleyel', she wrote. 'But little do I care if, to attain the proper effect, I use means that were not exactly those available to Bach.'[31] The essence of Landowska's art, as Virgil Thomson once observed, lay in her ability to provide 'a musical experience that clarifies the past by revealing it to us through the present'.[32] Her position was clear and consistent, and while there were many who challenged it on historical or aesthetic grounds, her genius as an artist was beyond dispute.

Landowska's high standards of execution and scholarship brought her into demand far beyond the circumscribed borders of the early music world. She played regularly with major orchestras and soloists, on piano as well as harpsichord. Her stature was confirmed in 1913, when the Berlin Hochschule für Musik invited her to set up its first harpsichord class. Interned in Germany as a resident alien during the First World War, she returned to France in 1919 and threw herself into an arduous regimen of touring and recording. Like Dolmetsch, though, she soon grew tired of the peripatetic life. In 1927 she purchased a villa in the little town of St Leu-la-Forêt, on the outskirts of Paris. There she established the Ecole de Musique Ancienne, where she conducted master classes in interpretation and technique during the summer and winter months. Students arrived from all over the world – not only harpsichordists and pianists, but singers, instrumentalists, conductors and even dancers. St Leu became a meeting-ground for artists, writers, scholars and composers.[33] Surrounded by her priceless collection of books, scores and instruments, Landowska held court, a diminutive but authoritarian figure who expected her word to be taken as gospel. Students quickly learned that, as one of them put it, 'she never explained anything and one could not question her'.[34] Some thrived in this environment, others rebelled against it, but most swore by Landowska's methods. Among her many pupils who went on to distinguished careers were Alice Ehlers, Ruggero Gerlin, Rafael Puyana, Ralph Kirkpatrick, Eta Harich-Schneider, Isabel Nef and the pianist Clifford Curzon.

Each summer from May to July, Landowska presented Sunday afternoon concerts, or *fêtes pastorales*, in a small concert hall she had built behind her villa at St Leu. It was there, in 1933, that she gave the first complete performance of Bach's Goldberg Variations on harpsichord in modern times. There, too, she made many of the recordings that carried her name and the sound of her harpsichord around the world. The reverence that Landowska inspired in almost everyone who crossed her path is reflected in an appreciation that Léon Kochnitzky wrote in 1934. Aptly comparing Landowska to the great actress Eleonora Duse, he described the mesmerizing effect that her inimitable entrance made on the expectant audience:

A long silence. The musician glides in, wearing a house dress of a single colour and without 'frilly ornaments.' She stops in front of the harpsichord. Smiling, she looks around at the friends she knows and at those she does not know, but who are her friends because they have come at her summons . . . . Sometimes she says a few words . . . . Or perhaps she remains silent and allows the harpsichord to seduce us . . . . When one is listening to Wanda (such greatness makes this familiarity permissible), the famous debate over the harpsichord, clavichord and piano seems to have been definitively resolved. The organ itself must give way. The double keyboard of her admirable instrument permits the harpsichordist to create effects of intensity and expression, nuances and *sfumature* that an organist would strive after in vain.

The conversation often lingers on after the concert. The musician meets her pupils and a few of the audience around a snack table that unites for the least noble of the five senses the enchantment of Haydn and the delicacies of the orchard. Perhaps the confitures of plums, red currants and strawberries are immortal: *a joy forever.*[35]

Sensitive and highly strung, Landowska thrived on effusive adulation, but she had mixed feelings about her phenomenal popularity, sensing that many people came to concerts to watch her in action rather than listen to the music. 'The gluttony with which the public rushes to buy tickets to hear the Goldberg Variations saddens and discourages me', she wrote. 'Is it through love for this music? No, they do not know it. They are prompted simply by the base curiosity of seeing a virtuoso fight with the most difficult work ever written for the keyboard.'[36] No doubt many of Landowska's fans failed to appreciate the subtlety of her art and the depth of musical culture which informed even the simplest phrase she played. On the other hand, Landowska's 'star' quality gave an incalculable boost to the revival. Her name became virtually synonymous with the harpsichord and hastened its acceptance as a legitimate concert instrument. That such a large number of women have taken up the harpsichord professionally is due largely, for better or worse, to Landowska's example. 'Many a wealthy girl for whom the career of a concert pianist seemed out of reach, but for whom the purchase of a harpsichord was no problem, started boldly on the harpsichord, trusting in the efficacy of candle light and stylish eighteenth-century attire', Harich-Schneider wrote. 'It goes without saying that these opportunists of a new fashion did not contribute much of their own to the harpsichord renaissance, but just tried – at a respectful distance – to copy Landowska.'[37]

Landowska was the first early music celebrity, the first performer of undisputed international stature the movement had produced. Outside France, she exerted an especially strong influence in Germany, where harpsichord-makers like Neupert and Maendler produced their own versions of the 'Landowska' Pleyel. Harpsichords had been made in Germany since the turn of the century, but they were unabashedly modern in design, like the notorious 'Bach' harpsichord built by Wilhelm Hirl of Berlin. With its kaleidoscopic array of stops and timbres, purportedly modelled on one of Bach's own instruments, Hirl's harpsichord instigated an unfortunate trend. Not until the 1930s did German harpsichord-builders abandon metal frames and return to more historically faithful construction techniques. Maendler devised a harpsichord with a damper pedal and a special action enabling the player to vary the dynamics by touch, while other builders revived the pedal harpsichord, which was equipped with an organ-like pedal keyboard activating an independent set of strings. Such dubious modernizations became standard equipment on German harpsichords and set them apart from contemporary French and English models.

By the end of the nineteenth century, Germany had arguably abandoned its commanding position in the revival and lagged behind both England and France in the performance of early music. The musicologist Hugo Leichtentritt, surveying the activities of the Schola Cantorum, ruefully observed that Germany could muster neither the performing talent nor the public interest to sustain a similar institution.[38] The situation took a turn for the better in 1905 with the founding of the Munich-based Deutsche Vereinigung für alte Musik. Initially comprising five members (one singer and four instrumentalists), the ensemble soon expanded to a small orchestra of old instruments under the baton of Bernhard Stavenhagen. Baroque and early Classical music, predominantly German, formed the backbone of its repertoire. Inevitably, comparisons were drawn with the Casadesus family's Société des Instruments Anciens, which often visited Germany. German critics conceded that the French society was far more polished technically, but the Munich players consistently received higher marks for scholarship. Leichtentritt, for instance, praised the 'painstaking authenticity' of their performances and musical editions. One of his colleagues noted that in contrast to the French musicians, who normally performed in modern concert attire, the Germans wore costumes that 'took the taste of the eighteenth century into account, although the men could not bring themselves to sacrifice their moustaches in the cause of stylistic propriety'.[39]

Christian Döbereiner, co-founder of the Deutsche Vereinigung für alte Musik, was a key figure in Germany's early music movement. Trained as a violinist and cellist, he became so proficient on the gamba that the conductor Felix Mottl invited him to take part in performances of the St Matthew Passion in 1907 and 1908. Thanks to Döbereiner and the harpsichordist Max Seiffert, historical instruments regularly adorned the Bach festivals that proliferated in Germany in the early 1900s under the impetus of the Bach Gesellschaft. After the Munich ensemble disbanded during the First World War, Döbereiner conducted small-scale performances of Bach's orchestral works as well as staged productions of the oratorios. The Staatliche Akademie der Tonkunst in Munich allowed him to set up an experimental course in old instruments and chamber music in 1922.[40] Four years later the German cellist Paul Grümmer established a gamba class at the Cologne Musikhochschule. A long-time member of the Busch Quartet, Grümmer took up the gamba around 1910 and subsequently formed a trio with the harpsichordist Günther Ramin and Reinhardt Wolf on viola d'amore.[41] Döbereiner toured in the twenties and thirties with the violinist Anton Hüber and the harpsichordist Li Stadelman, as well as performing with a Baroque chamber orchestra in Hagen directed by the instrument-maker Hans Hoesch.[42]

Like most of their contemporaries, Döbereiner and Grümmer played the gamba in a modern style that would be considered inauthentic today. Their instruments were hybrid beasts, with cello pegs, modern bows, sharply angled necks and fretless fingerboards. Musical life between the wars offered little basis for comparison, though German musicians might well have gained some insight into historical performance practice by seeking out the

Dolmetsch family's recordings. Döbereiner passed his ideas on to his pupils, one of whom, Willi Schmid, founded the popular Munich Viol Quintet. F. T. Arnold was appalled when he heard them in 1931. 'They did all they could to modernize the music,' the musicologist wrote to Dolmetsch, '&, if one shut one's eyes, one might have been listening to a Schumann quartet, besides wh: they had a number of annoying, characteristically German mannerisms: e.g. on almost every accented note the Gambist gave a little backward jerk of his square closely cropped head that made me long to punch it, & the "leader" was always stretching himself forward (as if he was trying to get out of his clothes – a swallowtail coat & white waistcoat at 4 o'clock in the afternoon!) in a quite unnecessary attempt to "conduct" the others.'[43] It was Grümmer's pupil August Wenzinger who ultimately led the reaction against such unstylish gamba playing in the thirties and forties.[44]

Germany being the birthplace of modern musicology, early music naturally found a home on university campuses. Scholars seized upon the notion of re-creating the Baroque collegium musicum, an informal gathering of amateur and professional musicians who performed chiefly for their own pleasure and instruction. Hugo Riemann started the modern collegium movement at the University of Leipzig in 1908. A group of musicologists and amateurs met weekly to perform Baroque instrumental music under his direction outside class. The concerts were open to the public, although inevitably they drew mainly from the academic community.[45] The idea quickly caught on and spread to other campuses. Riemann's protégé Wilibald Gurlitt assembled a collegium at the University of Freiburg after the war. It gave three concerts in Karlsruhe in 1922, followed two years later by a week-long series in Hamburg.[46] These ambitious programmes, which ranged from early chant and organum to chansons by Dufay and Binchois, were among the first public performances of medieval music in Germany. The performers – all students in Gurlitt's musicology seminar – played modern replicas of viols and a set of recorders made especially for Gurlitt by a leading German organ firm. Soon collegium groups were established at universities throughout the German-speaking world under such eminent musicologists as Werner Danckert, Friedrich Blume, Curt Sachs, Max Schneider and Gustav Becking.

Closely related to the collegium movement was the Organ Revival (*Orgelbewegung*) that came to fruition in Germany in the twenties. Historical organ recitals had become commonplace since Guilmant and Karl Straube published their anthologies of early organ music around the turn of the century, but comparatively little attention had been paid to the instruments themselves. Dolmetsch argued in 1915 that it was 'a revelation to hear Handel's or Bach's music on a well-preserved old organ',[47] but where were such instruments to be found? Those few that had remained in something like their original condition were in constant danger of being renovated and modernized. Dolmetsch helped save the St Gervais organ in Paris from such a fate and rescue efforts led by Schweitzer and others achieved a modicum of success. Schweitzer lobbied zealously for modern builders to emulate the 'old, simple, tone-beautiful' instruments of the early nineteenth century and earlier periods. A survey that he conducted in 1909 for the International Musical Society revealed widespread support for his views. Schweitzer maintained that the mechanical 'defects' of the old organs made it undesirable to copy them in every detail. Instead, he urged organ-makers to strike a balance between historical and modern principles, striving above all to produce instruments of individual character as an alternative to the ubiquitous, mass-produced 'factory' organs.[48] Inasmuch as Schweitzer's ideas were conditioned by his predilection for Bach, the terms 'Bach organ' and 'Baroque organ' were adopted to describe the instruments that he, Straube, Ramin, Helmut Walcha and others increasingly favoured.

Yet the first practical attempt to reproduce the tone quality of the early organs was inspired not by an instrument of Bach's time but by a much older specimen. The Praetorius organ, installed in 1921 at the University of Freiburg, was based on plans taken from Michael Praetorius's seventeenth-century treatise *Syntagma musicum*. But Oscar Walcker, who built the organ at Gurlitt's request, compromised by incorporating an electro-pneumatic action and other modern features. Straube came from Leipzig to play the dedicatory recital — consisting entirely of German Baroque music – in the elegant, wood-panelled hall of the university library. Critics commented on the instrument's 'graphic clarity' and 'simplicity of colouring', so different from the plush, 'orchestral' sound of the Romantic organs.[49] Gurlitt, who had envisaged the Praetorius organ primarily as a teaching tool, was surprised by the excitement it aroused. Over the next two decades, dozens of Baroque organs were installed in Germany, Denmark, Holland, Scandinavia, the United States, England, France and Italy. At the same time, many old organs were misguidedly 'restored' to Baroque specifications, often with deplorable results. The original Praetorius organ was destroyed in an air raid in 1944 and rebuilt after the war, this time with mechanical action and mean-tone tuning. 'For the sake of scientific and artistic fidelity we have renounced every kind of compromise with present-day, neo-baroque organ ideals or arbitrary stylizing', Gurlitt explained.[50] Such a radical declaration chimed perfectly with musicological orthodoxy in 1956; thirty-five years earlier, it would have seemed merely eccentric posturing.

The Organ Revival should be seen against the background of the broad-scale musical reform movement that arose in Germany around the turn of the century. A group of nature enthusiasts calling themselves *Wandervögel* banded together for the purpose of promoting outdoor recreation and fitness. They created a special musical repertoire, consisting mainly of German folksongs accompanied by guitar or lute. A journal entitled *Die Laute* commenced publication in 1917, by which time the *Wandervögel* had been effectively absorbed into what was known as the Youth Movement. Like the Arts and Crafts Movement in England, the Youth Movement was an expression of growing disenchantment with the mechanized uniformity of the industrial age. Its goal was nothing less than the physical and spiritual rejuvenation of the German *Volk*.[51] Fritz Jöde, a prolific arranger of folksongs, and Richard Möller, editor of *Die Laute*, were its musical gurus. As Germans embraced the concept of *Hausmusik* (duly acknowledging their debt to Dolmetsch),[52] the Youth Movement and the early music revival became increasingly intertwined. Möller published articles about early lute music, complete with instructions for reading tablature, and even commissioned a luthier in Hamburg to make copies of gambas, viole d'amore, viole da braccia and other historical instruments.

The early instrument industry in Germany blossomed after the First World War, with dozens of small and medium-sized workshops scattered around the country. The Youth Movement's rediscovery of the gamba and lute opened up a lucrative market. In 1921 Peter Harlan began producing a line of old instruments – including lutes, viols, harpsichords and clavichords – at his workshop in Markneukirchen. Five years later Harlan visited the Haslemere Festival on a German government grant, brought back a set of Dolmetsch recorders and copied them, using a slightly different system of fingering. Although the so-called 'German fingering' was less flexible than the 'English' system (Harlan himself later disavowed it), the recorder was an instant best-seller in Germany and became the virtual trademark of the Youth Movement. Cheap, portable and easy to learn, it was an ideal instrument for amateurs and students alike. Harlan and other makers supplied recorders for schools and for Germany's burgeoning crop of early music societies, while carrying on a brisk export trade with England and other countries on the side.[53]

By the early 1930s the recorder movement had spawned its own journal, *Der Blockflötenspiegel*, published by Hermann Moeck in Celle. German music publishers had not overlooked the public's waxing enthusiasm for early music. The houses of Bärenreiter and Moeck, both established in the mid-twenties, printed quantities of early music and how-to books, in addition to manufacturing and distributing recorders. Bärenreiter's founder, Karl Vötterle, took a keen interest in the Youth Movement and was closely associated with Gurlitt and the Organ Revival.[54] Unlike Moeck, which specialized in recorder music, Bärenreiter threw its resources behind the revival of early choral music; Vötterle himself helped organize amateur choirs and choral festivals throughout Germany. The Singing Movement (*Singbewegung*) was largely responsible for the rediscovery of Schütz in the twenties and thirties, a phenomenon which had as much to do with politics as with music.[55] Schütz festivals sprang up around the country and soon became as familiar as the ubiquitous Bach and Handel celebrations. (The modern revival of Handel's operas on German stages will be discussed in Chapter 7.) The Neue Schütz-Gesellschaft, which Vötterle founded, got off to an unsteady start in 1930 with its first festival in Berlin. Alfred Einstein criticized the amateurish, Romanticized performances, complaining that 'never before have I heard so many wrong notes in two days'. But he praised Pius Kalt's Catholic Choir and Erwin Bodky's stylish playing on 'an excellent Steingräber pedal harpsichord'.[56]

On a professional level, Germany boasted a large assortment of choral ensembles, from Siegfried Ochs's Philharmonic Choir in Berlin to small groups like the Stuttgart Chamber Choir, which specialized in madrigal music. The most widely known German choir of the interwar period was that of the Thomaskirche in Leipzig, where Straube served as cantor from 1918 to 1940. Straube's weekly performances of Bach motets and his international tours with the *Thomaner* did much to shape the twentieth-century conception of Bach. Although Straube conformed to the prevailing Romantic style as a young man, he became interested in historical performance practice in the twenties and pioneered the use of smaller forces in Bach's vocal music.[57] Such chamber-sized performances soon became as common in Germany as in England. Upon hearing the B minor Mass performed in Flensburg by a choir of fifty voices and a twenty-five-piece orchestra in 1933, Hermann Roth predicted that 'the notion of using big masses for the performance of this work will sooner or later be given up by all'.[58]

Outside Germany, France and England, the early music movement followed a more erratic pattern in the first four decades of the century. Thanks to the increasing mobility of performers and scholars, the dissemination of early music in modern editions and coverage of events in scholarly and popular publications, the revival had become a truly international phenomenon. Choral directors like Daniël de Lange in Holland and Mogens Wöldike in Denmark earned enviable reputations as early music specialists. Prague had its 'Skroup' Singing Society, Budapest its Palestrina Chorus, Helsinki its 'Suomen Laulu' Choir and Rome its Società Polifonica Romana, all closely associated with the pre-Classical repertoire. Bach societies were active in Spain, Italy, Belgium, the Netherlands and elsewhere. Early music was promulgated by a variety of amateur, professional and academic organizations such as the Orfeó Catalá in Barcelona, the Society of Old Music Amateurs in Warsaw, the Libera Estetica in Florence and the Society for Netherlands Music History. Historical concerts, long familiar in the major European musical centres, spread to Madrid, Stockholm, Copenhagen, Vienna, Zurich, Oslo and other cities. Reports of concerts and conferences trickled in from such distant points as Bucharest, St Petersburg and Johannesburg.

In Belgium, a growing early music community carried on the work begun by Fétis, Mahillon and Gevaert, although it was not until the 1930s that the Quatuor Belge des Instruments Anciens, led by Landowska's pupil Aimée van de Wiele, began giving concerts on old instruments. Ironically, the most prominent early musician in the country was not a Belgian but a transplanted American. Born in Denver, Safford Cape moved to Brussels in 1925 to study piano and make his name as a composer. Reviewers noted 'the modernity of his language' as well as his fondness for contrapuntal devices gleaned from the pre-Classical repertoire. Cape fell in with a group of scholars and performers interested in early music, among them the musicologist Charles van den Borren, whose daughter he soon married. Van den Borren was only an indifferent pianist, but he was insatiably curious as to how old music sounded. His inquisitiveness must have rubbed off on his son-in-law, for, at the age of twenty-six, Cape abruptly renounced composition and devoted the rest of his life to the performance of early music – specifically, the medieval and early Renaissance repertoire which had been largely passed over by the revival.

'I threw myself headlong into researching the style ... trying to reconstitute, one by one, all the elements that predominated at the formation of rhythm, song and expression', Cape later recalled. 'I tried to grasp its laws from the inside. There was no model from which I could draw inspiration. I was working in the dark, groping, so to speak. The day of the early music ensembles had not yet dawned. For inspiration, I had only the notations of the old masters and the fervent love that I nourished for them.'[59] This does an injustice to Dolmetsch, Bordes, Casadesus, Gurlitt and the rest, although Cape may well have been unaware of their work. But on one score he was certainly right: no one before had made a serious and sustained attempt to perform the music of the thirteenth, fourteenth, fifteenth and early sixteenth centuries in a historical fashion. Generally considered too archaic and arcane for non-specialists to appreciate, this repertoire was relegated to music-ological congresses, university seminars and the occasional festival programme.[60]

Cape was convinced that medieval music, if properly presented, would appeal to more than a handful of initiates. In 1932, he organized a modern string quartet and a small vocal group for a concert of early sacred music broadcast by Belgian radio. The encouraging response prompted him to form a permanent ensemble. The Pro Musica Antiqua made its début at a musicology lecture in early 1933, performing Dufay's *Vergine bella*, the Kyrie from his Mass *Se la face ay pale* and Arnold de Lantins's *Tota pulchra es*. Soon the group's repertoire expanded to embrace Machaut, Binchois, Landini, Busnois, Obrecht, Perotin, Leonin, de la Halle, Compère, troubadour and trouvère lyrics, Pierre de la Rue, Brumel, Isaac, Josquin and much more. Many of the scores they used were edited by Van den Borren, who served as Cape's unofficial musicological adviser.

In June 1935 the Pro Musica Antiqua opened the Exposition Universelle in Brussels with a concert of fifteenth-century Flemish music performed by eight singers and ten instrumentalists playing reproductions of viols, recorders, lutes and other old instruments. Tours to Bruges, Liège, Luxemburg, Holland and France enhanced their reputation. The French critic Robert Brussel was struck by 'the simplicity, conscientiousness and fervour of their interpretations', while the composer Darius Milhaud praised the 'impeccable rightness' of the instrumental playing. Wider exposure came with the recordings the Pro Musica Antiqua made in the thirties for the *Anthologie Sonore* and later for Deutsche Grammophon's Archiv series. Cape's careful but undogmatic scholarship and his talent for compiling interesting programmes enabled him to ply a middle course between musicologists and popularizers. One critic noted that Pro Musica Antiqua audiences were composed not of 'savants' but of 'ordinary listeners',[61] a statement that remained valid through the four decades of the group's existence.

Coincidentally, it was another American expatriate who brought medieval music to the attention of French audiences in the 1930s. A native of Memphis, Tennessee, the musicologist William Devan moved to Paris, changed his name to Guillaume de Van and ran the Bibliothèque Nationale's music department during the Second World War. In 1936 he founded the Paraphonistes de St Jean-des-Matines, which, like Jacques Chailley's contemporaneous Psallette de Notre Dame, specialized in music of the thirteenth to the sixteenth centuries. The Société de Musique d'Autrefois was founded in 1926 by Geneviève Thibault, a scholar of old instruments who had studied with Pirro at the Sorbonne and with Galpin in England. Her ensemble presented two wide-ranging programmes a year, one sacred and one secular, whenever possible using instruments from her personal collection. The women performers (the society was almost exclusively female) wore pink party dresses and most of their concerts were very long. Activity was suspended in 1932, when Thibault departed for the Far East with her husband. Upon returning to Paris in 1955, she took charge of the Conservatoire's instrument museum and resuscitated the society, many of whose alumni went on to notable careers in the early music field.[62]

One of Thibault's goals, never achieved, was to 'create a permanent school permitting selected interested artists to learn and perfect the technique of old instruments'.[63] Thibault's studies with Landowska and Nadia Boulanger had instilled in her a respect for practical scholarship. Boulanger – with d'Indy, the most influential composition teacher in France in the twenties – was as likely to have a Palestrina motet on her piano as a score by Stravinsky. Her love of early music bore fruit in several outstanding recordings of Monteverdi and Rameau. Boulanger owned a clavichord but shied away from historical instruments as a rule: she used a piano on her famous 1937 recording of the Monteverdi madrigals. (Asked why she had not played the continuo on a harpsichord, Boulanger candidly replied, 'Because it did not occur to me.'[64]) Boulanger and d'Indy believed that early music was an essential part of a well-rounded musician's education, but neither was interested in historical performance practice per se. Students came to learn how music was put together, not how it might have sounded centuries before.

Indeed, apart from Landowska's Ecole de Musique Ancienne – which, in any case, was less a school than a series of master classes – no conservatory gave pre-Classical music more than a token berth in its curriculum. The Schola Cantorum, aspiring to provide an alternative to traditional conservatory training, had long since outgrown its narrow plainchant-cum-Palestrina origins. Dolmetsch had an excellent reputation, but, apart from the apprentices in his workshop, few full-time students came to Haslemere. Most collegium groups were designed to be demonstration laboratories for musicologists, not training grounds for professional performers. Early music in the 1930s was rapidly becoming a specialized field. There was an urgent need for a school that would allow students to investigate the pre-Classical repertoire from all angles – practical, historical and theoretical.

It was this need that August Wenzinger and Paul Sacher hoped to fill when they founded the Schola Cantorum Basiliensis in 1933. Basle, the home of the new academy, had a long tradition of early music performances. Moritz Heyne, a curator at the city's musical instrument museum, gave concerts on instruments from the collection in the late nineteenth century, and his successor, Karl Nef, launched Wenzinger's career by inviting him to demonstrate the gamba for a musicology seminar in 1924. Wenzinger later joined the recorder player Gustav Scheck, an early exponent of the Baroque flute, and the harpsichordist Fritz Neumeyer in a highly acclaimed chamber ensemble. Contemporary music was Sacher's field, but he had studied with Nef and conducted a fair amount of early music with his Basle Chamber

Orchestra. It was his idea to start a 'teaching and research institute for early music', a concept so novel that the musical press outside Switzerland and Germany at first virtually ignored it. However, readers of the *Revue musicale* were alerted to the Schola's existence in a report from Basle in 1934. 'It is the only institution in Europe', wrote the French composer Raymond Petit, 'dedicated exclusively and in a very general way to the study and practice (also from the point of view of early instruments) of early music from the Middle Ages to Mozart and embracing instrumental music as well as vocal, religious as well as secular ... This Schola seems to me to correspond to a pressing need of the hour.'[65]

The Schola's prospectus proclaimed the founders' intention 'to establish a lively interaction between musicology and performance'.[66] This fragile balance was reflected in the composition of the faculty, which included scholars like Nef and Arnold Geering as well as performers like Wenzinger and the tenor Max Meili. From the outset, though, the performers indisputably had the upper hand. Everything at the Schola was – and still is – geared toward the practical goal of fostering 'the revival of early works in the spirit of their time'. The Schola was conceived as a kind of half-way house between the ivory tower of the university and the seminarian atmosphere of the conservatory. Its curriculum owed much to the populist philosophy of the Youth Movement. Sacher and Wenzinger shared a conviction that early music should not be an élitist pursuit, open only to a guild of professionals, but part and parcel of everyday life. Yet they were equally determined to root out 'dilettantism' and inculcate their students with a more professional attitude. Landowska, naturally enough, was singled out as the paradigm of the well-rounded performer–scholar the Schola hoped to produce.

'The Schola Cantorum is no stable for scrawny philologist–hacks and pedants who horse around with manuscripts', wrote Heinrich Strobel in the *Berliner Tagblatt*. Performance was the Schola's *raison-d'être* and it did not take long for critics to notice the difference between what they heard there

SCHOLA CANTORUM BASILIENSIS
LEHR- U. FORSCHUNGSINSTITUT FÜR ALTE MUSIK / DIREKTION PAUL SACHER

Fig. 2 *Programme for three concerts given by the Schola Cantorum in June 1934*

and the run-of-the-mill early music concert. 'No one will come away from such a performance thinking that this is lifeless scholarship', Strobel commented in a review of a concert by Schola faculty in 1935. Close ties with the nearby instrument museum and the University of Basle gave Schola students access to a wide range of resources, and through the years the school's directors have seen to it that most of the leading figures in the early music field came to Basle for short or long stays. Unlike its French namesake, the Schola Cantorum Basiliensis placed no particular emphasis on choral or religious music, although both have been adequately represented on its programmes over the years. The new prominence accorded in its curriculum to instrumental repertoire and techniques reflected the changing priorities of the early music movement as it grew away from its roots in the nineteenth-century choral revival.

Swiss neutrality enabled the Schola to continue operating with some semblance of normalcy during the Second World War. Almost everywhere else, however, the political, economic and social cataclysms of the thirties and forties had a profound impact on the revival. In Germany, the collectivist and nationalistic mentality of the Youth and Singing Movements played into the hands of the fascists, who twisted the innocent idealism of the movements' leaders to their own propagandistic ends. Schütz and, to a lesser degree, Bach were transformed into emblems of German cultural supremacy. Handel's oratorios and operas were performed in 'Aryanized' versions sanctioned by the authorities. Popular marches like the 'Horst Wessel-Lied' were arranged for the Hitler Youth to play on recorders, and scholars wrote learned articles about the importance of music – the right kind, of course – in the formation of children's character. The Nazis' co-opting of the early music revival became ominously clear at the 1936 Olympic Games in Munich, when thousands of youthful gymnasts performed to music by Carl Orff featuring a large ensemble of recorders and percussion instruments.[67]

As the thirties drew to a close, it became apparent that early music was undergoing a changing of the guard. The Casadesus family's durable Société des Instruments Anciens finally disbanded in 1939. Dolmetsch died the following year and the Haslemere workshop was converted into a factory producing aeroplane parts for the duration of the war. Cape remained in Belgium but kept a low profile, working for the Resistance and copying out manuscripts in libraries. One by one, dozens of European performers and musicologists associated with the revival lost their posts and emigrated, many of them to the United States. Landowska arrived in New York as a refugee on Pearl Harbor Day in 1941. By the time Europe picked itself up again five years later, France and Germany had taken a back seat to the new early music centres emerging on both sides of the Atlantic.

1 (TOP) The soprano aria 'Aus Liebe will mein Heiland sterben', showing the markings that Mendelssohn pencilled in his copy of Bach's St Matthew Passion.   2 (ABOVE) A. F. J. Thibaut's amateur choir in Heidelberg sang music by Marcello, Handel and Palestrina in the early 1800s.

3 (ABOVE) *The Victorians preferred Baroque music on a grand scale, as in this engraving of the 1859 Handel Festival at London's Crystal Palace.* 4 (LEFT) *The brilliant and eccentric Arnold Dolmetsch, shown here with his family consort at Haslemere, founded the modern historical performance movement. The Elizabethan costumes were a Dolmetsch hallmark.* 5 (BELOW LEFT) *The English Singers revived the practice of performing madrigals around a table. This photograph was taken in 1925, shortly after the group made the first of its many recordings.*

6 (OPPOSITE TOP) *A Romanticized conception of Baroque stagecraft was seen in this 1908 production of Rameau's* Dardanus *in Dijon.* 7 (OPPOSITE CENTRE) *The Pro Musica Antiqua of Brussels, directed by the American Safford Cape, dispensed with costumes in its pioneering performances of medieval and Renaissance music beginning in the 1930s.* 8 (OPPOSITE BOTTOM) *The Chanteurs de St Gervais, shown here on a visit to Fontainebleau in 1904, won renown for their performances of Renaissance and Baroque music under the direction of Charles Bordes.*

9 (LEFT) Nadia Boulanger played a key role in the revival, as both teacher and performer.

10 (RIGHT) Francis Poulenc wrote his Concert champêtre for Wanda Landowska after visiting the harpsichordist at St Leu-la-Forêt in 1926. 11 (BELOW) The Casadesus family's Société des Instruments Anciens, led by the 'sympathetic rascal' Henri (far right), specialized in minor Baroque composers.

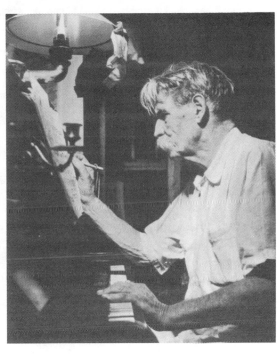

12　The spurious 'Bach' bow, nearly semi-circular in outline, was taken up after the Second World War by the Danish violinist Emil Telmányi.

13　Albert Schweitzer, a noted editor and interpreter of Bach's organ music, led the return to Baroque ideals of organ design.

14　A founding member of the Deutsche Vereinigung für alte Musik, the gambist Christian Döbereiner remained active into the 1950s.

15　Bravura temperament and technique made the English harpsichordist Violet Gordon Woodhouse a close rival to Landowska.

16   Edward J. Dent was one of many British
musicologists who took a practical interest in the revival.

17   Rev. Edmund H. Fellowes was largely responsible
for resuscitating the English madrigal repertoire in the
1920s and 1930s.

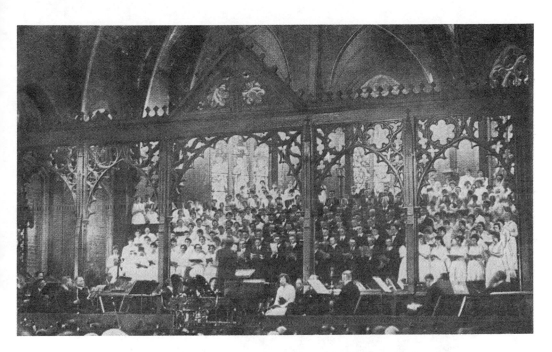

18 (ABOVE) *Bach's B minor
Mass at Bethlehem,
Pennsylvania, in 1917. A
visiting critic noted that everyone
he met in the town, from the
hotel porter to the trolly car
conductor, pronounced Bach's
name correctly.* 19 (RIGHT)
*Like the Casadesus ensemble, the
American Society of Ancient
Instruments was very much a
family affair and cultivated a
lush, Romantic style of playing.*

20 (RIGHT) *Paul Hindemith
(far right) wore several hats in
the revival as conductor,
instrumentalist, teacher and
composer. The Yale University
Collegium Musicum, which he
directed from 1940 to 1953,
produced many of America's
leading early musicians.*

21 *The New York Pro Musica's production of the medieval* Play of Daniel *in 1958 sparked renewed interest in pre-Baroque music. Noah Greenberg's flair for colourful instrumentation and scenic investiture set the group apart from more conservative ensembles like the Pro Musica Antiqua of Brussels.*

4

'BACK TO BACH'

*Modern Composers Rediscover Early Music · Stravinsky, Hindemith, Busoni
and Others · Neoclassicism, For and Against · Neue Sachlichkeit and
Anti-Romantic Tendencies · New Music for Historical Instruments ·
Forgeries, Pastiches and Misattributions · The 'Harpsichordized'
Piano, 'Bach' Bow and Other Spuriosities · Stokowski's Bach
Transcriptions · Toscanini and the New Puritanism.*

'KREISLER REVEALS "CLASSICS" AS OWN; FOOLED MUSIC CRITICS FOR 30 YEARS.'

THE FRONT-PAGE HEADLINE in the *New York Times* on 8 February 1935 rang
down the curtain on one of the longest-running musical hoaxes in
history. Years before most of his fellow violinists had rediscovered the pre-
Classical repertoire, Fritz Kreisler had been in the habit of featuring a group
of short pieces by seventeenth- and eighteenth-century composers on his
recitals. Critics and even a few scholars duly applauded his modest
contribution to the early music revival. Little did they suspect that more than
a dozen of the pieces by sundry 'old masters' that Kreisler had popularized
over the years had been penned by the great violinist himself.

Why did Kreisler dissemble? He explained, unapologetically, that he had
needed pieces to fill out his recitals as a young man and adopted various
pseudonyms because he considered it 'impudent and tactless to repeat my
name endlessly on the programmes'.[1] Certainly he made only a half-hearted
attempt to mask his fraudulent identities and readily pleaded guilty when
Olin Downes of the *Times* accidentally stumbled onto the secret. (Several of
Kreisler's musician friends had apparently been in on it for years.) But
Kreisler was not above having a bit of fun at the expense of the experts, and he
obviously relished thumbing his nose at the 'snobs . . . who judge merely by
name and who draw upon musicians' lexicons for their enthusiasm for us'.

Perhaps the most telling aspect of the Kreisler affair was that it was deemed
newsworthy at all. When Fétis practised what Weckerlin indulgently called
his 'innocent deceptions' almost a century earlier,[2] no great hue and cry was
raised in the musical world, let alone the popular press. Nor was Berlioz
censured for facetiously passing off the Shepherd's Chorus in *L'Enfance du*

73

Christ as the work of a fictitious seventeenth-century composer. (One had to be 'as ignorant as a fish', Berlioz said, to believe the date he assigned to the piece.)[3] Kreisler, like Berlioz, was both amused and aghast to find his bogus compositions accepted at face value by people who should have known better, especially in view of his frank admission that he had 'made no endeavor to stick closely to the style of the period to which they were alleged to date'.[4] While most critics took Kreisler's prank in good part, Ernest Newman indignantly attacked the violinist's behaviour as unethical and likely to discredit *bona fide* arrangements of old music. The virulence of Newman's accusations caught Kreisler by surprise. On the contrary, he retorted, he had done the musical world a service, for 'who ever had heard a work by Pugnani, Cartier, Francoeur, Porpora, Louis Couperin, Padre Martini or Stamitz before I began to compose in their names? They lived exclusively as paragraphs in musical reference books, and their work, when existing and authenticated, lay mouldering in monasteries and old libraries.'[5]

Henri and Marius Casadesus could scarcely enter the same plea in their defence. So cleverly did they mimic Handel, Mozart, C. P. E. Bach and other well-known composers that their counterfeits went undetected (or at least were not conclusively exposed) for decades. Saint-Saëns reacted incredulously to rumours that the repertoire of the Société des Instruments Anciens Casadesus consisted largely of ersatz classics. 'I replied', he assured Henri in 1907, 'that in that case you would have to have been composing before you were born, and that no matter who wrote this music, it is a flawless specimen of seventeenth- and eighteenth-century composition.' Henri's most successful forgery was the 'Handel' Viola Concerto; Marius's was the *Adelaide* Concerto, long attributed to Mozart. Musicians were loath to believe that such a charming and plausibly Mozartean work was a fake, even though the musicologist Alfred Einstein had seen through it immediately, calling the concerto 'a piece of musical mystification à la Kreisler'.[6] Not until Marius went to court years later to assert his legal rights as author of the *Adelaide* was the mystery finally cleared up.

The market for such 'spuriosities', whether created for profit or merely for the pleasure of hoodwinking the experts, kept pace with the public's ever-growing demand for early music. In his autobiography, Thomas Beecham tells of reviving Fletcher's *Faithful Shepherdess* in London in 1923. The conductor mischievously hired a young Italian composer 'who had a pretty knack of writing in some of the old styles' to compose new songs for the play, 'which we ascribed to fictitious composers and which were hailed by the cognoscenti as authentic period pieces'.[7] Then there were the professional forgers like Tobia Nicotra, who earned a footnote in the history of the early music revival with his convincingly executed 'autographs' of Palestrina,

Handel, Gluck, Mozart and others. Nicotra sowed further confusion by publishing two undistinguished pieces under Pergolesi's name. Pergolesi was an easy target for counterfeiters, as his music remained popular throughout the eighteenth and nineteenth centuries. It has taken scholars decades to sort out the hundreds of fakes and misattributions in the Pergolesi canon.[8] Fascinating though it is, this musicological imbroglio would have only marginal relevance to our story had not Igor Stravinsky innocently wandered into it when he borrowed some of Pergolesi's music for his ballet *Pulcinella*.

For Stravinsky's purposes, of course, it mattered little that only about half of the eighteen pieces he appropriated for his score were genuine Pergolesi. The rhythmic and formal characteristics that drew him to Baroque music were precisely the elements that made it, in Newman's words, 'as easy to imitate as the average political speech today'.[9] When Serge Diaghilev suggested he write a Pergolesi ballet for the Ballets Russes in 1919, Stravinsky's initial reaction was lukewarm. He held the Italian Baroque composers in low esteem and knew little of Pergolesi's music. (Later he let it be known that *Pulcinella* was the only 'Pergolesi' he had ever really liked.) In the event, however, Stravinsky came to consider the ballet a pivotal work in his career. '*Pulcinella* was my discovery of the past,' he told Robert Craft, 'the epiphany through which the whole of my late work became possible.'[10] Stravinsky's discovery had far-reaching consequences, for *Pulcinella* ushered in the era of Neoclassicism, the creative recycling of old forms and compositional techniques that was to become one of the dominant musical forces of the mid-twentieth century.

Diaghilev's happy suggestion was occasioned by the recent success of Vincenzo Tommasini's *Good-Humoured Ladies*, the precursor of a seemingly endless supply of ballets in the interwar years modelled on Scarlatti, Handel, Couperin and other Baroque composers. Unlike the vast majority of these works, however, *Pulcinella* was neither a simple pastiche nor a straight-forward arrangement; Stravinsky ever so subtly transformed what he took to be Pergolesi's music by infusing it with his own harmonic and rhythmic style.

I knew [the composer wrote] that I could not produce a 'forgery' of Pergolesi because my motor habits are so different; at best, I could repeat him in my own accent. That the result was to some extent a satire was probably inevitable – who could have treated *that* material in 1919 without satire? – but even this observation is hindsight; I did not set out to compose a satire and, of course, Diaghilev hadn't even considered the possibility of such a thing. A stylish orchestration was what Diaghilev wanted, and nothing more, and my music so shocked him that he went about for a long time with a look that suggested The Offended Eighteenth Century. In fact, however, the remarkable thing about *Pulcinella* is not how much but how little has been added or changed.[11]

The eighteenth century's musical language, with its formal symmetries and clear-cut harmonic planes, needed little alteration to suit Stravinsky's requirements. Whereas the nineteenth-century composers had looked to the Renaissance and Baroque masters for spiritual sustenance, Stravinsky and his contemporaries resurrected the eighteenth century as a specific antidote to Romanticism and all that it connoted. Clarity, balance, objectivity and economy were their watchwords; 'back to Bach' was their slogan. (Had it not been for Bach's special mystique, Mozart, Couperin, Scarlatti or Handel would have served their purpose equally well.) This was not, of course, to be taken literally, although a few composers, like the Palestrina sound-alike Don Lorenzo Perosi, did seem eager to turn back the clock. At best, Neoclassicism was not a recipe for shallow historicism or slavish imitation; it prescribed a deeper affinity for the music of the past. Stravinsky explained that he 'attempted to build a new music on eighteenth-century classicism using the constructive principles of that classicism'.[12]

Later in life, Stravinsky was to become a keen student of early music, in part through his contacts with specialist performers like Safford Cape and Noah Greenberg.[13] But his espousal of Neoclassicism in the 1920s had nothing to do with the historical performance movement of the day. It was dictated, instead, by his own artistic imperatives, which had themselves been shaped by forces long at work in the musical world. It was Ferruccio Busoni who coined the term *Junge Klassizität* (Young Classicism), which he defined as 'the mastery, the sifting and turning to account of all the gains of previous experiments and their inclusion in strong and beautiful forms'.[14] The *Fantasia contrappuntistica*, Busoni's answer to Bach's *Art of the Fugue*, expressed his desire to write music that would be 'old and new at the same time'. (Busoni described this densely contrapuntal work as 'something between César Franck and the *Hammerklavier* Sonata, but with an individual nuance'.)[15] His arrangements and transcriptions of Bach's keyboard works, running to eight volumes, are crammed with suggestions for phrasing, interpretation and even cuts. Busoni was a Romantic to the tips of his fingers. When he played the first prelude of Bach's 'Forty-Eight', Edward J. Dent recalled, 'it became a wash of shifting colours, a rainbow over the fountains of the Villa d'Este; he played the fugue, and each voice sang out above the rest like the entries of an Italian chorus until at the last *stretto* the subject entered like the trumpets of the *Dona nobis* in the Mass in B minor, though in the middle of the keyboard, across a haze of pedal-held sound that was not confusion but blinding clearness.'[16]

A pianist capable of giving that sort of performance does not, on the face of it, seem likely to sympathize with the spreading fashion for performing Bach on the harpsichord. Yet on an American concert tour in 1910, Busoni sought out Dolmetsch in Cambridge, purchased one of his instruments and shipped it back home to Berlin. The harpsichord subsequently made a brief appearance in his opera *Die Brautwahl* and left a mark on his Third Sonatina of 1915, which, despite its decidedly pianistic character, is designated *pro clavicembalo composita* (composed for harpsichord). Busoni's open-mindedness in this regard contrasts with the attitude of his fellow Bach-worshipper Max Reger, who had no use whatsoever for the harpsichord. In 1903 Reger and Karl Straube added a third voice to Bach's Two-Part Inventions and published them as organ exercises, thus incurring the opprobrium of several prominent musicologists. Reger, however, had no patience for the detached, analytical methods of the historicists. Bach, he declared, 'was a man of flesh and blood, full of vitality and strength, and no cold formalist.'[17]

It was, however, precisely the formal elements in Baroque music that appealed to Stravinsky, and this emphasis on structure set the Neoclassicism of the twenties apart from earlier efforts to hybridize the musical past and present. Arnold Schoenberg chided Stravinsky for 'wearing a wig just like Papa Bach' in works like *Pulcinella*, the Duo Concertante and the Dumbarton Oaks Concerto.[18] Schoenberg himself had used eighteenth-century dance forms in his Piano Suite op. 25 and other works, but the often flippant eclecticism of the Neoclassicists was alien to his nature. 'Classical perfection. ... To question it is not right. ... That is the latest style', the chorus sings in his 1925 cantata *Der Neue Klassizismus*, a satirical jab at Stravinsky and his followers. Curiously enough, Schoenberg seems to have borrowed a page from Stravinsky's book in his Cello Concerto of 1932, a whimsical stylistic hotch-potch based on a harpsichord concerto by the Austrian Baroque composer Matthias Georg Monn. In a letter to the cellist Pablo Casals, Schoenberg explained that he had been

> mainly intent on removing the defects of the Handelian style (prevailing in the original work). Just as Mozart did with Handel's *Messiah*, I have got rid of whole handfuls of sequences ..., replacing them with real *substance*. ... I think I've succeeded in making the whole thing approximate, say, to Handel's style. In harmony I have sometimes gone a little (and sometimes rather more) beyond the limits of that style. But nowhere does it go much further than Brahms, anyway there are no dissonances other than those understood by the older theory of harmony; and: it is nowhere atonal.[19]

Stravinsky, somewhat idiosyncratically, recognized three branches of Neoclassicism: his own and that of his imitators ('noted for their rhythms, their *ostinatos*, their "dissonances", and for their final C-major chords with B natural or A in them'); Schoenberg's ('obsessed by an artificial need to abnegate any suggestion of triadic "tonality" '); and the Hindemith school (characterized by 'its interminable 9/8 movements, its endless fourths, and its fugues with subjects at least thirty-two bars long').[20] Paul Hindemith was the golden boy of German music in the twenties, the composer who most unequivocally upheld the virtues of the *Neue Sachlichkeit* (New Objectivity) and the break with pre-war Romanticism. Unlike Schoenberg and Stravinsky, he maintained close ties with the early music world and performed regularly on his viola d'amore, for which he wrote a sonata in 1922. A friend of Fritz Jöde, Hindemith worked enthusiastically on behalf of Germany's Youth Movement, which he viewed as a potentially powerful force for revitalizing contemporary music. 'Out of the rebirth of ancient polyphony has grown an increasingly strong connection between this movement and the creative powers of our time', he and Jöde declared in a joint manifesto. 'These two tendencies are now confluent. Leading composers are purposely and affirmatively busying themselves with music for youth, since here a rich soil has been prepared by systematic education, an attitude which, nourished on old music, has sought to assimilate the music of the present.'[21]

Works like the song cycle *Das Marienleben* and the Kammermusik series attest to Hindemith's deepening involvement with pre-Classical music. But his concept of *Gebrauchsmusik* (functional music) led him down a different path from that of Stravinsky and Schoenberg in the late twenties and early thirties. His *Sing- und Spielmusik* (music to sing and play) was aimed at the same amateur market that Dolmetsch was trying to tap with his instruments. For a youth festival at Plön in 1932, Hindemith wrote a slight but attractive Trio for recorders, hoping to wean the Youth Movement from its unvarying diet of Renaissance polyphony and folksongs. Although he soon broke free of the limitations of *Gebrauchsmusik*, Hindemith continued to mine the riches of the pre-Classical era in such works as his opera *Mathis der Maler*, the ballet *Nobilissima Visione* and the monumental *Ludus Tonalis* for piano.

One of the Neoclassicists' hallmarks was their fondness for fugues, passacaglias, partitas, concerti grossi, canons and other characteristically Baroque musical forms. Carl Engel argued in 1928 that 'the smaller form is always the favorite during an interregnum' because 'it lends itself better to tentative methods'.[22] The fashionable miniaturism of the twenties and thirties, foreshadowed in isolated works like Prokofiev's *Classical Symphony* and Satie's *Sonatine bureaucratique*, illustrated what Engel termed 'a recoiling from complexity into simplicity', a revolt against 'the endless music-dramas and long-winded symphonies' of the Romantics. As musicologists were quick to point out, the Neoclassicists' fondness for titles like sonata, chaconne and concerto grosso did not in itself betoken a return to what Stravinsky called the 'constructive principles' of the Classical or Baroque styles.[23] But Alfredo Casella predicted that the revival of these time-honoured forms would eventually lead to the true synthesis of new and old that the Neoclassicists professed to desire. Stravinsky, who viewed tradition as 'a living force that animates and informs the present', showed how such a synthesis might be achieved. Other composers, cast adrift in the shifting currents of early-twentieth-century music, took heart from his example. 'If we mount toward the sources of antique musical art we shall be able to project ourselves with greater strength into the future, avoiding the abyss of the chaotic present', Gian Francesco Malipiero wrote in 1932.[24]

Paul Dukas had used similar words forty years earlier when he wrote that the time had come 'when music, so as not to lose itself in sterile repetition, must seriously retrace its steps and go back towards the springs from which it burst spontaneously'.[25] The Neoclassical spirit is already astir at the turn of the century in Dukas's Variations, interlude et final sur un thème de Rameau, Debussy's Hommage à Rameau and Ravel's Menuet antique, Pavane pour une infante défunte and Sonatine for piano. In his elegiac Tombeau de Couperin, Ravel drew upon not only eighteenth-century dance forms like the forlane and rigaudon, but a still older tradition of musical epitaphs. (One recalls Pierre Lalo's acid remark: 'It's nice, but how much nicer would be Le Tombeau de Maurice Ravel by Couperin.'[26]) In 1919, the year the Tombeau was first performed, Georges Jean-Aubry called attention to the bond between the modern and Classical French schools: 'The avoidance of all that is redundant; knowledge without the desire to display it; a horror of pedantry; a taste for pleasantry and for wit; these are the features that may be found as clearly and as constantly in the pieces of Couperin, Dandrieu, or Daquin as in those of Ravel, Roussel, or Séverac.'[27]

Essentially a reaffirmation of traditional Gallic virtues, fortified by a strong admixture of nationalistic fervour, Neoclassicism quickly took root in the France of d'Indy, Boulanger, Landowska and the anti-Romantic composers known as 'Les Six'. One of Poulenc's earliest Neoclassical works was the Concert champêtre, which he wrote for Landowska after visiting St Leu in 1926. For all its unmistakable modernisms – shifting metres, 'wrong-note' harmonies and so forth – the concerto's sound world is very much that of the eighteenth-century style galant. Richly embellished with grace notes, rolled chords and flourishes in the Baroque style, the harpsichord solo enmeshes the orchestra in what Landowska called a 'quivering and scintillating sonorous web'. Poulenc's music is nostalgic but not reactionary; like

Pulcinella, the *Concert champêtre* evokes the past in a modern accent. Henri Hell rightly called it 'a homage, and not a pastiche.' Although Poulenc authorized performances on the piano, it is the harpsichord's brittleness that gives the music its zesty, pins-and-needles sharpness. 'Baroque style and the surprises of modern harmony are volatilized in the sounds of the harpsichord' was another critic's apt comment.[28]

The harpsichord, intrinsically suited to counterpoint and sharply-etched rhythms, was the Neoclassical instrument *par excellence*. Earlier composers had begun to show an interest – Debussy, for instance, was planning a sonata for harpsichord, oboe and horn when he died – but its popularity really soared in the twenties. Falla used a harpsichord in his puppet opera *El Retablo de Maese Pedro* in 1923 and repaid Landowska for her services with his Concerto for harpsichord, flute, oboe, clarinet, violin and cello. (Landowska seldom played it: the harmonic astringencies of the Spaniard apparently pleased her less than Poulenc's wistful pastoralism.) The list of composers who enriched the harpsichord repertoire in the ensuing years – Ernst Krenek, Carl Orff, Rudolf Moser, Bohuslav Martinů, Wolfgang Fortner, Darius Milhaud, Hugo Distler, Lou Harrison, Vittorio Rieti and Florent Schmitt, to name just a few – attests to its widespread appeal. The less talented composers opted for what one critic called 'a kind of cute novelty that reduces the instrument of Frescobaldi and Couperin to a species of musical costume jewelry';[29] others, presumably more familiar with the piano, wrote into their music crescendos and other effects that are not available on the harpsichord. But the finest works of that period – such as the Falla Concerto, Frank Martin's dour *Petite symphonie concertante* and Walter Piston's jazzy Sonata for violin and harpsichord – use the instrument in ways that are at once idiomatic and innovative.

At a time when composers were busily experimenting with novel sonorities and textures, the fresh and evocative sounds of old instruments were eagerly welcomed as an extension of the traditional tonal palette. The recorder, with its chaste, uncomplicated timbre redolent of a simpler age, enjoyed a revival almost as robust as the harpsichord's. It spread from England, where Robin Milford first used it in his oratorio *A Prophet in the Land* in 1930, to the Germany of Hindemith and other members of the amateur-oriented *Hausmusik* school. Initially, neo-Baroque confections were the order of the day; not for some time did composers begin casting recorder music in a more modern mould. Meanwhile, other early instruments were making comebacks on a smaller scale. The dulcet-toned clavichord sang again in the music of Ernst Pepping and Herbert Howells, whose *Lambert's Clavichord* was described by Christopher Palmer as 'the work of a Tudor composer whose musical . . . language happens to be that of the twentieth, not the sixteenth century.'[30] The Finn Yryö Kilpinen composed a suite for gamba and piano in 1939. Even the lute underwent a renaissance of sorts, principally at the hands of the German composer Johann Nepomuk David. Ezra Pound's assertion that 'few contemporary composers have given more to today's music than has Arnold Dolmetsch' proved true in more ways than the poet could have foreseen when he made it in 1917.[31]

Not all historical instruments owed their new lease on life to Dolmetsch, however. A small band of enthusiasts had championed the viola d'amore throughout the nineteenth century, and Meyerbeer, Charpentier, Massenet, Puccini and Janáček used it as an orchestral seasoning in their operas. *La Mort de Tintagiles*, a ripe, impressionistic work written in 1900 by the Alsatian–American composer Charles Loeffler, features a long solo for the viola d'amore; though seldom heard today, it remained in the repertoire of performers like Henri Casadesus for many years. Richard Strauss exploited the instrument's soft, shimmering sound in his *Sinfonia domestica*, as did Prokofiev in his second *Romeo and Juliet* Suite (where it is marked 'ad libitum' and consequently seldom heard). Only gradually did the viola d'amore re-emerge as a solo instrument in works like the Hindemith Sonata and Kammermusik no. 6, Frank Martin's *Sonata* da chiesa (where it is combined with organ) and Mátyás Seiber's Four Medieval French Songs (with soprano, viola da gamba and guitar).

Many composers used early instruments to impart an archaic or exotic flavour to opera scores. In his unfinished epic *Nerone*, Arrigo Boito called forth the grandeur of ancient Rome with a vast orchestra that included six lutes and antique Roman trumpets. Riccardo Zandonai used a lute and viola pomposa to conjure a medieval atmosphere in *Francesca da Rimini*. The silvery timbre of the viola d'amore is among the special effects that Hans Pfitzner used in *Palestrina* 'to bring the sixteenth century nearer to the listener'.[32] Even Strauss contemplated using a harpsichord in the divertissement that he and Hugo von Hofmannsthal wrote to accompany a performance of Molière's *Le Bourgeois Gentilhomme* in 1912. Ultimately Strauss used a piano instead, but his appetite for historical allusion was not sated. In the various transformations of *Ariadne* – first into the opera *Ariadne auf Naxos*, then into incidental music for the Molière play, later still into an orchestral suite – more and more of Lully's original music for *Le Bourgeois Gentilhomme* made its way into Strauss's score. *Ariadne*, like the Mozartean *Rosenkavalier* of 1911, was a harbinger of the Neoclassicism that flourished after the war. Strauss was caught up in the movement to the extent that he orchestrated a set of harpsichord pieces by Couperin as a ballet and quoted from Rameau and Gluck in his last opera, *Capriccio*, from which he extracted a harpsichord suite in 1944.[33]

By this time Neoclassicism was firmly ensconced on the modern operatic stage, as composers revived the concept of the old-fashioned 'number opera', with its self-contained arias and ensembles, in contrast to the through-composed works of the Wagnerians. The Italians, led by Busoni, drew upon the Florentine monodists, Monteverdi and the liturgical *laude* of the Middle Ages, not only for the music but also – in works like Pizzetti's *Rappresentazione di Abram e d'Isaac*, Malipiero's *San Francesco d'Assisi* and Casella's *Favola d'Orfeo* – for the subject matter of their operas. The Germans naturally looked to Handel and Mozart, as did Stravinsky in his opera–oratorio *Oedipus Rex* and *The Rake's Progress*, the crowning work of his Neoclassical period. Stravinsky shared with Carl Orff the vision of a non-naturalistic, epic music theatre which had much in common with Baroque opera. Taking his cue from Monteverdi, Orff sought to make his musical language forceful and direct, pruning away all that was dramatically superfluous and highlighting the words in sharp relief. Whether Orff's bare-bones monophony and obsessive primitivism fall under the Neoclassical rubric is debatable – Stravinsky, never one to mince words, dubbed him a 'neo-Neanderthal'[34] – but *Carmina Burana*, *Die Kluge* and *Der Mond* undeniably partook of the anti-Romanticism that swept across Europe and America in the wake of the First World War.

The Organ Revival and the rediscovery of Schütz had a strong influence on the musical outlook of many of Orff's compatriots. Hindemith's teacher, Arnold Mendelssohn, set an example by openly emulating Schütz in his unaccompanied choral music, heeding the dictum enunciated by Brahms's friend Heinrich Freiherr von Herzogenberg: 'An age that has so successfully understood Heinrich Schütz and has experienced at first hand the expressive intensity of a Brahms can no longer content itself with Philistine hypocrisy; it can and must bring forth from its bosom works that in seriousness and magnitude of expression reflect the great figures of the past.'[35] Heinrich Kaminski imitated Baroque 'terraced dynamics' in an organ toccata in 1923, while composers like David, Pepping, Distler and Fortner – protégés of the indefatigable Straube – wrote choral music of a markedly archaic character. Bach-like chorale settings proliferated in the thirties, along with cantatas, histories, passions and organ music variously indebted to Germany's Protestant heritage. A sense of spiritual inwardness, a turning away from the turbulence of the outside world, suffuses many of these works. Distler's *Geistliche Chormusik* (1934–41) and David's Symphonic Variations on a Theme of Schütz (1942), to choose two of the better-known, movingly attest to the composers' withdrawal into the cocoon of the past.

Like Straube, Richard Terry served as midwife to British composers, whose offspring often bore the stamp of his conservative musical taste.

Howells's Mass in the Dorian Mode and Vaughan Williams's Mass in G minor (Tudor-inspired, as were his earlier Tallis Variations and his later *Job*) were among the contemporary works that Terry performed at Westminster Cathedral.[36] As the Elizabethans' popularity waned in the thirties, Purcell supplanted them as a model for younger musicians. Tippett admired 'the constructional power' of Purcell's ground basses,[37] modern descendants of which are found in his opera *The Midsummer Marriage* and in Britten's *Holy Sonnets of John Donne*. So strongly did Britten identify with Purcell that one suspects he saw himself as a second 'British Orpheus'. His enduringly popular *Young Person's Guide to the Orchestra*, a set of variations on a Purcell theme, and the numerous realizations of Purcell songs that he performed with the tenor Peter Pears testify to this lifelong fascination. Only Dowland, in Tippett's opinion, rivalled Purcell in setting the English language to music. Tippett's cantata *Boyhood's End*, written for Britten and Pears, owed much to the vocal music of Purcell and Monteverdi, which Tippett frequently performed at Morley College in the 1940s.

While editing the Tudor Church Music series in the early twenties, Terry observed that 'his most able helpers in the transcription and editing of old music were often young musicians with ultra-modern tendencies. Those who revelled in Scriabin and Stravinsky were usually the most ready to appreciate 16th-century works, whereas the musician who had stopped short at Schumann and Brahms saw nothing in it.'[38] One of the composers Terry must have had in mind was Peter Warlock (Philip Heseltine's alter ego), who is remembered today chiefly for his exquisite songs. An authority on the Elizabethan composers and Gesualdo – whose music, along with that of Bartók and Schoenberg, figured prominently on the Sackbut Concerts that he helped organize in the twenties – Warlock made ingenious use of sixteenth-century dance tunes in his effervescent *Capriol Suite*. Warlock's influence rubbed off on Constant Lambert, who edited the symphonies of William Boyce and flirted with Neoclassicism in his ballet *Pomona* and *Summer's Will and Testament*, a 'masque' for chorus, orchestra and baritone solo to words by the Elizabethan poet Thomas Nashe.

His *corantos* and *intratas* notwithstanding, Lambert firmly disassociated himself from the stylistic *potpourris* of the Neoclassicists. He likened them to surrealistic paintings in which incongruous elements were thrown together purely for effect. In his witty book *Music Ho!* of 1934, Lambert decried the 'age of pastiche' and the eagerness of his contemporaries to bask in 'the pale reflected glory of being true to whichever past composer is credited at the moment with having possessed the Elixir of Life'. The Stravinsky of *Pulcinella*, he wrote, 'is like a child delighted with a book of eighteenth-century engravings, yet not so impressed that it has any twinges of conscience about reddening the noses, or adding moustaches and beards in thick black pencil.' Lambert's devastating critique of Stravinsky's first Neoclassical score bears quoting at length:

> *Pulcinella* combines the chic of today with the chic of the eighteenth century – always a safe period to consider 'good taste'. Yet there is something touchingly naïve about Stravinsky's attitude toward Pergolesi. His thematic material is all there for him, he does not even have to vamp up a pseudo-Russian folk song, and yet by giving the works a slight jolt, so to speak, he can make the whole thing sound up to date and so enjoy the best of both worlds. The jolt he gives the machine consists, on the whole, in a complete confusion between the expressive and formal content of the eighteenth-century style. In Stravinsky's adaptation the expressive element is treated in a mechanical way and purely conventional formulae of construction are given pride of place. Like a savage standing in delighted awe before those two symbols of an alien civilization, the top hat and the *pot de chambre*, he is apt to confuse their functions.[39]

Lambert was by no means alone in dismissing Stravinsky as a *poseur* and *Pulcinella* as a caricature of eighteenth-century Classicism. Stravinsky's weakness, Ernst Krenek decided, was that he hid behind so many other composers that his own personality was obscured. (Years before, Saint-Saëns had warned the young Charles Bordes of the dangers of immersing himself in the past: 'Early music is an ocean upon which one can make an eternal voyage of discovery. You may find everything you are looking for there, but you will lose yourself.') Virgil Thomson cautioned that a daily intake of old music was bad for a composer's digestion and wrote Neoclassicism off as 'a cocktail of culture'.[40] Edgard Varèse, who conducted choral performances of early music for many years (having acquired a taste for it as a student at the Schola Cantorum), regarded Neoclassicism as dangerously escapist. 'It takes the parkways and not the lonely and uncharted roads through the wilderness; it gives up adventure, effort, research, experimentation. It is a real menace to the art and science of music', he told Olin Downes in 1948. 'There is too often, in this return to Bach, Scarlatti, Pergolesi, Couperin, Mozart, and so forth, a mixture of superficial musicology and intellectual sycophancy or pure indolence. When music or any other art begins to look back over its shoulder it is because it is out of touch with reality.'[41]

Krenek's opposition to Neoclassicism was predicated on moral as much as on artistic considerations. In his view, there was a direct link between the *Wandervögel* movement, Hindemith's 'concerto grosso style' and the Hitler Youth, the common denominator being 'a tendency to whittle down, a reduction of music from a spiritual art to a professional craft'.[42] Neoclassicism did indeed dovetail neatly with the fascists' emphasis on law and order, and with the efforts of the Italian and German régimes to exploit their cultural heritage for propaganda purposes. (It is no accident that musicians like Stravinsky and Casella were strong admirers of Mussolini.) Nevertheless, Italian composers of all stylistic persuasions took pains to distance themselves from German influences. Casella wrote that he was 'taking a position definitely contrary to the seductions of the symphonic poem' (which was 'not ours at all, but French or Nordic') in his *Roman Concerto* of 1926. In his ballet *Scarlattiana*, Casella staked out 'a harmonious meeting ground between the eighteenth and the twentieth centuries', deliberately eschewing 'any residue of nineteenth-century chromaticism'.[43] How differently Neoclassicism reacted upon the Italian and German tempers can be seen by comparing Respighi's three suites of *Ancient Airs and Dances* (1917–32) with Orff's Little Concerto for harpsichord and winds of 1927. Both are more or less faithful transcriptions of early lute music, but Respighi's lush orchestrations contrast strikingly with Orff's pellucid austerity.

Krenek's views are significant because he spoke for a substantial body of musicians, those who were historically aware but rejected Neoclassicism as an intellectual bromide. He claimed that the Neoclassicists had perversely misinterpreted Busoni's call for clarity and economy. Their music, he implied, was not so much simple as simple-minded.[44] Like Schoenberg, Krenek believed that atonality had a more legitimate claim to kinship with the eighteenth century because it preserved 'the essence of classicism, the compactness and balance of its construction'. He asserted that 'the twelve-tone school tried to revive the spirit of the old forms, while neoclassicism presented replicas of their façades with interesting cracks added'.[45] Not surprisingly, Krenek was drawn less to Baroque music than to the labyrinthine counterpoint of the fifteenth-century Flemish master Ockeghem. Modern composers, he predicted, would be influenced by Ockeghem's 'unusual and imaginative treatment of dissonance, by his boundless freedom in rhythmic and metric matters, and by his capacity for spinning forth tirelessly vibrating melodic lines over extraordinary spans'. The cross-fertilization that Krenek envisioned was subtler and more probing than any of the Neoclassicists had attempted:

Present-day composers who practice the twelve-tone technique will be interested in the ways in which Ockeghem used his 'basic patterns', the cantus firmi, to create structural unity in large musical areas. One of the most inspiring elements should be observation of the sovereignty with which Ockeghem mustered his resources, switching from the forceful discipline of elaborate contrapuntal techniques to unrestricted interplay of melodic forces, never committing himself to any rigid method.[46]

Of course, Krenek's fellow twelve-tone composers had not overlooked the lessons that pre-Classical music had to offer. Schoenberg treated the past as a vast repository of musical resources which were not simply to be pirated but reinterpreted in light of modern composers' needs. Schoenberg was profoundly indebted to Bach's contrapuntal procedures, his use of chromaticism and treatment of large-scale musical structure. Berg recycled the past in a different way when he used Baroque forms as the subliminal structure of his opera *Wozzeck* and quoted a Bach chorale in his Violin Concerto to give the music an extra tonal and psychological dimension. Webern's transcription for orchestra of the six-part ricercar from Bach's *Musical Offering* is a textbook illustration of what Schoenberg called *Klangfarbenmelodie*, in which the melody ricochets from one instrument to another, creating the impression that one is listening to a 'tone-colour melody'. So successfully did Webern translate Bach's music into his own spare, pointillistic language that the *Fuga à 6* is tantamount to an original work.[47] Stravinsky later performed a similar operation in his arrangement of Bach's 'Vom Himmel hoch' and, to a lesser degree, the *Monumentum pro Gesualdo* and *Tres Sacrae Cantiones*.

Webern's and Stravinsky's approach to transcription as a creative act is controversial, to say the least, in an age preoccupied with questions of originality and authenticity. But before the era of sound recordings, when popular compositions circulated in arrangements for various instruments, few musicians worried about the ethical issues involved. Most nineteenth-century composers felt no qualms about touching up another artist's work; in fact, they felt they were doing the old masters a favour by bringing their music up to date. Busoni did not go quite that far, but his contention that 'notation itself is the transcription of an abstract idea'[48] implied that an arrangement could capture the essence of the composer's conception as accurately as the original work. Hindemith, on the other hand, considered the art of transcription on a level with 'providing a nice painted skirt and jacket for the Venus de Milo', declaring that 'an arrangement is artistically justified only when the arranger's artistic effort is greater than the original composer's'. This is arguably true of *Pulcinella* and perhaps even Webern's *Fuga à 6*, but where does one draw the line between transcription and recomposition? Hindemith does not address this question, contenting himself with lambasting the laxity of his contemporaries. 'You are not permitted to sell unsanitary macaroni or mustard, but nobody objects to your undermining the public's mental health by feeding it musical forgeries.'[49]

Few transcriptions, no matter how skilful or conscientious, would meet Hindemith's exacting standards for adulteration. Nevertheless, the part they played in the early music revival, particularly in the nineteenth and early twentieth centuries, is far from negligible. Hamilton Harty's reorchestration of Handel's *Water Music*, Myra Hess's piano reduction of Bach's *Jesu, Joy of Man's Desiring* and Leopold Stokowski's Bach transcriptions – to cite some familiar examples – introduced pre-Classical music to millions of listeners who knew nothing of Dolmetsch or Landowska. Virtually every major concert artist in the early twentieth century had a selection of such arrangements in his repertoire, and distinguished composers made transcriptions of Baroque music as a matter of course. If anyone objected, they pointed out that they were merely following the example of Bach and his contemporaries, who thought nothing of borrowing and arranging one another's music. And besides, who would fault them for trying make Baroque music accessible to a larger audience?

This attitude was clearly conducive to the chicanery of Kreisler and the brothers Casadesus. Indeed, the difference between their pseudo-Baroque and -Classical concoctions and countless arrangements of early music produced by other reputable musicians early in this century is often hard to define. It was one thing, however, for Percy Grainger to transcribe a Willaert motet or a Machaut ballade for the wind bands that he conducted on his American tours – just as Willaert or Machaut might have done under similar circumstances – and quite another for a composer to attempt to improve upon his predecessors' work in the way that Hindemith seems to have meant. In the latter category falls, among many such examples, Mahler's arrangement of selected movements from the Bach orchestral suites, which his biographer Donald Mitchell describes as a 'disconcerting mixture of devotion, penetrating insight and the weirdest notions of, as it were, updating Bach in terms of turn-of-the-century resources and sonorities'.[50]

Since a conventional harpsichord could hardly compete with Mahler's high-powered orchestral machine, a curious contraption known as a 'harpsichordized' piano was substituted at the first performance of the Bach–Mahler suite in 1910. This was created by inserting thumb-tacks or similar devices into the piano hammers, producing a metallic sound not unlike that of the modern French and German harpsichords. These musical mongrels – it is tempting to call them the instrumental equivalents of transcriptions – came in several varieties and anticipated the experiments that John Cage later carried out on his 'prepared piano'. Ravel used a tack-piano in *L'Enfant et les Sortilèges*, and Reynaldo Hahn called for one with brass tongues placed between the hammers and the strings in his operetta *Mozart*. The electronically amplified harpsichord was a later invention. One of the earliest models, the Thienhaus-Cembalo, designed in Germany in the late thirties, had two built-in microphones to ensure that it could be heard in large concert halls or even outdoors.

Instrument-makers had been experimenting with various hybrid keyboard instruments since the late eighteenth century, attempting to combine the piano's hammer action with the plucking jacks of the harpsichord. Modern technology gave such efforts fresh impetus. Around 1930 the German musicologist Werner Danckert designed a 'cembalochord', which, according to a contemporary report, 'reproduces the original harpsichord sound without any metallic side-effects'.[51] Some twenty years earlier a Belgian named Georges Cloetens had invented the *orphéal*, an ordinary piano with a tube attachment which mimicked the sounds of various instruments, among them the regal, cornemuse, musette, viola d'amore, gamba and oboe da caccia. Another short-lived novelty was the harp-lute, designed by Gustave Lyon (it was a modification of his newly-introduced chromatic harp) and touted as a practical substitute for the lute.[52] Since lutenists were perennially in short supply, easier-to-play instruments like the *Lautenklavier* – a gut-strung harpsichord that sounded like a lute – were often used instead.

Perhaps the most notorious of these organological freaks is the so-called 'Bach' bow which had a brief vogue in the middle of this century. Albert Schweitzer and others were perplexed by the polyphonic passages in Bach's solo violin works: how could three or four notes be sustained at the same time? Schweitzer decided that an outwardly-curved bow, almost semicircular in shape, was the solution to the problem. The tension of the bow-hair could be regulated by thumb pressure – slack for chordal passages, allowing the bow to wrap around the strings, and taut for single-line melodies. Schweitzer began championing his 'Bach' bow as early as 1905, but it was not until the thirties that the German violinist Ralph Schröder put the idea into practice; the Dane Emil Telmányi picked it up and modified it a few years later. Interesting as these experiments were, Schweitzer's prediction that violinists one day would play with both a 'round' and a modern convex bow proved wildly off-target. The concave bows used by Baroque string players today have less in common with Schweitzer's spurious prototype than with the more gently curved bow that Dolmetsch used when playing the Baroque violin.[53]

To ears and minds conditioned by the late twentieth century's attitude toward historical performance practice, such attempts to conflate past and present may seem misguided. But they reflect a sincere and open-minded desire to reconcile a growing interest in pre-Classical music and instruments with the dictates of modern concert life. Whether early music needed to be up-dated was debatable, but a strong case could be made that modern instruments were, on the whole, superior in design and construction to their predecessors. If Bach had only had a modern piano, it was said, surely he would not have hesitated to use it. But the fact is that Bach did *not* play a modern piano and could hardly have conceived of music for an instrument that had not yet been invented. Whether his music sounds better on a harpsichord or a piano is a question of aesthetics, not history. In the 1980s we tend to be much more dogmatic about such things than musicians in the early twentieth century, who, by and large, felt that compromise with strict historical accuracy was not only permissible but essential in order to bring early music across more vividly to modern listeners.

The most prominent exponent of this viewpoint, as far as the musical public was concerned, was the conductor Leopold Stokowski. Trained as an organist of the Romantic school, Stokowski had little interest in authentic sonorities and dismissed those who attempted to re-create historical performance practice as pedants. 'Naturally those whose minds are concerned with the written and literal aspects of music who do not fully realize the importance of music as it *sounds* – in our imagination – will not admit the constant evolution of music and the never-ending growth of its expression', he declared.[54] In his unblushing faith in musical progress, Stokowski was very much a child of the nineteenth century, and one has to admire the consistency of a man who clung to his beliefs from the time of his first famous Bach transcription in 1914 to the end of his life more than six decades later.

Stokowski conceived Bach's music in pictorial terms, a habit that was anathema to the younger generation of musicians, the Nèoclassicists above all. When Stokowski listened to Bach's D minor Toccata and Fugue, for example, he visualized 'a vast upheaval of Nature', replete with 'great white thunderclouds', 'the towering majesty of the Himalayas' and 'massive Doric columns of white marble'. In his dozens of orchestral transcriptions, Stokowski sought to convey this sense of architectonic grandeur by exploiting to the full the colours and sonorities of the Romantic orchestra. Although his Bach transcriptions are often derided as grotesquely unstylish extravaganzas – an image that Stokowski's flowery language and equally flamboyant behaviour did nothing to dispel – they are no less faithful to Bach's originals than, say, Respighi's 'orchestral interpretation' of the C minor organ Passacaglia. Stokowski's enriched orchestrations went hand in glove with his predilection for slow tempos in pre-Classical music. A revealing anecdote is told about Stokowski's performance of a Vivaldi concerto grosso in a modern orchestration by Sam Franko. In his memoirs, Franko recalls suggesting to the conductor that one of the movements might be more effective if it were taken at a livelier tempo. 'No, my dear friend, you're mistaken', Stokowski supposedly replied. 'This music belongs to the sixteenth century and can't be played slowly enough.'[55]

Arturo Toscanini was no more historically inclined than Stokowski, but whereas the latter remained oblivious to musicological concerns, Toscanini's music-making has to be considered in the context of the search for textual accuracy and 'work-fidelity' that overtook the scholarly field in the late 1800s. Like Stravinsky, Toscanini believed passionately that it was the performer's sacred duty to play precisely what the composer indicated in his score, nothing more and nothing less. 'Com'è scritto' (as it is written) was his constant refrain. This served him well enough in the nineteenth-century repertoire, but the imprecision of older musical notation makes it problematical to play simply what is written (which may explain why Toscanini so seldom performed Baroque music). Toscanini's legendary literalism was a healthy corrective to the abuses commonly committed in the name of interpretative licence, but it could also provide a convenient excuse for failing to come to grips with questions of performance practice, questions that required a broad knowledge of history and musical styles. In 1936 David Ewen cited, as an illustration of Toscanini's extraordinary memory, an incident that occurred during a rehearsal of a Vivaldi concerto. At a certain point the conductor turned to the first violins and demanded: 'Can't you see that those four notes are marked *staccato*?' The leader pointed out that no such marking was to be found in the violin parts. A score was fetched from the orchestra library; again, no *staccato* markings. Toscanini was unswayed. The next day he triumphantly brought in an older score that contained the markings as he had remembered them. It did not occur to him to question whether such markings had any basis in Baroque performance practice; it sufficed that they appeared in a printed score.[56]

There was, of course, a broad expanse of middle ground between the extreme positions of Toscanini and Stokowski. Ernest Ansermet, a thinking man's conductor if ever there was one, rejected the literalism of Toscanini and Stravinsky (although he was closely associated with the latter's music and conducted the premiere of *Pulcinella*) in favour of a more sophisticated (or perhaps merely sophistical) blend of scholarship and interpretative freedom. 'One never plays "what is written"', he insisted, 'but one must play nothing which is not in keeping with the *musical meaning* of the text.' This search for the sense of the music behind the notes, as it were, led Ansermet to initiate a detailed correspondence with Dolmetsch in the late twenties concerning the rhythmic interpretation of Baroque music.[57] Ansermet was atypical, however; the conducting profession was rife with pseudo-scholarship. In the late forties the American harpsichordist Putnam Aldrich played Bach's Fifth Brandenburg with Pierre Monteux and the San Francisco Symphony

Orchestra. 'At a preliminary rehearsal with the flute and violin soloists,' he recalled:

> I began straightway realizing the figured bass of the opening *tutti*. The conductor interrupted: 'What are those chords you are playing? Bach wrote no chords here!' I tried to explain that the figures under the cembalo part stood for chords, but he said, 'If Bach wanted chords he would have written chords. This is to be an authentic performance. We shall play *only* what Bach wrote!' And in an aside to the other musicians he said, 'You see, musicologists have always their noses in books and forget to look at what Bach wrote.'[58]

Monteux may have been misinformed, but he was not deaf. In the second movement, scored for the three soloists alone, he was forced to admit that the unharmonized bass line was insufficient, and gave Aldrich permission to 'add a few discreet chords'. Aldrich also tells of a 1935 performance of the *St John Passion* with the Boston Symphony Orchestra. The conductor, Serge Koussevitzky, had taken care to obtain the services of players on period instruments – harpsichord, viole d'amore, oboi d'amore and gamba – but the overweight string section played havoc with the orchestral balance. (By contrast, Koussevitzky performed the Brandenburgs with a chamber orchestra and employed a reduced ensemble for Mozart.) The idea that Baroque music should be played by a chamber-sized orchestra of authentic size was by no means as widely accepted fifty years ago as it is today. Reduced forces were (and by some still are) felt to trivialize the big Baroque choral works. Wilhelm Furtwängler spoke for many of his peers when he decried the trend toward small-scale performances of the Bach passions. 'As if polyphony were a problem of numbers and not of interpretation, as if one could not be just as "polyphonous", given enough space, with a choir of 500 as with one of fifty members, as if an orchestra could not be as polyphonous as a string quartet.'[59]

Furtwängler elaborated on this topic in an essay entitled 'Observations on the Performance of Early Music', published in 1932.[60] It was necessary, he said, to distinguish between the nineteenth century, which sought a reflection of itself in old music, and the twentieth century, which valued the past for its own sake. 'We want to reproduce Bach and Handel just as they themselves wanted to be performed.' But Bach and Handel, he reasoned, would never have tolerated hearing their music played by thirty or forty musicians in large concert halls like Berlin's Philharmonie. Furthermore – and on this point Furtwängler was surprisingly in tune with later musicological thought – to be really authentic, performers of Baroque music would have radically to change the listening habits and perceptions of twentieth-century audiences. Since this was clearly out of the question to Furtwängler – as it was to Beecham, Stokowski, Toscanini and virtually every other major conductor of the time – nothing was to be gained by belabouring the issue of authenticity or by indulging in protracted musicological debates over fine points of historical interpretation that had no practical relevance to twentieth-century performance.

Notwithstanding Furtwängler, a growing number of conductors in the twenties and thirties was in fact attempting to alter the way audiences listened to pre-Classical music. It is worth noting that many of them were actively involved with contemporary music and so approached the older repertoire with a broadened historical perspective nurtured, in part, by their experience of Neoclassicism. Ansermet was one; others were Paul Sacher in Switzerland, Paul Collaer in Belgium, Roger Desormière in France, Boyd Neel in England and Adolf Busch in Germany. The clarifying effect that conductors like these had on modern-instrument performances of early music was analogous to the impact the Neoclassicists made on composition. The proliferation of chamber orchestras between the wars offered an alternative to the orchestral behemoths bequeathed by the nineteenth century. Many such ensembles, like the Boyd Neel Orchestra, played roughly equal amounts of Baroque and contemporary music, while others, such as Claude Crussard's Ars Rediviva in France, specialized in eighteenth-century repertoire. The Basle Chamber Orchestra was one of the most wide-ranging, playing music of every period except the nineteenth century. Many of the contemporary works written for and performed by Sacher's orchestra, especially in its early years, had a strong Neoclassical flavour. Names like Hindemith, Stravinsky, Bloch, Roussel, Casella, Ghedini, Milhaud, Malipiero, Pepping and Martinů turned up regularly on the orchestra's programmes.[61] Indeed, so eagerly did Swiss composers like Martin, Honegger, Conrad Beck and Willy Burkhard embrace Neoclassicism in their reaction against Germanic Romanticism that it became virtually a hallmark of the modern Swiss school of composition.

Surveying concert life in the twenties and thirties, one is struck by the extent to which the early music movement overlapped with mainstream musical culture. It was possible for a pianist like Harriet Cohen, for example, to pursue a dual career as a specialist in contemporary music (primarily Bax and Vaughan Williams) and as a noted interpreter of Purcell and Byrd. Hugues Cuénod, the Swiss tenor who took part in Boulanger's Monteverdi recordings in the late thirties, had a repertoire ranging from Couperin and the English lute-song composers to Stravinsky and Milhaud. Just as transcriptions played an important part in disseminating pre-Classical music, so the revival owed a great deal to performers who were not early music specialists.

How many people were introduced to early music by the legendary Bach recitals that the pianist Harold Samuel gave in London in the early twenties, by Pablo Casals's performances of the Bach solo cello suites, or by the transcriptions of Renaissance and Baroque lute music that Emilio Pujol and Andrés Segovia featured on their guitar recitals? Shaw once suggested to Dolmetsch that if Segovia could be persuaded to take up the lute, the whole world would accept it as a legitimate instrument.[62] One might argue conversely, however, that Segovia performed a greater service by playing early music on the guitar and thus undoubtedly reaching a bigger audience.

The way 'back to Bach', then, led down many divergent paths. The early music movement itself was split into at least two camps. One, descendants of the nineteenth-century revivalists, insisted on fidelity to the spirit of the music but took a softer line in matters relating to historical authenticity. The other rejected this vestigial Romanticism and preached a new objectivity and work-fidelity. Neoclassicism, with its emphasis on purity of line and depersonalization of musical utterance, was as much a philosophy of performance as a compositional aesthetic. Stravinsky and Toscanini considered the ideal performer to be the composer's mouthpiece, the faithful transmitter of a musical text. With the blessing of the younger generation of musicologists, this new puritanism became the guiding spirit of the historical performance movement after the Second World War. As practised by its more fanatical adherents, it led to performances of a peculiarly neutral character, so that it often seemed to make little difference whether they were playing Vivaldi or Webern. Ironically, by reducing all music to a common stylistic denominator, they were doing precisely what they professed to be rebelling against in the Romantic tradition. Yet if the 'back to Bach' movement left a mixed legacy, the Janus face of Neoclassicism, encompassing past and present in one eclectic glance, still stands as an apt metaphor for the early music movement in the 1980s.

5

OLD MUSIC IN
THE NEW WORLD

Boston's Handel and Haydn Society · Theodore Thomas · The Bethlehem Bach Choir · The Musical Art Society of New York · Sam Franko's Orchestral Concerts of Old Music · Dolmetsch and Landowska in the United States · The American Society of Ancient Instruments and Other Ensembles · American Instrument-Makers · The Diaspora of European Early Musicians · Hindemith's Collegium Musicum at Yale · The New York Pro Musica.

NINETEENTH-CENTURY America imported the bulk of her musical culture from Europe, and early music was no exception. Immigrant musicians, notably those of German origin, transplanted their traditions and institutions wherever they settled. By the same token, many Americans acquired an appreciation for the old masters when they crossed the Atlantic to polish their musical training. The seeds of revivalism flourished in American soil. The United States even produced an indigenous early music revival of sorts, focusing on the archaic hymns of the Yankee tunesmiths – a movement that men like Kiesewetter and Choron would have found easy to understand.[1] The secularization of religious life was as much a matter of concern to Americans as to Europeans. As late as 1918, a writer in the *Musical Quarterly* complained that 'music used in the church of to-day differs but little from that of the concert-hall or the opera'. Deploring the neglect of Palestrina, Victoria, Bach and other old masters, he urged choir directors 'to make a comprehensive study of the music of the early church, antedating the introduction of instrumental accompaniment'.[2]

Religious reformers, the adulation of Bach and Handel, the Cecilian movement, historical concerts, instrument collectors – the ingredients of the early music revival were much the same in the New World as in the Old. Every American city, no matter how small or isolated, with any pretensions to 'high culture' boasted an amateur choral society dedicated to cultivating the Classical and pre-Classical repertoire. The grandfather of these organizations, Boston's Handel and Haydn Society, traces its origins to 1815, when a hundred citizens gathered on Christmas night to pay homage to the society's eponymous composers in a community sing. *Messiah*, destined to become a holiday ritual throughout the land, was introduced in 1818, followed closely by *Samson, Solomon, Israel in Egypt*, the Dettingen Te Deum and other Handel oratorios. Among the society's early conductors was Charles Edward Horn, whose father had been one of Wesley's Bach commandos in England. But it was not until the 1870s, at the instigation of the German-born conductor Carl Zerrahn, that the society began presenting Bach's oratorios in a reasonably complete form for the first time in America.

Bach's instrumental music had found its way into American musical life somewhat earlier, though it proved not to be to everyone's taste. Bostonians heard the Concerto in C for three keyboard instruments (pianos, of course) in 1853. 'Let no one henceforth talk of Bach as dry and learned,' declared *Dwight's Journal*, the leading musical periodical of the day, 'for here every movement was full of charm and humanity and poetry and wisdom'.[3] But it was sheer wishful thinking for *Dwight's* to assert, a short time later, that 'the Bach bug-bear [was] already vanishing'. The average music-lover would no doubt have agreed with a rival journal's description of the Bach A minor Violin Concerto as 'very heavy and uninspired'. Yet Bach had his proselytizers, as well, some of them in unexpected places. The American premiere of the *St John Passion* took place not in New York or Boston but in Bethlehem, Pennsylvania. It was the brainchild of John Frederick Wolle, an American organist who had come to love Bach's music while studying in Munich with Joseph Rheinberger. After conducting the *St John* in 1888 and the *St Matthew Passion* four years later, he boldly fixed his sights on the B minor Mass. Only a recalcitrant choir, apparently balking at the prospect of scaling this musical Everest, prevented him from realizing his ambition then and there.

Wolle persevered, however, and in 1900 he finally presided over the American premiere of the Mass, conducting a choir of eighty and an orchestra of thirty amateur instrumentalists. News of the event quickly spread in the United States and abroad. 'Nothing finer has ever been done to develop a Bach cult in America', H. E. Krehbiel wrote in a dispatch to the *Musical Times* in London.[4] Arthur A. Stanley, the director of the University of Michigan School of Music, attended the second Bethlehem Bach Festival in 1901. In a long and enthusiastic report for the *Zeitschrift der internationalen Musikgesellschaft*, he elaborated on the special atmosphere that drew pilgrims to this unlikely shrine from far and wide:

On one side of the Lehigh River lies South Bethlehem, the seat of the Carnegie Steel Works in which the largest steel forgings of modern times are made. Here all is bustle and excitement; thousands of workmen hurry to and fro in the heat and turmoil of the shop; the air is filled with the smoke of scores of furnaces, and the scene is a perfect picture of that aspect of American life supposed by foreigners to be the ideal of existence on this side of the Atlantic. Crossing the river from the railroad station by a quaint old covered bridge, such as one rarely sees now-a-days, and ascending the gentle slopes covered with a luxuriant growth of fine trees, one comes to the sleepy old town of Bethlehem, founded by the Moravians in 1741. The very air is redolent of tradition; the impelling forces are those of culture and art; on every side are met traces of that veneration for the past which is, unfortunately, no longer considered an evidence of appreciation among us, but which is on the other hand too often held to be indicative of mental weakness.[5]

By this time Wolle's choir had swollen to some 110 singers, not counting a large contingent of boys, and the orchestra had grown commensurately. All the performers hailed from Bethlehem and its environs. As one admiring visitor observed, 'There are the workers, the daughters and wives of the workers. There are the foremen, the managers, there are the millionaires in the chorus. There are the pupils and teachers from the university. Nearly every family in Bethlehem is represented.'[6] Against all odds, Wolle succeeded in moulding this motley crowd of trained and untrained voices into a disciplined and responsive ensemble. 'There are better choruses in this country, some distinguished by a nobler quality of tone, some by more flexibility of style, and some by more delicacy of shading', W. J. Henderson wrote in the *New York Times*.[7] 'But there is no chorus which excels this [sic] in decisiveness of manner, in vigor, and masculinity of style.' In keeping with tradition, Wolle invited the audience to join in the chorales; many of them knew Bach's music so well that they closed their programme books and sang from memory. Everyone Henderson met in Bethlehem, from the hotel porter to the trolly car conductor, talked incessantly of Bach – 'and all', he added somewhat superciliously, 'pronounced his name correctly'.[8] A later and equally incredulous visitor declared that it was as if 'the subway crews of New York were heart and soul in a plan to raise a monument to Dante [or] the longshoremen of Hoboken were madly in love with the ninety teachings of Confucius'.[9]

By all accounts Wolle's performances were remarkable, in spite of his old-fashioned habit of inserting drawn-out ritardandos into the music at every opportunity. (Henderson counted twenty-six in the first half-hour of a *St Matthew* performance.)[10] Critics described Wolle's Bach as vivid, virile and dramatic, in the manner of Rheinberger and Schweitzer. Scholarship was not his forte and he had little interest in speculating how Bach might have performed his own music. Thus he took the trouble of obtaining reproductions of oboi d'amore, but accompanied the recitatives on a modern grand piano and routinely simplified the orchestra parts for his players. Such was the nature of the Bach cult in Bethlehem for the duration of Wolle's régime, which lasted – with a six-year hiatus before World War I, when he tried unsuccessfully to transplant the festival to California – until his death in 1933.[11]

If Bach and Handel predictably dominated the revival in the United States, Palestrina was by no means ignored, thanks to the missionary work of organizations like the American St Cecilia Society in the late 1800s. His masses and motets figured in the programmes of Leupold Damrosch's Oratorio Society of New York in the seventies, and more prominently still in the repertoire of the chorus that Leopold's son, Frank, founded in 1894. Modelled on the Henry Leslie Choir in London and the Berlin Singakademie, the Musical Art Society consisted of a core of 55 to 70 paid professional singers, enabling Damrosch to present works that were too difficult for the average amateur choir. Bach's 'Singet dem Herrn', two seventeenth-century Italian songs, a chorus from Gluck's *Alceste* and the Palestrina–Wagner *Stabat Mater* were heard on the society's first concert at Carnegie Hall. Damrosch's musical tastes were impressively catholic   he conducted everything from Adam de la Halle to Elgar – but his chief claim to fame was as an interpreter of the Renaissance and Baroque polyphonists, especially Bach, Handel, Palestrina, Lassus, Josquin, Sweelinck, Victoria, Arcadelt and Lotti.

Charles Bordes was scouting out the same territory at the turn of the century, and Damrosch naturally availed himself of the Schola Cantorum's useful editions, supplementing them with a number of his own. Gustave Schirmer, whose firm published them, loyally brought his family to the Musical Art Society's concerts, an experience that his daughter recalled as being 'more like going to church or school' than a performance.[12] Something about Damrosch's programmes prompted even hardened critics to adopt a reverential tone. One wrote that a certain concert 'was in every respect uplifting and peculiarly gratifying, as an evidence that a serious and beautiful spirit still prevails in music in spite of the tendency toward vulgarity, licentiousness and silly slop in other forms of entertainment.'[13] As if to accentuate the aura of aristocratic refinement, Damrosch prevailed upon his friend Krehbiel to provide extensive notes on the music for inclusion in the society's sumptuously printed programme books. When the choir was forced to disband for lack of funds in 1920, Richard Aldrich wrote that 'there has been no other such society that has held up higher ideals, has accomplished more remarkable results, has revealed more of unfamiliar beauty, buried from the last generation, to New York music lovers'.[14]

Damrosch's work was not restricted to the field of choral music; the Musical Art Society followed the common practice of interlarding its programmes with instrumental selections featuring distinguished guest soloists. In 1896, for example, one reads of Bach's Sixth Brandenburg being played on a set of old string instruments – five gambas and a violoncello piccolo – lent by Morris Steinert. An optician by trade and a musician by vocation (he founded both a prosperous piano company and the New Haven Symphony Orchestra), Steinert was a typically American combination of aesthete and entrepreneur. On a trip to his birthplace in Bavaria, he began buying antique keyboard instruments, shipped them back to Connecticut and restored them to playing condition, 'firmly convinced', as he wrote in his autobiography, 'that the old instruments were the right ones for a true interpretation of the old masters'.[15] Like his friend A. J. Hipkins in England, Steinert was a proficient player and enjoyed demonstrating his harpsichords and clavichords for anyone who cared to listen. He seldom declined a request to send them, often at his own expense, to cities as distant as Vienna (for the 1892 Exhibition of Music and Drama) and Chicago (for the 1893 World's Fair). In a characteristically public-spirited gesture, Steinert donated his collection to Yale University, where it was put to good use by later generations of early musicians.

America's first great popularizer of Baroque instrumental music was yet another German immigrant, the conductor Theodore Thomas. A charter subscriber to the Bach Gesellschaft, Thomas began performing the Brandenburgs, orchestral suites and shorter works as early as the 1860s on his tours throughout the East and Midwest along the celebrated 'Thomas Highway'. Visiting London in 1880, Thomas attended the Crystal Palace Handel Festival and noted matter-of-factly in his diary that 'it would be desirable to have a Handel cult in all countries'.[16] The United States had nothing to compare with the Handel Festival, but Thomas's performances of Baroque music were on nearly the same scale. In 1881 he brought together a 500-voice chorus and the entire New York Philharmonic to perform Bach's cantata *Ein feste Burg*. Critics took his massive orchestrations in their stride. 'Great as are the changes which he was obliged to make,' the *New York Tribune* assured its readers, 'there is not in the entire work a single effect which is not indicated in the original score, a single phrase which is not wholly characteristic of Bach, or a single passage in which the pure flavor of the original is not preserved with the utmost fidelity. It is a triumph of technical skill, pure taste, and entire sympathy with the spirit of the composer.'[17]

The obligatory invocation of the composer's 'spirit' served to justify any number of questionable practices; Thomas was no more guilty than any of his contemporaries of inflating Baroque music out of proportion. It was left to his younger colleague Sam Franko to point the way toward a more historically authentic manner of performing early orchestral works. Leader of the Thomas Orchestra from 1884 to 1891, Franko had studied violin with Joachim in Berlin and with Vieuxtemps in Paris, an experience that greatly broadened his musical horizon. Convinced that New York audiences were surfeited with nineteenth-century music, and dissatisfied with the Romanticized treatment that Thomas and other conductors gave to the older repertoire, he determined to try a different approach with his newly formed American Symphony Orchestra. Instead of adapting Baroque and Classical works for a large modern orchestra, he declared his intention of performing them 'in the character of the time' – that is, 'in a small hall with a small orchestra'.[18]

This revolutionary manifesto sent a small but discernible tremor of excitement through the musical world. 'The musical Schliemann', as the critic H. T. Finck dubbed Franko, conducted the first of his 'Concerts of Old Music' in 1900 at New York's Lyceum Theater. The programme was decidedly off the beaten track, consisting of the overture to Gluck's *Iphigenia in Aulis*, a violin concerto by Viotti, a pair of dances by Monsigny and a Haydn symphony. Franko did not choose pieces simply for novelty's sake. 'It was necessary to find old works worthy from the historian's point of view, but such as still had sufficient interest for a mixed modern public', he explained. With this goal in mind he made regular expeditions to Europe, where he enlisted Gevaert and Saint-Saëns to help track down scores in libraries and archives. Lully, Rameau, Mozart, Marcello, Hasse, Philidor, Dittersdorf, Cimarosa, Vivaldi, Bach and many other composers found a home in Franko's concerts. He soon built up a large and loyal following. Aldrich praised him for presenting Mozart's early G minor Symphony and the First Brandenburg 'as they may have sounded to Mozart and Bach', with an orchestra 'based on six first violins and five seconds'.[19] So successful was Franko in educating his listeners that one critic took him to task for disregarding his own advice. 'Had Mr. Franko reproduced the old forces, – a small band of strings and two harpsichords, which instruments are now to be had to prove that a revival of archaic things in music is in progress, – there can be no doubt that the effect would have been much greater.'[20]

Franko was ahead of his time – not for another two or three decades did scaled-down performances of early orchestral music become at all common in the United States – but even if he had accomplished nothing else, he would still deserve mention here for introducing Arnold Dolmetsch to American audiences. Dolmetsch's début with the American Symphony Orchestra in 1903, assisted by his wife Elodie on harpsichord and his wife-to-be Mabel Johnston on gamba, stirred considerable interest. Aldrich admired 'the rectitude of style, the fluency of technique and the lovely enthusiasm of the three performers', noting that their playing 'exercised an unbroken fascination upon their listeners'.[21] Other critics were more ambivalent, expressing appreciation of the performers' abilities but remaining sceptical of the value of such historical exercises. Dolmetsch and his entourage spent a month on the East Coast, giving fourteen concerts which elicited such a gratifying response that a second tour was immediately arranged for the following year. This time Dolmetsch travelled with Mabel and the harpsichordist Kathleen Salmon. (He and Elodie had been divorced in the meantime.) Aldrich had had second thoughts about Dolmetsch. His reputation in London, the critic surmised, was based 'less on his proficiency as a player than on his work in restoring the old instruments to practicability and re-establishing the methods of playing them – matters, indeed, deserving of high appreciation'.[22]

If Dolmetsch cut a quaint figure in *fin-de-siècle* Bloomsbury, it is not difficult to imagine the impression his unconventional wardrobe and lifestyle – to say nothing of the music he played – made on American audiences as the threesome worked its way westward from Boston to Chicago. An invitation from Ben Greet to provide music for a series of Shakespeare productions prompted Dolmetsch to consider staying in the United States indefinitely. By the time he signed a contract with Chickering in 1905, he was already a man to be reckoned with in musical circles, and *Musical America* gave prominent coverage to the announcement of his appointment. During the five years he lived in Cambridge, Dolmetsch did more than anyone before him had done to whet Americans' appetite for early music and instruments. Reaction to his work was by no means consistently positive – wherever he went, Dolmetsch seemed to attract large numbers of disparagers and admirers – but the 75-odd harpsichords, virginals, spinets, clavichords, viols and lutes that he produced for Chickering are, by common consent, among the finest instruments of their time. And it is surely no accident that Boston and New York, the two American cities where Dolmetsch was most active, soon blossomed into thriving early music centres.

Of the many American pupils and protégés who tended Dolmetsch's flame after he returned to Europe, none was more influential or devoted than the composer Arthur Whiting. In a widely circulated article entitled 'The Lesson of the Clavichord', first published in the *New Music Review* in 1909,[23] Whiting wrote that 'the reproduction of the Clavichord and Harpsichord is as important to the present-day students of keyboard music as are some recent discoveries of the antique to archaeologists'. But Whiting was a creative artist, not an antiquarian, and he applauded Dolmetsch for undermining musicians' 'sense of superiority to the past'. The clavichord would teach musicians 'to make the greatest effects with the smallest means – to cultivate the art of suggestion'. Whiting buttressed his arguments with performances on his Chickering harpsichord, in which one critic discerned 'unsuspected qualities of sweetness and delicate elegance'. Another wrote that the instrument's 'brittle and sparkling sounds' gave Bach's G minor English Suite 'a peculiar piquancy which could not be obtained from a piano of to-day'.[24] Whiting followed in Steinert's footsteps by instituting a series of educational concerts at Ivy League schools, in which he was later joined by the New York Philharmonic's principal cellist, Paul Kéfer, who had become a convert to the gamba after buying a Dolmetsch instrument.

To be sure, Americans did not attend early music concerts purely to be edified or instructed: performers' personalities were an important attraction. In 1906, for instance, *Musical America* reported that Olive van Wagner had arrived from Europe to give a recital of old French songs in period costume, 'emulating the example of Arnold Dolmetsch'.[25] Her eighteenth century French harpsichord was said to have cost ten thousand dollars – many times the price of one of Dolmetsch's reproductions. Yvette Guilbert, who landed in New York a few days later, announced she would sing a similar programme dressed in costumes of various periods, one of which reportedly cost thirty thousand francs.[26] This sartorial one-upmanship had nothing to do with music, of course, but it undoubtedly helped sell tickets. Stage settings, the more extravagant the better, were certain to go down well. When Frances Pelton-Jones, one of Dolmetsch's better-known American harpsichord pupils, played a concert of seventeenth- and eighteenth-century consort music at New York's fashionable Plaza Hotel in 1910, the room was decorated in the style of a Louis XVI salon, a touch of Old World elegance that the hotel's proprietors were no doubt eager to offer their affluent guests.[27]

The vaguely exotic atmosphere conjured by the words 'early music' owed much to the steady influx of European musicians who visited the United States in the early years of the century. At the 1915 Panama-Pacific International Exposition in San Francisco, Saint-Saëns delivered a lecture entitled 'On the Execution of Music, and Principally of Ancient Music', which was largely devoted to a rather superficial discussion of historical performance practice. The Alsatian musicologist Jean Beck, an authority on troubadour and trouvère songs, emigrated to Philadelphia and became the darling of high society. The English Singers, the Société des Instruments Anciens Casadesus, the Società Polifonica Romana, the Aguilar Lute Quartet of Spain and other well-known European ensembles criss-crossed the country in the teens and twenties. At the same time, American collectors and museums were scouring Europe for old instruments as avidly as for old master paintings. The Boston Symphony Orchestra's purchase of Henri Casadesus's instruments in 1926, shortly after the Museum of Fine Arts acquired the Galpin collection, made Boston pre-eminent in the early instrument field. Only a handful of other institutions – including Yale, the Metropolitan Museum in New York, the University of Michigan in Ann Arbor and the Smithsonian Institution in Washington – possessed comparable resources.

The widespread availability of historical instruments, both originals and copies, gave rise to America's first flush of early music groups in the twenties and thirties. The Philadelphia-based American Society of Ancient Instruments was founded by a Dutch violinist named Ben Stad, who had once been associated with the Casadesus Société in Europe. Both French and American groups consisted of harpsichord and viols, with singers and other instrumentalists added as needed. At a time when Americans often seemed oblivious to home-grown talent, Stad's ensemble made several recordings, took part in the dedication of the Folger Shakespeare Library in Washington in 1932 and sponsored a festival ambitiously modelled on Haslemere.[28] Another Society of Ancient Instruments was formed in the late thirties by members of the Boston Symphony Orchestra. While the Philadelphia society concentrated on the medieval and Renaissance repertoires, the Boston group was known for its highly polished performances of Baroque music. Alfred Zighera, the group's director, cultivated a smooth, sustained style of playing that made his gamba sound like a cello. He and Stad seem to have been influenced more by Continental groups like the Munich Viol Quintet than by the thinner, more 'archaic' sound of the Dolmetsch school.

The revival of pre-Classical choral music in the United States continued apace after the demise of the Musical Art Society. Groups like Kurt Schindler's Schola Cantorum in New York, Archibald T. Davison's student choirs at Harvard, Nicola Montani's Palestrina Chorus and Henry S. Drinker's Accademia dei Dilettanti di Musica in Pennsylvania made the music of Palestrina, Victoria, Monteverdi, Byrd and Bach part of the basic choral repertoire. Here, too, European musicians seized the initiative. Margarete Dessoff, an Austrian conductor who came to the United States in the early twenties, was one of the first choral conductors to specialize in medieval and Renaissance music. The Dessoff Choirs performed a wide range of literature from fourteenth-century motets to Vecchi's madrigal comedy L'Amfiparnaso (of which it gave the American premiere in 1933). Upon returning to Europe in 1936, Dessoff turned the choir over to the Swiss-born conductor Paul Boepple, who had a special interest in early vocal technique.[29] Boepple had already founded a group called the Cantata Singers, which likewise became known for its historically aware performances of early music under such scholar–conductors as Arthur Mendel, Alfred Mann and Thomas Dunn. Another notable group in the late thirties was Lehmann

Engel's Madrigal Singers, which performed early American music as well as European polyphony.

Beginning in the mid-thirties, Bach festivals sprang up across the country, from Florida to California. While none matched the special aura of Bethlehem's, the festival that Albert Riemenschneider founded at Baldwin-Wallace Conservatory in Ohio became an important centre of Bach scholarship. A number of composers also became involved with early choral music as conductors. Ernest Bloch was associated with a community chorus set up by the People's Music League in New York at the end of World War I to study early polyphonic music. This experiment in proletarian music-making was soon abandoned for lack of interest, leaving the critic Paul Rosenfeld with 'the memory of a marvelous absorption on the platform; of a man hearing golden alleluias and seraphs' hymnings; pleading, explaining, cajoling; and not being able to believe the mystic carolings not every tittle as present and luminous to other ears as to his own'.[30] Edgard Varèse had greater success with the choirs he directed in New York (and earlier in Paris and Berlin). Reviewing a programme rather catchily titled 'Modern Music of the Sixteenth and Seventeenth Centuries' (Grigny, Couperin, Monteverdi, Charpentier, Frescobaldi, Schütz and Grandi were the composers), Olin Downes praised Varèse's 'penetrating musicianship' and 'communicative enthusiasm', adding that the performances were 'refreshingly earnest, intelligent and unprofessional in spirit'.[31]

In America as in Europe, however, it was Landowska who really fired the public's imagination and rescued early music from the limbo of historical concerts and lecture-demonstrations. Arriving in New York in November of 1923 with four harpsichords in tow, she made her Carnegie Hall début with Stokowski and the Philadelphia Orchestra playing two concertos on harpsichord (one of Handel's op. 4 and Bach's unaccompanied *Italian*) and one on piano (by Mozart). Having thus presented her credentials as a well-rounded musician, she devoted her next programme three weeks later with the New York Symphony entirely to Baroque harpsichord music. Richard Aldrich thought her 'an exceedingly skillful player' and praised her clean articulation and beautiful tone,[32] but the tenor of his colleagues' reviews was more respectful than enthusiastic. Not for some time did the United States accord Landowska the recognition to which she had long been accustomed in Europe. Some months after her first appearance, Downes reflected on the vogue for old music that centred around this deceptively demure-looking woman:

Would she have found as sympathetic audiences in an earlier day? Last Tuesday night the Philadelphia Orchestra performed almost a whole

Fig. 3   Wanda Landowska

program of delightful old music. Bruno Walter of the New York Symphony produced a week since a charming symphony of Johann Christian Bach. Three days previously Mme. Landowska gave a performance of Mozart's E flat piano concerto, which was not only one of a round dozen of the greatest musical experiences this writer ever had, but was greeted with clamorous enthusiasm by a very large and democratically constituted audience. More and more the artistic world is becoming aware of the wealth of beautiful music that preceded the romantic era, and its intolerance of nearly everything that went before. . . . It is possible that the next fifty years will see a new and much better balance in the cultivation of music of all periods, and that researches into the musical literature of the centuries preceding the last one will bear constantly richer fruit and establish a broader appreciation.[33]

Downes's prediction came true, perhaps sooner than he expected. Within little more than a decade of Landowska's first visit, the United States could lay claim to a number of noted harpsichordists, among them Frances Pelton-Jones, whose 'Salons Intimes' in New York continued into World War II; Gavin Williamson and Philip Manuel, a much-recorded harpsichord duo from Chicago; and Putnam Aldrich, who played frequently with the Boston Society of Ancient Instruments. The most distinguished was Ralph Kirkpatrick, who taught himself to play as an undergraduate at Harvard and gave his first recital on the university's Chickering harpsichord in 1930. The next year he went abroad on a fellowship, studying with Landowska in Paris, Dolmetsch in England and Ramin in Germany. Kirkpatrick's star rose swiftly. In Berlin he performed with Eta Harich-Schneider's collegium, earning a glowing review from Alfred Einstein. He played for Bernard Berenson at I Tatti near Florence, demonstrated the clavichord to his compatriots Elliott Carter and Roger Sessions, and taught at the Mozarteum in Salzburg.[34] By the late thirties, when Kirkpatrick began touring extensively in the United States, both alone and with the violinist Alexander Schneider, the concert circuit had become more congested. A crowd of American harpsichordists – Melville Smith, Claude Jean Chiasson, Daniel Pinkham, Sylvia Marlowe, Rosalyn Tureck – was now vying for attention alongside transplanted Europeans like Alice Ehlers, Yella Pessl, Edith Weiss-Mann and Ernst Victor Wolff.

The birth of a domestic harpsichord industry in the thirties and forties was a natural outgrowth of this activity. After Chickering shut down their early instrument department in 1910, no harpsichords seem to have been built commercially in America until 1931, when John Challis returned from a four-years' apprenticeship at Haselemere and set up shop in Ypsilanti, Michigan. Challis had heard Landowska on her first American tour and was deeply impressed; his ideas about harpsichord sound and design reflected her influence as much as, if not more than, Dolmetsch's. Challis was not interested in copying historical models. He disliked the sound of the eighteenth-century instruments he had heard and saw no reason to perpetuate their shortcomings by reproducing them. Nor did he hesitate to take advantage of the newest technology and synthetic materials. Steel frames (which Dolmetsch had tried and rejected), bakelite pin blocks, hard rubber jacks and nylon tongue springs were standard equipment on Challis harpsichords. He contracted with a piano manufacturer to supply heavy laminated wooden cases for his instruments and even experimented with metal soundboards to give them greater stability in extreme climates. In a sense, Challis was merely carrying some of Dolmetsch's more controversial innovations to their logical conclusion. He was a quintessentially American figure, part Yankee tinkerer, part consummate artisan, hailed as a genius by some, by others spurned as an apostate.[35]

Another young American made the pilgrimage to Haslemere some twenty years after Challis and underwent a different sort of conversion. Frank Hubbard began studying old instruments in Boston while nominally a graduate student in English literature at Harvard. His first mentor was Chiasson, who since before World War II had been manufacturing harpsichords of an eclectic design, incorporating certain features of the 'Landowska' Pleyel. Hubbard, however, had different ideas: he proposed to copy extant historical instruments as meticulously as possible, down to the finest detail. While learning his trade at Haselemere in the late forties, Hubbard travelled around Europe taking measurements of antique harpsichords in museums. In 1949 he opened a workshop in Boston with William Dowd, a fellow Harvard student who had been apprenticed under Challis. They parted ways nine years later, but the 'Boston school' of harpsichord-making that they founded, predicated on authenticity of design and materials, would revolutionize the reproduction of harpsichords and other historical instruments in years to come.[36]

The impetus toward authenticity manifested itself in other fields of instrument-making as well. The European Organ Revival, for example, had begun to influence organ design in the United States as early as the mid-thirties. E. Power Biggs's recordings and broadcasts on the small, two-manual organ installed in 1937 at Harvard's Germanic Museum (later the Busch-Reisinger), and the recordings that Carl Weinrich made on similar instruments at the Westminster Choir School, carried the sound of the modern 'Baroque' organ from coast to coast. The recorder, too, was making inroads in America, with craftsmen like David Dushkin, William Koch and Friederich von Heune leading the way. Although the United States had nothing to compare with Germany's Youth Movement in sparking an interest in folk music and archaic instruments, the recorder's value as a teaching tool was nonetheless recognized by American educators. Carl Dolmetsch's annual concert tours (beginning in 1936) and performances by ensembles like the Trapp Family Singers laid the groundwork for a popular recorder movement. The American Recorder Society was founded in 1939, with Suzanne Bloch, the composer's daughter, as president. Bloch had studied with Dolmetsch in England and performed regularly in New York as a lutenist, singer and virginalist. At a time when early instruments (excepting, perhaps, the harpsichord) were generally regarded as exotic playthings, she convinced many American musicians that they deserved to be taken seriously. Under Bloch and her successor Erich Katz (Wilibald Gurlitt's former assistant in Freiburg), the Recorder Society flourished and became a significant factor on the American early music scene after World War II.[37]

In the twenties and early thirties, scores of American musicians had traversed the Atlantic to study with experts like Dolmetsch and Landowska or, as with Safford Cape and Guillaume de Van, to make their careers abroad. Now the tide was turning. European exiles entered the United States in droves, carrying whatever possessions they had been able to salvage from the impending holocaust. Landowska, forced to abandon most of her famous library and instrument collection at St Leu to the Nazis, arrived at Ellis Island in 1941 with little to her name besides a Pleyel harpsichord that a devoted student had managed to ship out of occupied Paris.[38] Ten weeks later, she played the Goldberg Variations at Town Hall before an audience that constituted 'virtually a social register of professional musicians'.[39] This time the critics unanimously hailed her as a conquering hero. Virgil Thomson called Landowska's playing 'one of the richest and grandest experiences available to lovers of the tonal art'. This triumph ushered in a period of intense and productive activity. Eventually Landowska moved away from New York into a rambling country house in Lakeville, Connecticut, a placid retreat not unlike her beloved St Leu, where she spent the last dozen years of her life teaching, writing and making recordings.

Boston, since Dolmetsch's day the intellectual capital of America's early music movement, extended a warm welcome to many European refugees and émigrés. Boulanger arrived in 1938 at the invitation of Radcliffe College, where she taught a course called 'Early and Modern Music – A Comparative Study' and continued to perform both from time to time.[40] The following year Alfred Einstein took up a professorship at Smith College, the site of a series of famous Baroque opera productions in the twenties and early thirties (see Chapter 7). The college availed itself of Einstein's expertise in presenting a four-day festival of sixteenth- and seventeenth-century music in 1941. *Musical America* commented that while most people would not choose a steady diet of early music, 'the rareness with which it is ever heard and the beautiful way it was sung in Northampton make it not only interesting but a privilege to hear as well'.[41] In neighbouring Cambridge, the musicologist and harpsichordist Erwin Bodky, recently arrived from Germany, inaugurated a series of early music concerts at Harvard. Out of these grew the Cambridge Collegium Musicum, later known as the Cambridge Society for Early Music, which Bodky directed until shortly before his death in 1958. The society provided a platform for a number of prominent artists, including the composer–harpsichordist Daniel Pinkham and the recorder virtuoso Bernard Krainis, although as a rule performances were given on modern instruments.[42]

The impact that musicians like Boulanger, Bodky and Einstein had on American musical life is hard to overestimate. As part of the European diaspora of the thirties and forties, they helped change the direction of American musical scholarship and hence, indirectly, of performance. The presence on American campuses of Willi Apel, Manfred Bukofzer, Hans T. David, Otto Gombosi, Paul Henry Lang, Curt Sachs, Leo Schrade, Edward Lowinsky, Karl Geiringer and Hans Tischler, to name only the most prominent of the expatriate musicologists, made America a significant force in the study and practice of early music. A thriving tradition of applied musicology, a concept still viewed with suspicion in some parts of Europe (though not in England), gave the United States an advantage in the comparatively young discipline of historical performance practice. The relaxed interaction between scholars and performers in the American academic world fostered the growth of European-style collegium groups, such as Apel's at Harvard and Siegmund Levarie's at the University of Chicago.

The Yale Collegium Musicum, the most renowned of these academic ensembles, was organized shortly after Hindemith joined the faculty in 1940. It was originally conceived as an informal reading group for Schrade's musicology class, but Hindemith had more ambitious plans. Under his direction, the collegium's annual concerts soon attracted attention beyond the university community. Hindemith's versatility (his main instrument was the viola, but he also played viola d'amore, gamba, recorders and bassoon) qualified him to coach performers on almost any instrument. Some of the instruments the collegium used were salvaged from the Steinert Collection; others came from nearby museums. For a performance of Dufay's Mass *Se la face ay pale* in 1946, Hindemith's friend Emmanuel Winternitz, curator of the Metropolitan Museum's instrument collection, arranged the loan of a set of medieval instruments, including a harp, psaltery, rebec, vielle, lute, tromba marina, cornett, crumhorn, natural trumpet, sackbuts and portative organ. 'This is the first time that such an authentic orchestra of the 15th century has ever been assembled in this country for actual performance', a press release for the concert announced.[43]

Hindemith was neither an antiquarian nor a purist by temperament. He realized that only historical instruments could re-create the sound-world of pre-Classical music, but his primary purpose was identical to that envisaged earlier by Riemann and Gurlitt: to broaden the horizons of young musicians and give them first-hand experience of the music they were studying. The Yale Collegium in effect offered a survey of Western music from the Notre Dame School of the twelfth century to the great Renaissance masters, with a smattering of Baroque works thrown in for good measure. Hindemith's overriding interest in early musical forms and compositional techniques caused him to discount certain aspects of performance practice. He was not above performing Monteverdi madrigals with a chorus of seventy, adding Romantic *portamenti* to a Renaissance motet, or altering tempos and dynamics to make a piece more dramatically effective – solecisms for which stricter colleagues gently chided him. But early music for Hindemith was living art, part of the ongoing tradition to which he as a composer belonged, and he approached it as one on intimate terms with the old masters. 'Damn!' he was once heard to mutter after a rehearsal of an Isaac mass. 'To think that music has lost this!'[44]

Like Brahms's performances of early music in the nineteenth century, Hindemith's were characterized by a firm projection of musical structure and an irrepressible vitality, qualities that stand out on the recordings the Yale

Collegium made in the early fifties. After his farewell appearance with the group at the Metropolitan Museum in 1953, Jay S. Harrison wrote in the *New York Herald Tribune*: 'Not a phrase was mislaid nor a color blurred. It was eloquent, elegant, passionate rendering. It was serious, devout. And it served to remind us of an ideal in performance that is easily forgot in this day of last minute preparation and resultant mediocrity.'[45] Hindemith aimed to entertain as well as edify his listeners. He had no qualms about dressing up medieval monophonic dances with improvisatory instrumental parts, long before this became common practice, and he scrapped the conventional mixed-bag concert format in favour of programmes carefully designed to cast light on a central theme. All of which explains why Hindemith exerted such a powerful influence on America's fledgling crop of early musicians. Many of his students at Yale went on to direct other academic collegium groups (notably George Hunter at the University of Illinois) or, like the harpisichordist Albert Fuller and the lutenist Joseph Iadone, to perform professionally with early music ensembles.

Most of the instrumental groups active in the immediate post-war years – those directed by Bodky, Zighera, Marlowe, Pessl and Harich-Schneider, for example – were primarily devoted to Baroque repertoire. Medieval and Renaissance instrumental music was still, for the most part, an unknown quantity as far as the American public was concerned. But in 1953, the very year that Hindemith returned to Europe, a group called the Primavera Singers made its début on a small American record label. To everyone's surprise, the recording – a selection of Banchieri madrigals – was something of a hit, catapulting the ensemble and its director, Noah Greenberg, into the spotlight. Greenberg swiftly recruited a corps of instrumentalists and rechristened his ensemble the New York Pro Musica Antiqua, after Cape's long-established group in Brussels. The 'antiqua' was soon dropped to avoid confusion, but there was little danger that the ensembles would be mistaken for each other. Despite the similarity of their repertoires, both focusing on music written before 1700, the performing styles of the two Pro Musicas were as different as the personalities of their directors. Cape's understatement and Old World suavity contrasted sharply with the virile, outgoing showmanship of Greenberg, who, like Hindemith, believed that early music should sound as fresh as if it had been composed the day before.

Greenberg had no pretensions to scholarship or virtuosity. But he was a man of keen enthusiasms, a born communicator, and early music was his passion. As a machinist in the Merchant Marine, he had shopped around for scores and recordings on port calls overseas. Upon returning to New York in 1949, he took a job organizing choruses for the International Ladies' Garment Workers Union, one of which specialized in early music.

Greenberg's common touch made him an effective ambassador for the all-but-unknown composers whose music he had discovered on his voyages. But in casting musicological caution to the winds and adopting a more robust, down-to-earth approach to early music, Greenberg did not lose sight of the manifold problems involved in deciphering and performing old scores. Throughout his career he relied on the counsel of scholars like Gustave Reese and Edward Lowinsky, who were as excited as he was to hear – not just with their inner ears, but physically – the music they had studied for so long. Indeed, one senses a hint of envy in their admiration for Greenberg's obstinate refusal to be hedged about by scholarly scruples. His procedure was forthright: he sought the best advice available, evaluated it by his own criteria, and then proceeded to do what he felt would be most effective. Inevitably, Greenberg's risk-taking elicited both praise and censure, and never more so than in the Pro Musica's most brilliant single achievement, *The Play of Daniel*.

Greenberg conceived the idea of reviving the work after coming across the music in Coussemaker's anthology of medieval liturgical dramas. But the nineteenth-century edition – consisting of a single melodic line in neumatic notation, with no indications as to instrumental accompaniment or tempo – could only serve as a springboard for a performance. Greenberg asked the medievalist Rembert Weakland to transcribe the music into modern notation; he himself edited it for voices and a panoply of early instruments. *Daniel* was presented in 1958 at the Cloisters, the Metropolitan Museum's medieval wing. Lincoln Kirstein's staging, a visual spectacle replete with prancing lions and a fire-eater, was far more elaborate than anything spectators in the thirteenth century are likely to have seen. Nor did W. H. Auden's English verse narrative, delivered by an actor costumed as a monk, have any basis in medieval practice. But Greenberg's *Daniel* was never meant to be a historical re-creation. It was an attempt to bring a small part of the Middle Ages to life for modern audiences, and as such the Pro Musica's production became an instant classic, what one critic called 'an astounding exercise of creative scholarship'.[46] A recording was issued forthwith and Oxford University Press published Greenberg's edition of the score the following year. *The Play of Daniel* was repeated so often in the United States and abroad that it became the Pro Musica's calling card.

In 1963 Greenberg resurrected another medieval liturgical drama, *The Play of Herod*, this time with the collaboration of the British scholar William L. Smoldon. It was devised in much the same spirit as *Daniel*, though initially Greenberg dispensed with an interpolated text. (Archibald MacLeish was later commissioned to write a verse narrative.) Once again, the production was enthusiastically greeted as 'a living document of bygone times that comes across with fire, passion, affection and wit'.[47] Equally significant in the long run was the substantial ($465,000) grant that the Ford Foundation awarded the Pro Musica that year, in part to underwrite *The Play of Herod*. This, too, was a milestone for America's early music movement, which hitherto had subsisted on the fringes of respectability. Such generous subvention helped compensate for the lack of patronage by radio networks and recording companies that many of the Pro Musica's European counterparts enjoyed. In short, the early music revival in the United States had finally come of age.

Greenberg's untimely death in 1966 left the movement temporarily bereft of leadership. The New York Pro Musica continued to perform for a further eight years, but his successors proved unable to sustain its momentum. Greenberg's legacy manifested itself, instead, in the subsequent efflorescence of American early music ensembles: the Waverly Consort, the Boston Camerata (which had been in existence since 1954), Concert Royal, Pomerium Musices, the Ensemble for Early Music, Music for A While, the Musicians of Swanne Alley, Calliope and many more, all built on the sturdy foundations he had laid down. The Pro Musica's accessible style, with its occasionally glitzy overtones, was perfectly mated to its time and place. Greenberg showed that a serious early music group could appeal to a mass audience without compromising its artistic or scholarly integrity. The Pro Musica's colourfully imaginative performances fell out of favour for a while, but recent years have seen a willingness to re-evaluate them on the basis of their superb and richly communicative musicianship. Greenberg adroitly steered his ship between the Scylla of fashionable gentility and the Charybdis of academic pedantry. If Dolmetsch ushered the revival into the twentieth century, Greenberg gave it a new lease of life. The unprecedented success that the Pro Musica achieved under his guidance was an unmistakable sign that the early music movement was at long last emerging from the deep shadow cast by Haslemere.

6

'TO OPEN WIDE THE WINDOWS'

*Early Music in the Mass Media · Recordings and Broadcasts · Some
Recorded Anthologies · The BBC's Third Programme · The Electronic
Media as Patrons of Early Musicians · Pre-Classical Music in Films, on
Television and in Literature · The Post-War Vivaldi Craze · Jazz and
Popular Treatments of Early Music.*

IT seems appropriate that Noah Greenberg's first exposure to early music
came via the recordings he picked up on his journeys overseas. For he
belonged to a new generation: children of the media age, he and his
contemporaries were attuned to the enormous potential that modern
communications technology offered for disseminating music. Especially in
the United States, with its culturally diverse and geographically far-flung
audience, the mass media were a crucial factor in the early music revival, as
Greenberg acknowledged in his contribution to the Reese *Festschrift*:

> Amazingly enough, it was not the givers of conventional concerts who
> opened up their programs to the repertory of early music, but the record
> companies – and, for the most part, not the large record companies (who
> could easily have afforded to do it) but the small ones, who could not
> afford to hire the virtuoso ensembles and artists needed to sell recordings
> of the standard repertoire . . . . Not only is the general public now familiar
> with sonorities and repertory both of which were largely unknown two
> decades ago, but what began as a curious interest in new music and timbres
> has now broadened and deepened into a cultivated awareness of musical
> styles. Today there is a new tolerance in public listening and understand-
> ing, a tolerance that may even be extending itself into a demand for the
> curious novelties of contemporary sounds. Certainly the tyrannical
> monopoly of the standard repertory has been seriously weakened.[1]

Rapid developments in recording and broadcasting in the first decades of
the twentieth century enabled early musicians to reach an audience beyond
the wildest dreams of the movement's pioneers. The sixty thousand people

who had an opportunity to hear the Chanteurs de St Gervais at the 1900 Paris Exposition represented a mere fraction of the potential audience for the New York Pro Musica's concerts, recordings and broadcasts in the fifties and sixties. Interestingly, the Pathé company approached Bordes in 1900 with a plan to record a selection of Gregorian chant. He must have given the proposal serious consideration, for Pathé got as far as preparing a catalogue, though no cylinders seem to have been made.[2] That record companies viewed chant recordings as commercially viable can be inferred from the fact that similar proposals had been advanced as early as 1891.[3] Yet the first recordings that the Sistine Chapel Choir made between 1902 and 1905 contained but a single specimen of chant – the Alleluia from the Mass of the Assumption – along with unaccompanied pieces by Viadana, Mozart, Meluzzi, Capocci and Stehle.

In 1904, however, the Gramophone Co. sent its engineers to Rome to a congress commemorating the thirteenth centenary of the death of Gregory the Great, traditionally held to be the codifier of the chant repertoire. Among the participants were several prominent figures in the restoration of historical chant performance, including Dom Joseph Pothier and Dom André Mocquereau from Solesmes. It is the range of interpretations of the so-called Solesmes method, which the Vatican had officially sanctioned only the year before, that makes these acoustically primitive recordings so extraordinarily fascinating.[4] Rhythm is the crux of the matter: the choirs sing with varying degrees of metrical freedom under the five directors, Mocquereau's performances being the most supple and speech-like, Dom Antonio Rella's the most rigidly accentual. Whatever their respective merits as musical renditions, these early recordings are invaluable historical documents, particularly when compared with later recordings by the Solesmes monks, Richard Terry's Westminster Cathedral Choir and groups representing other schools of chant interpretation.

Around the same time, according to Mabel Dolmetsch, the music publisher Robert Cocks brought a recording apparatus to Arnold Dolmetsch's house in Dulwich and 'made some beautiful recordings on wax cylinders'.[5] Alas, these tantalizing mementos have not survived, nor is it known what music they contained. In the event, Dolmetsch's recording career was deferred for some two decades, thus depriving posterity of a chance to hear him in his prime. In 1903 Landowska made a set of piano rolls for Welte-Mignon of pieces by Bach, Daquin, Francesco Durante and others, but early recordings were notoriously unkind to instrumentalists and consequently few were made. To understand what pre-Classical music sounded like before the First World War, one must turn instead to the recordings of singers like Alessandro Bonci, Nellie Melba, Maria Barrientos,

Andrew Black, Giuseppe Anselmi, David Bispham and Blanche Marchesi. If their performances of arias by Handel, Scarlatti, Pergolesi and Bach are predictably Romanticized, they nevertheless yield some exquisite surprises. Bispham, for instance, delivers the coloratura passage-work of Handel's 'O ruddier than the cherry' in a limpid, unforced tone that any bass might well envy. Such recordings tell us a great deal about turn-of-the century attitudes toward Baroque vocal music. But for anyone interested in the evolution of historical performing styles, it is cause for regret that no record company saw fit to preserve performances by Louis Diémer, the Chanteurs de St Gervais, the Deutsche Vereinigung für alte Musik, Daniël de Lange's Amsterdam A Capella Choir or any of a dozen other ensembles in the forefront of the revival at the beginning of the century.

Admittedly, the gramophone companies were not entirely to blame for this lacuna in the historical record. They simply gave the public what it wanted to hear, and not for some years did an appreciable quantity of pre-Classical music fall into that category. The expansion of early music activity in the twenties coincided with major advances in recording technology. The Gramophone Co. (HMV) in England launched an ambitious programme in 1920 when it invited the harpsichordist Violet Gordon Woodhouse to record short pieces by Bach, Purcell, Couperin, Rameau, Scarlatti and others. Despite the primitive acoustic-era sound – Compton Mackenzie later recalled that 'there was something fascinating about a pre-electric recording of the harpsichord, a kind of ghostliness which suited the past it was reviving'[6] – one cannot help being impressed by the magisterial technique and grand manner which made her Landowska's most formidable rival. In an article written for Mackenzie's magazine *The Gramophone* in 1923, Woodhouse recounted her delight upon discovering how well recordings captured the harpsichord's sharp attack and clear, ringing tone.[7] Evidently HMV judged her initial albums a success, for Woodhouse made two more batches of recordings in 1922 and 1923, including a substantial portion of Bach's B flat Partita and Handel's *Harmonious Blacksmith*. In 1927, after the introduction of electrical recordings, she committed Bach's *Italian* Concerto to disc in a characteristically bracing, bravura reading. Woodhouse's recordings have stood the test of time remarkably well, but sadly she never returned to the studio after 1928, although she was preparing to record Bach's 'Forty-Eight' at the time of her death in 1948.[8]

Columbia, HMV's chief competitor, was somewhat slower off the mark in the early music field. The Dolmetsch family made several records for the label in 1921, but for some reason – perhaps because viols and recorders did not reproduce satisfactorily – they were never released. Dolmetsch, however, pronounced himself well satisfied. 'They don't sound as loud as Caruso's, but they are, I think, quite loud enough', he wrote. 'They might interest only a small section of the public, but from the educational point of view they are worth having.'[9] Unfortunately, the qualities that made Dolmetsch a stimulating and magnetic performer in the flesh – at least in the eyes of his admirers – all too often vanished on recordings. What did stand out, more glaringly than ever, were the blemishes and amateurishness that marred many of his performances. But the Dolmetsch name was too famous to ignore, and from 1929 various members of the family were constantly active in the recording studio. Percy Scholes, Dolmetsch's old friend (and sometime critic), commissioned recordings of viol pieces by Morley and Dering for Columbia's *History of Music by Ear and Eye*. In the last decade of his life Dolmetsch recorded a wide range of music, from medieval organum to Welsh folksongs and Beethoven's *Moonlight* Sonata (probably the earliest version on fortepiano). The first album of a projected recording of Bach's 'Forty-Eight' on clavichord appeared in 1933 to decidedly mixed reviews. Mackenzie argued, rather tepidly, that the recordings should be welcomed for their 'personal and historical interest' in consideration of Dolmetsch's advanced age and declining health.[10] But such special pleading failed to quell the increasingly harsh criticism meted out to the Dolmetsches (excepting Rudolph, whose performances on harpsichord were consistently singled out for praise). Alec Robertson wrote scathingly of a 1939 recording of John Jenkins's Fantasy for three viols (played by Carl, Cécile and Nathalie) and the *Moonlight* Sonata: 'These recordings are so poor that the ordinary standards of gramophone criticism can hardly be held to apply to them. If the admirers of the Dolmetsch family really have to sit through such dry and scraping sounds as are emitted by the two treble viols and the viola da gamba in Jenkins' pleasing Fantasy, then I am sorry for them.'[11] An American reviewer encouraged his readers to buy the Dolmetsches' records provided they were willing 'to make allowances for technical deficiencies in the light of the fact that any better presentation of this material is unlikely'.[12]

This may well have been true of the instrumental consort music heard at Haslemere, but recordings of early vocal and harpsichord music offered a considerably wider choice. It was not uncommon to find two or more competing versions of popular pieces like Morley's 'Sing we and chant it', 'Sumer is icumen in' or Rameau's 'Le Tambourin' listed in the catalogues. The major British and Continental record companies catered liberally to the early music audience in the twenties and thirties. One of the most sought-after groups was the English Singers, which made dozens of recordings – chiefly of Elizabethan madrigals – between 1921 and 1955.[13] The lack of rhythmic definition in their earliest efforts is no doubt partly attributable to the fact that they were recorded with 'six noses crowded into the single horn', as Steuart Wilson recalled. The group's electric recordings, including a dozen discs made in 1927 for Roycroft in New York, were a distinct improvement, though one's enthusiasm is tempered by the flaccid rhythms and unfocused tone. Recordings were in large part responsible for the international reputations enjoyed by Anselm Hughes's Nashdom Abbey Singers, Henry Expert's Chanterie de la Renaissance, the Leipzig Thomanerchor under Straube, Terry's Westminster Cathedral Choir, Kennedy Scott's Bach Cantata Club, Henry Washington's Schola Polyphonica, Sacher's Basle Chamber Choir, Ochs's Berlin Philharmonic Choir, Rudolph Mauersberger's Dresden Kreuzchor, Luis Millet's Orfeó Catalá and Davison's Harvard University Choir.

Pre-electric recording technology favoured smaller ensembles, and the chamber-choir movement that sprang up in the teens and twenties, especially in Germany and England, was tailor-made for the studio. The five discs of Byrd's music that the English Singers recorded for the composer's tercentenary in 1923, with one voice to a part, have a presence that most choral recordings of the period lack. The muddy recording of Palestrina's *Confitebor tibi* that Raffaele Casimiri and the Sistine Vatican Choir made at roughly the same time illustrates the difficulty of performing complex polyphonic music with a large group. Yet the remarkable thing is that composers like Byrd, Lassus, Palestrina and Schütz were represented at all on disc, as the demand for such esoteric items was undoubtedly quite small. On the other hand, recordings of the Bach and Handel oratorios could always be counted on to sell well. By the early thirties, nearly complete versions of the B minor Mass and *Messiah* were available, conducted by Albert Coates and Thomas Beecham, respectively. No attempt to record an entire Handel opera seems to have been made until the early fifties, but there is no dearth of recorded evidence of the early German revivals. Singers like Lotte Lehmann, Eva Liebenberg, Gerhard Hüsch, Emmi Leisner, Maria Olszewska and Heinrich Schlusnus recorded their interpretations of Handel arias, while the Italian and French repertoire found champions in the likes of Reinald Werrenrath, Martha Angelici and Ralph Crane. While these vintage recordings for the most part sound dated today – for one thing, almost none of the singers seems to have realized that Baroque music without ornamentation is, as Robert Donington says, 'mere bones unclad' – the singers' ease of vocal production, fluid coloratura and extraordinary breath control have an authentic quality that transcends their stylistic shortcomings.

The popularity of Woodhouse and Landowska (by far the most prolific harpsichordists in the recording studio) opened the doors for Anna Linde, Li Stadelman, Régina Patorni-Casadesus, Pauline Aubert, Marguerite Roesgen-Champion, Erwin Bodky, Lewis Richards, Simone Plé, Paul Brunold, Alice

Ehlers, Ruggero Gerlin and other harpsichordists of lesser renown. In 1929 Brunswick issued the first complete recording of the Brandenburg Concertos, performed by the London Chamber Orchestra under Anthony Bernard. Rudolph Dolmetsch played the harpsichord in all but the fifth concerto, which featured the pianist Walter Gieseking as keyboard soloist. Bernard, well aware of the microphone's inability to capture high frequencies, explained that 'the Second Brandenburg Concerto with the very high trumpet part could not be given exactly as written by Bach; both microphone and wax would have rebelled. Even in the fourth concerto the high notes of the flute had to be controlled in all forte passages.'[14] By the mid-thirties, when Adolf Busch recorded his acclaimed Brandenburg set for Columbia, the technology had progressed so dramatically that even the stratospheric piccolo trumpet part in the second concerto emerged in full sonic splendour.

'The repertoire that is available today for students and gramophone enthusiasts will amaze those who have not kept pace with its recent extension. Not only have virtually all the standard works been recorded, but much [sic] of the rarest works of the past, known only by name to many musicians and music lovers, have now been transferred to the discs.' So wrote Lawrence Gilman in his foreword to the first edition of The Gramophone Shop Encyclopedia of Recorded Music in 1936.[15] The 'society' issues that HMV's Walter Legge initiated in the early thirties encouraged record companies to become more audacious in their choice of repertoire. Legge's idea was simple: by soliciting subscriptions from listeners interested in a specific composer or musical work, HMV (and later its competitors) could recoup in advance the cost of recordings that would not otherwise have been commercially attractive. Among them were Landowska's accounts of the Goldberg Variations, Couperin and Scarlatti sonatas; Edwin Fischer's recording of the 'Forty-Eight' on piano (HMV's answer to the abortive 'Forty-Eight Society' which Columbia had created for Arnold Dolmetsch),[16] Albert Schweitzer's sampler of Bach organ music, and Pablo Casals's performances of the Bach solo cello suites. Emboldened by the success of these ventures, record companies enriched their catalogues in the thirties with Nadia Boulanger's album of Monteverdi madrigals, Landowska's Italian Concerto, Handel's op. 6 Concerti Grossi (excerpts conducted by Ansermet and the entire set played by the Boyd Neel Orchestra, both using harpsichord continuo), early choral music performed by the Orfeó Catalá of Barcelona, chant sung by the Solesmes monks, and smatterings of Lully, Rameau, Josquin, Palestrina, Schütz, Victoria, the Elizabethan composers and others. In England, the National Gramophonic Society was formed to promote recordings of unusual music, and in 1935 Decca lavished £20,000 on an uncut recording of

Purcell's *Dido and Aeneas*, issued by subscription on seven twelve-inch discs.[17]

Another of the recording industry's innovative schemes, historical anthologies, provided additional outlets for pre-Classical music. Columbia led the way in the early thirties with its *History of Music by Ear and Eye*, five eight-disc volumes, each accompanied by an illustrated booklet, surveying Western music from Gregorian chant to Varèse. The project was master-minded by Scholes, one of the first musicologists in England (or anywhere else) to take recordings and radio seriously as purveyors of concert-hall music. Among the participants in the recordings were Terry, the Dolmetsch family, the St George's Singers (conducted by Edmund Fellowes), the Bach Cantata Club, the contralto Doris Owens and the pianist Harold Samuel. No sooner had the Columbia set appeared than Parlophone brought out its *Two Thousand Years of Music*, a German production supervised by Curt Sachs, then director of the state instrument museum in Berlin. The scale of this undertaking was more modest – a mere dozen 78 rpm discs to cover everything from ancient Greek music to the High Baroque – but, whether by accident or design, the two anthologies complemented each other neatly. Columbia's reflected a distinctly British bias, while Parlophone's was weighted in favour of the German and Franco-Flemish masters. Judged purely by the calibre of the performances, however, the English anthology ranks several notches above the German. The Parlophone records make for exceedingly tedious listening today, while many of the performances in the Columbia *History* have worn remarkably well.

Sachs, having been stripped of his academic posts by the Nazis, emigrated to Paris in 1933 and embarked upon a vastly more ambitious project, the *Anthologie Sonore*, which was conceived as 'a living museum of music' employing the best performers available. 'Each epoch of history might be said to have its own sonority', wrote René Dumesnil in a pamphlet outlining the programme of the society. 'This derives from the instruments, which provide the timbre, and even more from the style, which is the reflection of the manners and the spirit of the time.'[18] Authenticity received high priority in the *Anthologie Sonore*, although it could not always be strictly observed; for example, modern brass and wind instruments had to be used, as historical reproductions were not yet widely available. The roster of performers was conspicuously more cosmopolitan than either Columbia's or Parlophone's. It included Cape's Pro Musica Antiqua, the Basle Chamber Choir, the tenor Max Meili and the baritone Yves Tinayre, Expert's Chanterie de la Renaissance, Henryk Opienski's Motet and Madrigal choir, Erwin Bodky on clavichord and Gerlin on harpsichord, the organists Marcel Dupré and André Maréchal, the lutenists Emilio Pujol and Herman Leeb, the gambist

Eva Heinetz and Guillaume de Van's Paraphonistes de St Jean-des-Matines. The anthology was open-ended and the recordings were issued in no particular sequence. (When the Haydn Society later reissued them on LPs, they were methodically rearranged by period.) Eventually the series spanned the centuries from Gregorian chant to Beethoven, providing a more or less comprehensive overview of pre-Classical music for generations of music lovers, professionals and students. Response to the *Anthologie Sonore* was keen, particularly in the United States, where it was hailed as 'a unique kind of recording enterprise in which an ideal, but all too rare, team work is maintained between the executives and technicians of a recording society, the artist, and the scholar – all uniting in the service of the composer and his music'.[19] Mackenzie regretted that none of the English record companies had had the idea first, but added wryly, 'we may perhaps be thankful that it has escaped the peculiar stamp of English academic culture'.[20]

Not until the early fifties did England produce, in HMV's lavish *History of Music in Sound*, a worthy companion to the *Anthologie Sonore*. Historical anthologies, large and small, had proliferated in the interim. Tinayre's *Seven Centuries of Sacred Music* on the Lumen label surveyed the song literature from Notre Dame organum to Mozart. For American Columbia, Tinayre recorded four discs of sacred and secular music from the twelfth to the seventeenth centuries. The American Society of Ancient Instruments recorded two volumes of Renaissance and Baroque music for Victor. The Czechs launched their monumental *Musicae Bohemicae Anthologia* and the Italians their *Musiche Italiane Antiche* (containing, *inter alia*, an abridged version of Monteverdi's *Orfeo* recorded in Rome in 1943). In addition, the catalogues swelled with dozens of shorter collections by Boris Ord's Cambridge University Madrigal Society, the Trapp Family Choir, Mogens Wöldike's Danish Radio Madrigal Choir, André Maréchal, Alice Ehlers and others. In the mid-thirties the Editions de l'Oiseau-Lyre (sometimes referred to by its English name, the Lyrebird Press) began issuing records to accompany its highly regarded publications of early music. Founded in 1932 by Louise B. M. Dyer, an Australian amateur musician and patron of the arts, L'Oiseau-Lyre established itself as one of the foremost purveyors of early music when its recording operation was absorbed by Decca after the Second World War.

A further fillip to the revival was provided by specialist record shops catering for listeners with off-beat tastes. A handful of them, such as the Boîte à Musique in Paris and the Gramophone Shop in New York, issued recordings of unusual music, new as well as old, under their own imprints. By the late thirties the American recording industry was recovering from its Depression-induced slump and producing recordings by a wide array of early musicians, foreign and domestic. Prominent among them were Ars Rediviva, the Boyd Neel Orchestra, Hermann Diener's Collegium Musicum, the London Chamber Orchestra, the Marcel Couraud Vocal Ensemble, the Busch Chamber Players, Lehman Engel's Madrigal Singers, Suzanne Bloch, Max Goberman's New York Sinfonietta, Ralph Kirkpatrick, Yella Pessl, Ernst Victor Wolf, Carl Weinrich, E. Power Biggs and Nicola Montani's Palestrina Chorus.

In 1940 the American critic David Hall reflected that 'the phonograph within the last few years has been the chief means of bringing old music to the modern listener'.[21] Had he lived in Europe instead of the United States, Hall might have been inclined to add that radio provided an equally important forum for the revival. From the early thirties, the volume of early music broadcast in Germany, England and France made it possible to speak for the first time without exaggeration of a mass audience for pre-Classical repertoire. The British Broadcasting Company (later Corporation) commenced regular transmissions in 1922 and other European countries soon set up their own broadcasting entities. As with recordings, early experiments in musical broadcasting left much to be desired. A Gibbons service transmitted from Canterbury Cathedral in 1925 threw the *Musical Times*'s 'wireless' correspondent into a quandary. While the church bells could be heard quite distinctly, he reported, 'the music itself came through so vaguely that one would not be justified in expressing an opinion on the more complicated music or its performance'.[22] The BBC persevered nonetheless, offering its listeners some remarkably venturesome fare in the late twenties, including broadcasts from the Haslemere Festival, an English-language performance of Monteverdi's *Ritorno d'Ulisse in Patria*, a series devoted to Bach's church cantatas and, in 1928, a programme of medieval choral music commemorating the fortieth anniversary of the Plainsong and Mediaeval Music Society. The quality of radio transmission improved steadily. Reviewing a pair of concerts by the Société des Instruments Anciens Casadesus in 1928, the *Musical Times* called them 'programmes of unique interest, both musical and historical, beautifully performed, and broadcast to perfection. So good was the transmission, in fact, that one speculated whether it was due to the special character of the instruments. If so, the B.B.C. may do much to bring about a revival in the making and playing of some delightful instruments that have been regarded as obsolete.'[23]

Radio did indeed make a vital contribution to the early music movement. Nowhere was this more apparent than in Germany, where the significance of the new medium was quickly grasped and its educational potential keenly debated. In 1932 the *Zeitschrift für Musikwissenschaft*, Germany's leading musicological journal, aired a telling exchange of views between the conductor Ernst Latzko and Richard Baum, Karl Vötterle's colleague at Bärenreiter.[24] Latzko argued that radio, as the 'natural centre' of the revival, had been largely responsible for 'the intensive and systematic cultivation of early music' in Germany. The sounds of the old instruments lent themselves perfectly to electronic reproduction, above all the harpsichord, which, in Latzko's vivid phrase, made 'a triumphal march through the transmitter'. Baum was not convinced. Whatever else radio engineers may have achieved, he countered, they had yet to prove themselves capable of reproducing the fine nuances of timbre which distinguished historical instruments from modern ones. Furthermore, he questioned whether the essentially passive medium of radio was an appropriate vehicle for music that was not meant to be heard in a concert hall. Like many of his associates in the Youth Movement, Baum believed that participatory music-making – the very essence of the *Hausmusik* ideal – was inherently more worthwhile than simply listening to music, whether on radio or on records. (Many musicians, fearing that electronic reproductions would supplant live performances, at first refused to accept the new media as legitimate.) The only point on which Latzko and Baum found themselves in accord was that radio offered an unprecedented opportunity to reach millions of listeners who might otherwise remain untouched by the revival.

German radio took its educational mission seriously. As early as 1930 Westdeutscher Rundfunk in Cologne (then, as later, an enlightened patron of early music) formed an early music society comprising violin, viola d'amore, gamba, flute and harpsichord.[25] In the early thirties the network's audiences heard contemporary harpsichord music performed by Li Stadelman, the *St Matthew Passion* broadcast from the Thomaskirche in Leipzig, Latzko's Collegium Musicum, Alice Ehlers playing a newly discovered harpsichord concerto by J. C. Bach, a recital on an eighteenth-century organ at Rothab, and a concert of 'unknown' Bach including a performance of the sixth solo cello suite on a viola pomposa. Particularly notable were the weekly broadcasts of Bach cantatas performed by the Thomanerchor under Straube. These were relayed to France, England and other countries, boosting their potential audience far beyond the more than 3.5 million radio listeners in Germany itself.[26]

Just as modern modes of transportation were binding together the musical world, so radio, by chipping away at the bastions of provincialism, hastened the transformation of the early music movement into a truly international community. The French musicologist Henry Prunières, on hearing a Bach cantata broadcast from the Gewandhaus in 1932, exclaimed: 'I thought I was in the vast Leipzig hall, so faithfully were the atmosphere and the resonance of the building transmitted to me over the airwaves, and the singing, too, came across with ideal purity'.[27] Although he complained that France lagged behind other European countries in broadcasting outstanding musical events, Prunières conceded that 'not a week goes by but that one can hear a great work, old or modern, never before performed in Paris'. He was impressed by Landowska's broadcast of a Haydn concerto from Zurich in 1932, noting that the microphone conveyed the sound of her Pleyel harpsichord splendidly. 'It is not distorted as the piano's sound too often is. I have no doubt that the T.S.F. is contributing in large measure to familiarizing the general public with the rich sonorities of this magnificent instrument that Landowska has done so much to revive.'[28] Already in 1930 the *Revue musicale* had devoted an entire issue to *musique mécanique*,[29] in which the writer observed that Bach's transparently contrapuntal music was especially well served by the microphone. The article was illustrated with a photograph showing Falla at the harpsichord playing his concerto in a recording studio.

American radio networks, philosophically inclined to entertain rather than educate their listeners, plied a less adventurous course than their European counterparts. Instead of an 'intensive and systematic cultivation of early music', American audiences were offered sporadic and almost invariably brief broadcasts by the likes of the Handel and Haydn Society, the English Singers and the Aguilar Lute Quartet from Spain. Not until the late thirties and early forties did artists like Kirkpatrick, Biggs, Bloch and Landowska begin broadcasting with any regularity. During the war, NBC's University of the Air produced a series of 110 programmes tracing the development of music in the Americas over several centuries, but such substantial presentations were few and far between. As a result, American early musicians never looked to the radio networks for support as did ensembles like the Basle Chamber Orchestra, the Brussels Pro Musica Antiqua and the London Chamber Orchestra.

In England, the BBC Singers and the Fleet Street Choir continued to broadcast a fair amount of early music during the Second World War. But it was in 1946, with the creation of the Third Programme, that the BBC made its greatest contribution to the revival. Devised by a team of distinguished musicologists including Anthony Lewis and Denis Stevens, the Third Programme was pitched at 'the alert and receptive listener, who is willing to make an effort to select his programming in advance and then meet the performer half-way by giving his whole attention to what is being broadcast'.[30] By its very nature the new service appealed to a minority audience (estimated at two-thirds of a million listeners at the outset),[31] but the exposure it provided for early music and its performers was of inestimable value. By the early fifties Third Programme listeners were being escorted down little-known byways of the repertoire in series devoted to early medieval music,

Tallis, Dufay, Dunstable and the Eton Choirbook. A seventy-part survey of European art music, launched in 1948, formed the basis of HMV's highly successful *History of Music in Sound*. Elizabeth Roche has calculated that works written before 1700 accounted for nearly a third of the music broadcast on the Third Programme in a single week in 1953.[32] Reacting to the inevitable charges of élitism, the BBC soon signalled a retreat from this bold policy, but there was no stopping the growth of English early music groups that the Third Programme had precipitated. The BBC's experiment had demonstrated conclusively that early music deserved to be part of every listener's experience and not, as Roche put it, 'merely aural furniture for an ivory tower'.

The electronic media's patronage of early music in the post-war period gave rise to a new phenomenon: the early music ensemble organized specifically for the purposes of broadcasting or recording. As we have seen, both Cape's Pro Musica Antiqua and Greenberg's New York Pro Musica grew out of groups originally assembled for studio work. In 1954 Westdeutscher Rundfunk formed the Cappella Coloniensis, a descendant of its earlier Society for Early Music. Directed by August Wenzinger and Eduard Gröninger, the Cappella was the first early-instrument chamber orchestra to gain wide exposure on radio and recordings, as well as making concert tours throughout the world.[33] A decade later Franzjosef Maier founded a similar ensemble, the Collegium Aureum, to record the Baroque and early Classical repertoire for the Harmonia Mundi label; it, too, soon branched out into giving concert performances.[34] Christopher Hogwood's Academy of Ancient Music, the most popular early-instrument orchestra of the 1980s, likewise emerged from the studio to become one of the most prolific early music groups on records. When one considers how many radio orchestras and choirs have devoted a significant portion of their time to pre-Classical music over the years, the role the radio networks have played in building an audience for early music takes on even greater importance.

Television, by contrast, has contributed comparatively little to the revival. Greenberg's broadcasts with the New York Pro Musica on America's excellent 'Omnibus' series in the late fifties and early sixties demonstrated that early music could be successfully adapted to the medium, but television executives have understandably been wary of filling their screens with musicians wielding viols, crumhorns and Baroque flutes, no matter how gifted or telegenic they may be. Consequently, early music has featured only fitfully on television as accompaniment for theatrical productions (notably the Early Music Consort of London's soundtracks for the BBC series *The Six Wives of Henry VIII* and *Elizabeth R*), in special presentations like Nikolaus Harnoncourt's Monteverdi opera cycle of the 1970s, or on educational series like Granada's survey of music history (television's belated answer to the monumental recorded anthologies of yesteryear).

Similar limitations apply to cinematic applications of early music. One sympathizes with the *Musical Times* correspondent who was scandalized to hear the 'Et incarnatus' from Bach's B minor Mass accompanying a love scene in a 1928 silent film.[35] Yet such travesties at least fostered an awareness of early music, if only subliminally, as did Alice Ehlers's cameo appearance playing the harpsichord in the ballroom scene in Laurence Olivier's *Wuthering Heights* of 1939. In the early thirties the Dolmetsch family recorded soundtracks for two feature-length adventure films on historical subjects,[36] anticipating by some four decades the music that David Munrow wrote and performed for such films as John Boorman's science-fiction fantasy *Zardoz* and Joel Santoni's *La Course en tête*. Early music has served as an aural backdrop for works of art in films like André Cauvin's *L'Agneau Mystique* (played by Cape's Pro Musica Antiqua) and Ernst Marischka's *St Matthew Passion*. When Ernest Irving arranged the music for *The Great Mr Handel*, a 1942 fictionalized biography of the composer, he borrowed a pair of Kirckman harpsichords and had the orchestra switch to gut strings to make them sound more authentic.[37] Several of Miklós Rózsa's film scores, notably *Quo Vadis?* and *Diane*, incorporate old instruments and music. Bach has inspired a number of feature and documentary films, including Jean-Marie Straub's *Chronicle of Anna Magdalena Bach*, which was distinguished chiefly by Gustav Leonhardt's first (and, to date, his only) screen appearance as the composer.

Whether good, bad or indifferent, such creations attest to early music's gradual absorption into twentieth-century mass culture, much as literature did at an earlier phase of the revival. Literary allusions to pre-Classical music and performers occur with increasing frequency from the time of Mendelssohn's *St Matthew* revival, which made a deep impression on Goethe and his contemporaries. References to early music abound in German Romantic literature and fictionalized accounts of pre-Classical composers' lives were perennially popular in Europe. Typical of the genre are the novellas by Stéphen de la Madelaine that appeared in the *Revue et gazette musicale* in the 1830s, the libretto to Flotow's opera *Alessandro Scarlatti*, and Albert Emil Brachvogel's novel *Friedemann Bach*, which a modern commentator describes as 'a catch-all of historical fact, scurrilous anecdote, frenetic imagination, and bare-faced sentimentality'[38] (no doubt a highly saleable combination then as now). A recent descendant is Laszlo Passuth's novel *Madrigal* about Gesualdo, whose sensational career has always provided good copy. Victor Hugo's invocation of *puissant Palestrina*, the 'father of harmony', in his poem *Que la musique date du seizième siècle* reflects his interest in Fétis's historical concerts.[39] The hero of Gabriele d'Annunzio's *Il Fuoco* experiences a vision in which he hears a woman singing Monteverdi's *Lamento d'Arianna* while accompanying herself on the harpsichord. D'Annunzio met Dolmetsch in Rome in 1897, shortly before the novel was written, but his breathless description of the work's climax suggests a Wagnerian love-death rather than a typically relaxed Dolmetsch performance: 'Suddenly their souls were ravished by a power that seemed the lightning-like eagle by which Dante in his dream was ravished up to the flame. They were burning together in undying truth, they heard the world's melody pass through their luminous ecstasy.'[40]

Like many of his contemporaries, d'Annunzio espied a link between the theories of the sixteenth-century Florentine Camerata, from which Monteverdi's operas sprang, and Wagner's *Gesamtkunstwerk*. This theme is more fully developed in George Moore's *Evelyn Inness*, and it is no accident that the other major writers whom Dolmetsch inspired – Yeats, Pound, Joyce – all traced the roots of their art back to the Renaissance and beyond. The figure of the musician who is at once in touch with the pre-Romantic past and avowedly, even defiantly, progressive recurs frequently in turn-of-the-century literature, a well-known representative being the eponymous hero of *Jean Christophe* by the French music critic Romain Rolland. Although he was well-disposed professionally toward the Schola Cantorum, the opinions that Rolland put into his fictional composer's mouth are often highly critical of d'Indy. 'The *Schola* had tried to let in fresh air, and had opened the windows upon the past. But only on the past,' Rolland writes. 'The windows were opened upon a courtyard, not into the street. And it was not much use. Hardly had they opened the windows than they closed the shutters, like old women afraid of catching cold. And there came up a gust or two of the Middle Ages, Bach, Palestrina, popular songs. But what was the good of that? The room smelt of stale air. And if they knew more music than other people, they also denied more in art. Their music took on a doctrinal character: there was no relaxation: their concerts were history lectures, or a string of edifying examples.'[41]

The modern artist's ambivalent relationship with tradition is a central theme of two extraordinary musical novels published in the 1940s, Hermann Hesse's *Das Glasperlenspiel* and Thomas Mann's *Doktor Faustus*. Hesse's hero, Joseph Knecht, belongs to a hermetic order of intellectuals whose passion for the glass-bead game is equalled only by their love of pre-Classical music. Hesse posits the theory that the true contemporary feels at home in every epoch and should therefore be able to perform music of any period as if it were modern. Among the League of the Journeyers to the East were itinerant instrumentalists and minstrels who performed early music 'as though all later refinements, fashions and virtuosities were still unknown'.[42] Hesse had mused on the purity of early music as early as 1913 in a short story entitled *Alte Musik*,[43] but his retreat into the past assumed more cosmic dimensions in the nostalgic fantasizing of *Das Glasperlenspiel* (written in neutral Switzerland during the war). Mann was annoyed by Hesse's 'pious antiquarianism', alleging that he saw 'nothing fine after Purcell'.[44] Mann's own sympathies lay with the progressive composers, but, as Alex Aronson has pointed out, the narrator of *Doktor Faustus*, Serenus Zeitblom, would not have been out of place in Hesse's novel.[45] An amateur on the viola d'amore, Zeitblom is often prevailed upon 'to regale the company with a chaconne or sarabande from the seventeenth century, a *'plaisir d'amour'* from the eighteenth, or to perform a sonata by Ariosti, the friend of Handel, or one of Haydn's written for the viola di bordone but quite possible for the viola d'amore as well'.[46] Mann's composer–protagonist Adrian Leverkühn attends a concert by Paul Sacher's Basle Chamber Choir consisting of 'Monteverdi's Magnificat, some organ studies by Frescobaldi, an oratorio by Carissimi, and a cantata by Buxtehude'.[47] (The programme actually took place on 14 November 1943, while Mann was living in the United States.) The many detailed references to early music in *Doktor Faustus*, counterpointing the primary discussion of Schoenberg's musical language, and the dialectical tension that Mann sets up between new and old, reveal how extensively the activities of the Schola Cantorum Basiliensis had permeated the world of ideas as well as music.

Early music figures more tangentially in a variety of lighter fictional works, from the description of a Landowska recital in Christine Weston's novel *The Dark Wood* to James Gollin's recent series of murder mysteries featuring an American early music ensemble called the Antiqua Players.[48] Given the fascination that early music and its performers have long exerted on men and women of letters, it is not surprising that the poet–musician Ezra Pound played a prominent role in the Vivaldi revival of the late forties and early fifties. The emphasis on Baroque music in the concerts that Pound organized in Rapallo in the thirties reflected not only his longstanding admiration of Dolmetsch but also his ultra-conservative political views. Hailing Vivaldi as a champion of 'Italian musical autarchy', Pound worked tirelessly to get his works published and performed.[49] In Vivaldi, the early music revival found a composer who appealed to laymen in a way that Bach, Schütz, Rameau, Purcell and the others whose names were frequently invoked in the cause of musical nationalism had never done. The rediscovery of his music (literally, for much of it came to light only in the late twenties and thirties) proved, as Robert Craft has said, 'as momentous for lovers of Baroque music as that of the Dead Sea Scrolls for students of religion'.[50] The 'Vivaldi craze' and the introduction of long-playing records after 1948 seem to have been made for each other. Vivaldi recordings flooded the market in the early LP era, a period which saw *The Four Seasons* become a perennial best-seller and turned Baroque chestnuts like the Pachelbel Canon into what someone called 'the Muzak of the intelligentsia'.

As Greenberg pointed out, the early music explosion was sparked by the small, independent record companies that proliferated just before and after the war, especially in the United States. Musicraft, Technicord, Vox, Westminster, Concert Hall Society, Esoteric, Lyrichord, Renaissance, Timely, Discophiles Français, Kantorei, Durium and the Neglected Master-piece Recording Society are but a few of the labels that catered for listeners in search of the unusual. By employing lesser-known artists, they were able to keep production costs down and compete with the major firms, most of which continued to focus on the standard bread-and-butter repertoire. A conspicuous exception was Deutsche Grammophon, whose Archiv series gave fresh impetus to the historical anthology in the fifties. Under the direction of Fred Hamel, a German musicologist who had studied with Arnold Schering and Friedrich Blume, Archiv Produktion aspired to be nothing less than a comprehensive survey of Western music from Gregorian chant to Mozart. Hamel agreed with Curt Sachs that recordings were a valuable educational resource, but earlier anthologies, he felt, had been 'more interesting scientifically than musically'.[51] He saw no reason to continue presenting early music in the short snippets required by the 78 rpm format. Instead Archiv committed itself to recording works 'in their complete authentic form', using specialist performers playing period instruments whenever possible. With Germanic thoroughness, the record-ings were grouped into twelve 'research periods' and decked out with scrupulous historical documentation. Deutsche Grammophon's imprimatur and resources ensured the success of the project and other firms soon developed their own early music lines, among them Telefunken's Das Alte Werk, L'Oiseau-Lyre's Florilegium and EMI's Reflexe series.

Both on records and in the concert hall, the revival of Baroque music expanded precipitately in the fifties. Yet despite the exposure that recordings gave to groups like the New York Pro Musica, the Brussels Pro Musica Antiqua, the Prague Madrigal Singers and the Deller Consort, medieval and Renaissance music fared much less well on records than the eighteenth-century repertoire. In a survey of sixteenth-century music available on records in 1958, Jeremy Noble pointed out that only five of Palestrina's 105 masses had been recorded, and only a single one by Lassus; the situation has changed very little in the last three decades. As for the medieval repertoire, Gilbert Reaney complained in 1957: 'It is a shock to anyone who does not believe music was invented around the year 1500 to find how little medieval music is available on gramophone records'.[52] For the most part, recordings of pre-Baroque music were confined to anthologies; Archiv was practically alone in offering a sustained look at the work of a single composer or school. Only in the sixties and seventies, when groups like Musica Reservata, the Studio der frühen Musik, Syntagma Musicum and the Capella Antiqua of Munich came to the fore, did record companies begin to redress the balance.

James Coover and Richard Colvig reported in 1973 that the amount of medieval and Renaissance music in American record catalogues had nearly doubled in the past decade, while the number of composers represented had almost tripled. In 1967 Judy Collins recorded Landini's *Lasso di donna* on a folksong album with an early-instrument ensemble directed by Joshua Rifkin – surely the first time medieval music had won a place on the 'pop' charts. Yet glaring gaps remained to be filled in such key areas as Renaissance sacred music. Howard Mayer Brown noted in 1975 that there was plenty of Palestrina, Josquin and Victoria to be heard, but very little of Isaac, Obrecht, Willaert, Lassus and other composers of comparable historical significance. He concluded that 'sacred music of the 16th century is so badly represented on recordings . . . that one can scarcely begin to get an idea of the riches that exist'. Elizabeth Roche, surveying a quarter-century of early-music record-ings in 1979, echoed Brown's complaint: 'For so large a period of musical history [up to 1650] to account for so tiny a proportion of record company activity should be no source of satisfaction to anybody.'[53]

Nevertheless, the revival had undeniably come a long way since the late thirties, when the musicologist Charles van den Borren was pleasantly shocked to hear a recording of a piece he had only imagined before in a 'mental reading'.[54] Indeed, as more and more early music became available, some musicologists began to fear that the permanence of recorded perfor-mances would lend a spurious authority to interpretations which were by their very nature tentative and experimental. 'Musical performance is still the most uncertain, the most controversial field of historical research', Otto Gombosi wrote in 1952. 'While up to now the enthusiastic dilettantism of groups playing old music on old instruments – often and notoriously not the right kind of old instruments – has done little harm and probably a small measure of good, the new situation confronts us with an emergency and there is danger that stop-gap measures will be taken for the final word of wisdom.'[55]

Gombosi's apprehension was not unfounded. Recordings like the New York Pro Musica's *Play of Daniel* and the Studio der frühen Musik's Arabic-flavoured *Carmina Burana* did indeed confer a kind of instant authenticity upon the highly personalized and controversial theories that lay behind them. As long as such experiments were conducted at musicological congresses and the like, scholars had a chance to discuss and vet them *in camera* before they entered the public domain. Modern mass-communication techniques short-circuited that process. Suddenly performances of early music were being touted as 'authentic' with all the resources the publicists had at their command. The commercialism of the recording industry added a new and unsettling factor to the performer–scholar–audience equation. 'Too often does one suspect that the market, more than historical fidelity and artistic taste and intelligence, is what pushes performances for recordings', an eminent musicologist has written. Armen Carapetyan went on to accuse record companies of peddling 'confusion, insufficient knowledge, sometimes plain ignorance, sometimes inexcusable carelessness, ill judgment and too often poor taste' in their treatment of early music. [56] On the other hand, musicologists have sown no small amount of confusion of their own over the years. Perhaps, after all, the haphazard policies of the recording industry simply reflect the problems the early music movement has had in coming to terms with its own success in the media age.

The ramifications of that quandary have become ever more apparent as performers and recording engineers enter into a more sophisticated partnership. Slowly and inevitably, early music has gone 'high-tech'. In the sixties the Swingle Singers doo-be-dooed their way to fame in jazzy Baroque arrangements and *Switched-On Bach*, intoned on the Moog Synthesizer by Walter (now Wendy) Carlos, became one of the best-selling classical albums of all time. Jazz and popular treatments of Baroque music were, of course, hardly new. Ralph Kirkpatrick and others had noted the aptness for dissonant harmonies and sharp rhythmic figures that commended the harpsichord to jazz composers like Duke Ellington and John Lewis. [57] Baroque music has been a strong force in modern jazz, from Jacques Loussier, Art Farmer, Benny Goodman and Alex Wilder to Claude Bolling, Bob James and Keith Jarrett. It has even infiltrated the rock world: witness the appropriation of Bach's 'Air on the G String' by the English group Procul Harum in 'A Whiter Shade of Pale'. In America the Mannheim Steamroller uses harpsichord, lute and recorders in a dreamy, soft-rock idiom, while the guitarist Frederick Hand has extended the scope of his jazz improvisations to embrace Machaut and the *Cantigas de Santa Maria*. Martin Best's easy-listening blend of folk and early music idioms has made him popular with a wide variety of audiences. We have heard Vivaldi and Bach played on traditional Japanese instruments (aptly dubbed 'well-tempura'd Bach'), rock versions of the Monteverdi operas, and *Dido and Aeneas* arranged for pop singers, saxophones and synthesizers, to say nothing of the apparently inexhaustible musicological travesties of P. D. Q. Bach.

For better or worse – perhaps for better *and* worse – twentieth-century mass media have radically transformed the early music movement. No longer are Monteverdi, Machaut, Byrd, Purcell, Vivaldi and the rest the private preserve of scholars and connoisseurs. Early music is in the air – literally as well as figuratively. Concerts and recordings of early music are reviewed regularly in the popular press. Partly as a result of this heightened publicity and competitiveness, standards of performance in the field have improved immeasurably. It is now taken for granted that early musicians should be as technically proficient as their mainstream colleagues. Early music, in short, has become a highly marketable commodity, with much-recorded performers like Frans Brüggen, Nikolaus Harnoncourt, Christopher Hogwood, Emma Kirkby, Gustav Leonhardt, Michala Petri and Sigiswald Kuijken in demand far and wide. The sheltered world of Bordes's Schola Cantorum and Dolmetsch's Haslemere seems increasingly remote. Landowska, the first of the early music superstars, spoke of the need 'to open wide the windows on our magnificent past' and weave early music into the fabric of everyday life.[58] Three decades after her death, the windows have been thrown open wider than even she might have imagined.

7

STAGING A COMEBACK

*The Baroque Opera Revival · Modern Stagings of Rameau, Lully, Purcell,
Monteverdi, Handel and Others · Germany's 'Handel Renaissance' ·
Arrangements and Updatings of Early Operas by Vincent d'Indy, Carl Orff,
Luciano Berio and Others · Baroque Dance and Stagecraft Resurrected ·
Alfred Deller and the Countertenor Renaissance · August Wenzinger,
Nikolaus Harnoncourt, Raymond Leppard, Alan Curtis, Nicholas McGegan
and Other Scholar–Conductors.*

Perhaps the major obstacle to reviving Baroque operas is the practical problem of assembling the ingredients. Performing a Handel trio sonata or a motet by Josquin is one thing; mounting a production of a seventeenth- or eighteenth-century opera, with all its elaborate trappings, is quite another. Nineteenth-century commentators and editors of early opera – men like Robert Eitner and Friedrich Chrysander – tended to be enthusiastic about the works themselves but dubious about putting them on stage. And so, apart from the handful of pre-Mozartean works that stayed more or less continuously in the active repertoire – *The Beggar's Opera*, Pergolesi's *Serva padrona*, Handel's *Acis and Galatea*, Gluck's *Orfeo* and *Armide* – the nineteenth century owed its acquaintance with early opera chiefly to bits and pieces parcelled out on concert programmes.

The first of Fétis's *concerts historiques* at the Paris Conservatoire, in 1832, included excerpts from two of the earliest operas, Peri's *Euridice* and Monteverdi's *Orfeo*, as well as works by Lully, Rameau, Handel, Keiser, Scarlatti, Pergolesi and Gluck.[1] It was a resounding success, certainly more so than the series of historical soirées that the Paris Opéra presented in 1880. Although the management took care to put a smattering of modern works into each programme, intermingled with fragments of Rameau, Lully and Gluck, many disgruntled patrons walked out in the middle of the performance. In Adolphe Jullien's opinion, the Opéra had erred by offering too little early music to satisfy the real connoisseurs and too much for the general public.[2] It was not the first time such a miscalculation had been made. When several scenes from Destouches's *Callirhoé* were given in 1875 at the Salle Taitbout in Paris, one critic complained that the effect was 'of an immense and monotonous recitatif'[3] (though one wonders whether he was criticizing the music itself or the performance). In Italy a few years later, the Società Musicale Romana presented a concert of *musica melodrammatica* from Peri to Rossini. The first three numbers – two concerted pieces by Caccini and Monteverdi's *Lamento d'Arianna* – were accompanied by an ensemble of antique viols, theorboes, archlutes, harps and harpsichord, similar to the instrumentation that Fétis had used in his *Orfeo* excerpts.[4]

Staged performances of Baroque opera were exceedingly rare in the nineteenth century, though admittedly it is sometimes difficult to ascertain from published reports whether the music was presented in concert form or, as must often have been the case, with a modicum of staging, sets and costumes. The production of Peri's *Euridice* in 1894 by students of Franklyn Sargeant's Academy in New York does not sound very elaborate, but the Hamburg State Theatre had greater scenic resources at its disposal for the condensed version of Handel's *Almira* that opened its week-long festival of German opera in 1878. This time monotony was avoided by mixing trumpets and reed instruments with the strings (33-strong 'to achieve the necessary fullness of tone', according to one report).[5] But Chrysander, whose editions of the Handel operas had recently begun to appear, grumbled about the 'philistine dismemberment' of the score[6] and the arranger's 'contempt for musical scholarship'.[7] Nevertheless, the production was repeated the following year in Leipzig (where the *Neue Zeitschrift für Musik* commented favourably on the singers' virtuosity but regretted that Handel's arias 'were not written with dramatic considerations in mind') and again in Hamburg as part of the Handel bicentenary celebrations in 1885.

An event of farther-reaching consequence occurred ten years later, when the first modern staging of Purcell's *Dido and Aeneas* was seen in London. 'The music is of the kind that exhilarates like the air of a frosty morning in spring', gushed the *Musical Times* of the performance by Royal College of Music students at the Lyceum Theatre.[8] No doubt the score lost some of its crispness in Charles Wood's lush orchestration, cited by the magazine's reviewer as an example of 'well-intentioned but mistaken zeal'. *The Times* sounded a chauvinistic note, averring that *Dido and Aeneas*, 'as compared with the conventional Italian operas of the Handelian period, merits the higher title of "music drama".' The paper praised the dancers and décor ('though in one scene an English country lane had to do duty for the depths of the Carthaginian forest') and predicted that the work would soon become part of the regular operatic repertoire.[9] A different kind of staging was essayed by Gordon Craig in 1900 for the newly formed Purcell Operatic Society at the Hampstead Conservatoire. Craig blithely announced that he had 'taken care to be entirely incorrect in all matters of detail'; *The Times* reported that his designs were 'calculated to alarm the most intrepid student of modern art'.[10] The music was arranged by the conductor, Martin Fallas Shaw, who likewise disregarded historical precedent in using a piano continuo. As for Purcell's other theatre music, King Arthur and The Fairy Queen were revived in concert around the turn of the century, though neither reached the stage until the 1920s. A student production in Boston of Milton's Comus in 1901, with period music, sets and costumes, testifies to a parallel interest in resuscitating the Tudor and Stuart masques.[11]

Exhumations of early dramatic works did not stop with the seventeenth century; medieval music theatre, sacred and secular alike, was ripe for revival as well. Adam de la Halle's Jeu de Robin et de Marion, which Coussemaker had published in a scholarly edition in 1872, was heard in a modernized version by Julien Tiersot and Emile Blémont at a festival honouring the composer at Arras in 1896.[12] Under Bordes and d'Indy, the Schola Cantorum seized the initiative in reviving the French Baroque operas. The first modern performance of Rameau's Platée, however, took place in Munich in 1901. The music was reorchestrated, apparently committee-style, by members of the Orchester-Verein, and, according to one report, an attempt was made to give the production a period look. 'The old stage with its "podium" was revived. The costumes, half Greek, half Louis XIV, as they were at the time of the first performance in 1749, were very successful.'[13] Emile Jaques-Dalcroze, the originator of eurhythmics, conducted Rameau's Hippolyte et Aricie in Geneva in the spring of 1903.[14] That summer Bordes led an alfresco production of La Guirlande in the courtyard of the Schola, prompting Constant Zakone to ask, 'Why are we so seldom allowed to hear a master who combines the best qualities of our race?' The sets were spare, consisting of 'false shrubbery and marbles' lit by pink lamps.[15]

As a rule, however, Schola productions were not staged, and the larger works – Rameau's Dardanus, Castor et Pollux and Zoroastre, Lully's Armide and Destouches's Issé – were typically given in fragmentary form. Despite their patriotic preference for French composers, d'Indy and Bordes were not blind to the genius of the first great master of the lyric stage. For the Schola's first production of Monteverdi's Orfeo in 1904, involving some 150 singers and instrumentalists,[16] d'Indy prepared a French translation and a new performing edition, which he candidly proffered as 'a work of art, not of archaeology'.[17] The first and last acts were summarily dropped and substantial cuts were made in the remaining three. D'Indy based his orchestra on Monteverdi's own – pairs of flutes, oboes and trumpets, five trombones, strings, harp-lute, chromatic harp, harpsichord and organ – but his realization of the continuo was thoroughly modernized. The production's success emboldened d'Indy to present L'Incoronazione di Poppea the following year. It, too, was well received, Louis Laloy declaring it 'a much more varied and lively work than *Orfeo*, whose nobility is not without some monotony'.[18]

In his review of *La Guirlande*, Zakone called for the establishment of a 'French Bayreuth' dedicated to the revival of the classic French operas. Bordes made a similar proposal, insisting that care be taken to employ a permanent stage director who would be 'more respectful of the old works than of the sometimes outdated and anti-natural traditions of the modern lyric theatre'.[19] In 1905 the *Tribune de St Gervais* announced that Bordes had formed an ensemble to perform medieval mystery plays, Monteverdi's *Orfeo* 'and other characteristic reconstructions'.[20] He did not live to see his idea brought to fruition, but he did conduct *Castor et Pollux* at Montpellier in January 1908. Eduard Perrin reported that the production 'succeeded beyond all expectations', in spite of weaknesses in the choreography and staging, and suggested that Rameau was more deserving than Gluck of the title of operatic revolutionary.[21] Meanwhile, the Paris Opéra was pressing ahead with plans to mount a production of *Hippolyte et Aricie* that very spring. The premiere took place in a blaze of publicity. Just before the opening, the *Bulletin français de la Société Internationale de Musique* published a long and copiously illustrated article by Georges Imbart de la Tour of the Conservatoire arguing that modern productions of Rameau's operas should adhere as closely as possible to Baroque stagecraft and musical style. Only this, the professor wrote, would convey the 'period atmosphere' which he considered 'indispensable' to the works.[22] In the event, the Opéra disregarded his advice and opted for conventional spectacle. Laloy deplored the 'display of loose-fitting lingerie which, since Talma's day, has given our *tragédies* the academic coldness of a David tableau'.[23] Henri Quittard was equally disappointed by the choreography and staging. 'The chorus and supers didn't act at all', he wrote. 'And when they did so by accident, one wished they had refrained. The ballets seemed to be governed by the same negligence.'[24] The most damning criticism, though, concerned the disfiguring cuts and revisions that d'Indy had made in the score. Laloy sarcastically chided him for bowdlerizing *Hippolyte et Aricie* in a misguided effort to tone down its livelier passages:

Too many dances, too many smiles, too many garlands and flowers! Modern virtue reproves such superfluous ornaments and unpardonable distractions. No matter what the cost, the old opera must don the cast-off garments of our sermonizing lyric drama. Recitative, which everyone agrees is its weak part, will be shunted to the foreground and doled out slowly, so that the monotony of its cadences may become unbearable. The airs, on the other hand, will be dashed off, since we are embarrassed today to abandon ourselves to the charm of the voice; above all, no runs, trills and vocalises, which were the old opera's attraction but are not lucky enough to please our arbiters of good taste, to say nothing of our singers. The famous Nightingale's Aria, in which the violin and flute give a bubbly imitation of a joyous voice, will be condemned without trial. Moreover, since the slowness of the recitative makes the work longer than usual, other sacrifices will be made, and several of those divertissements to which Rameau devoted the best part of his genius will be banished without regret. . . .

As for the performance, it will be by turns unsteady and disjointed, never unleashing those picturesque rhythms which are the very soul of such music. How hard it is for some of us to understand an art whose sole aim is to please, not to teach or even to move, us. We have utterly forgotten the character of early opera, which is a suite of dances tied together by dialogues and airs, and not, as in the nineteenth century, a dramatic plot decked out with festivities and parades.[25]

Quittard was particularly incensed by the singers' poor intonation. The conductor, evidently anticipating a problem, endeavoured to assist them by reinforcing the harpsichord with a double string quartet in the recitatives. Under the circumstances it may have been just as well that the idea of using a Baroque orchestra was never seriously considered, although Bordes and others had long been advocating such a step.[26] Even if, say, Eugène de Bricqueville's collection of Baroque instruments had been procured, practical objections could be raised to using them in an auditorium as large as the Palais Garnier. According to Quittard, even the specially designed Pleyel harpsichord used in Hippolyte et Aricie (apparently an early version of the 'Landowska' model) was barely audible.[27] Elsewhere, however, historical instruments were becoming so familiar in opera houses, especially as part of the continuo group, that their absence was likely to be remarked upon. When Giacomo Orefice edited Orfeo for a concert in Milan in 1909, he discarded both harpsichord and organ in favour of a 'harp-harmonium' and a conventional modern orchestra. An Italian newspaper critic defended his revisions, pointing out that Monteverdi's orchestra could not be revived because some of the instruments were no longer obtainable and that, in any case, the effect that the original scoring made on listeners in the seventeenth century could never be duplicated.[28]

Orefice's Orfeo quickly cornered the Italian market, but it was d'Indy's edition that was heard in the first modern stage performance of the opera at the Théâtre Réjane in Paris in 1911. Economy dictated that it be played against sets designed for the theatre's current production of Maeterlinck's L'Oiseau Bleu, an incongruity that merely served to sharpen the public's appreciation for the work.[29] *Orfeo* came to New York's Metropolitan Opera House in 1912 for a special Sunday evening performance, sung in English without sets or costumes. The *New York Times* noted that the audience 'was considerably nonplused by the work' and made 'only the faintest attempts at applause'.[30] Germany saw its first *Orfeo* in Breslau in 1913. It, too, was an extra event, segregated from the main opera season; few managements were reckless enough to subject their regular patrons to such esoteric fare. Nevertheless, several State Theatre singers took part and some of the music omitted by d'Indy and Orefice was apparently restored. The reviews were mixed. Max Schneider declared that the opera 'was really more outlined than performed', while Erich Freund found the edition by Hanns Erdmann-Guckel 'too luxuriantly contemporary'. Ernst Neufeldt was more favourably disposed but hedged his bets by wondering aloud how posterity would judge the production. 'Our nephews will no doubt laugh at our performances of early music, just as we laugh at those of the nineteenth century. We are still in the period of experimentation.'[31]

When *Poppea* returned to the boards in 1913 at the Théâtre des Arts in Paris, Emile Vuillermoz poked fun at d'Indy's 'fidelity to the cult of our ancestors', noting that 'the tomb of Monteverdi . . . is one of those that he honours with frequent libations and precious offerings'. Vuillermoz found the occasion more edifying than enjoyable. 'In spite of the involuntary stiffness and the majestic slowness of a somewhat overly solemn perform-ance, the glorious ancestor arose from his grave with surprising vivacity . . . . Unfortunately, he was in better shape than his interpreters, who were disconcerted to discover so much liveliness in an immortal. It is their fault, I fear, that the resurrection failed to produce the miraculous results that were anticipated; the intention was excellent but the effort left something to be desired.'[32]

Early opera revivals continued at a slow but steady pace through the first two decades of the century. The Liceo 'Benedetto Marcello' in Venice sponsored a performance of Galuppi's *Filosofo di Campagna* in 1907 and staged Marcello's *Arianna* five years later.[38] Gagliano's *Dafne* was given in Moscow in 1911 with scenery inspired by old engravings and a balalaika imparting a touch of ethnic colour to the continuo ensemble.[34] The Monte Carlo Opéra, under the enterprising leadership of Raoul Gunsbourg, mounted four Baroque works – *Orfeo*, Rameau's *Fêtes d'Hébé* and *Platée*, and Lully's *Armide* – between 1910 and 1918. All of this helped prepare the ground for the extraordinary 'Handel Renaissance' of the twenties and thirties. But the revival of Handel's operas and oratorios in Germany had as much to do with contemporary social and political issues as with musical trends. Just as politicians on the right and left were attempting to forge a new social order, German musicians were searching for new aesthetic principles to counteract the unrest that was gradually engulfing the country. Handel's works, with their firmly delineated musical and dramatic structure, nobility of expression and glorification of heroic exploits, answered the German people's yearning for stability and, more importantly, a sense of national pride.

Thus Oskar Hagen, the prime mover of the Handel opera revival, wrote of his desire to establish 'the most intimate contact with the spirit and form of [the] infinitely more capable past'.[35] Like d'Indy, Hagen was markedly unsympathetic to much contemporary music; his view of the eighteenth century was strongly tinged with nostalgia and idealism. Not a musician but an art historian by profession, Hagen subscribed to the Romanticized view of the past fashionable in certain artistic circles of the day. He first looked into Chrysander's editions of the Handel operas while recuperating from an illness in 1919. As soon as he was back on his feet, he asked his wife, the soprano Thyra Hagen-Leisner, to read through the scores with him on the piano. The more he heard the more excited Hagen became. Instrumentalist friends began dropping by several times a week to take part in informal reading sessions. The next step was to put the operas on stage. The authorities at the University of Göttingen, where Hagen taught, obligingly offered to underwrite a trial production of *Rodelinda*. Three performances were scheduled at the end of the school year in June 1920; a fourth was later added by public demand. Hagen himself conducted the university orchestra, as well as editing and translating the opera; his wife sang the title role, and Paul Thiersch, the director of the Staatliche Kunstgewerbeschule in nearby Halle and a close friend of Hagen's, designed the sets. It was, in short, a modest academic production of a fairly ordinary sort.

The reaction it elicited, however, was anything but ordinary. Reports of the performances appeared in some forty German newspapers; Hagen and his small band of Handel enthusiasts became celebrities almost overnight.[36] The next summer's production of *Ottone* (which Hagen rechristened *Otto und Theophano*) attracted still more attention at home and abroad. The vigour and spontaneity of the response strengthened Hagen's conviction that Handel's operas still had the power to speak to modern listeners. He approached them neither as a historian nor as a musicologist. Wielding his pruning shears with a ready hand, he altered the sequence of arias and whole scenes, transposed the castrato parts downwards to bring them within the tenor or baritone range, and added Romanticized dynamics and tempo markings. Hagen was perfectly candid about his editorial procedure, and historicism had nothing to do with it. He justified his wholesale cutting and rewriting of Handel's recitatives, for instance, by arguing that modern audiences were better behaved than Handel's and therefore needed no such musical filler to give them time to settle down.[37] Some of Hagen's ideas are patently absurd; others – such as his assertion that the timbre of the baritone voice was closer to the castrato than that of female altos – are neither demonstrably true nor untrue. But lest one judge too hastily, his productions must be viewed in the context of their time. If latter-day Handelians find many of his decisions unconscionable, they were by no means so egregious when one considers the high-handed tactics of respected musicians like d'Indy and Orefice.

Although none of the early Göttingen productions seems to have been recorded, the Handel albums made by the contralto Emmi Leisner (Hagen's sister-in-law) and other leading concert singers of the day – with their unvaried legato phrasing, virtually non-existent ornamentation, thickly orchestrated recitatives and ubiquitous ritardandos – convey a fair idea of what they must have sounded like. Hagen's published editions provide ample corroborating evidence. As Edward J. Dent wrote, his continuo realizations 'were conceived by someone accustomed to play Wagner's operas (and with vigorous enthusiasm) on a modern grand pianoforte'.[38] None of this disturbed critics overmuch in the twenties. Hagen's revivals proceded with a 1922 *Giulio Cesare* that did more than any other single production to secure Handel's niche in the modern repertoire. The ancient Roman was a hero with whom German audiences could readily identify. Hagen's edition of the opera speedily did the rounds, by one tally chalking up 222 performances on 33 stages in only five years.[39] In no time a veritable epidemic of Handel productions had broken out. Halle got into the act in 1922 with a production of the 'magic' opera *Orlando*, directed by the musicologist Hans Joachim Moser. The naturalistic, quasi-Baroque sets and costumes marked a significant departure from the spare, Expressionist style favoured at Göttingen. Hagen added *Serse* to his list in 1924, and other cities soon jumped onto the band-wagon. Karlsruhe and Leipzig saw *Tamerlano*; *Admeto* was given in Brunswick in a bilingual edition by Hans Dütschke, a Berlin gymnasium teacher, with the recitatives sung in German and the arias in the original Italian. By 1925, when Hagen departed for the United States to take up a post at the University of Wisconsin, 181 Handel productions had been seen in 37 cities, mostly in Germany. *Giulio Cesare*, *Rodelinda* and *Serse* were far and away the most popular, followed by *Ariodante*, *Alcina*, *Siroe*, *Radamisto*, *Muzio Scevola*, *Amadigi* and others.

Despite the proven effectiveness of his editions, Hagen was not without his detractors. The musicologist Rudolf Steglich, for example, protested that his cuts, shifts and transpositions played havoc with Handel's tonal schemes. *Rodelinda*, he wrote, was a carefully wrought piece of musical architecture, not 'a bundle of arias tied together with recitatives'. Hagen's ill-considered changes had begotten a stylistic monstrosity, 'a half-modern, half-Baroque hermaphrodite'.[40] Reviewing a production of *Ariodante* at Stuttgart in 1926, Hermann Roth spoke of a 'crisis' in the Handel opera revival and lashed out at 'trendy modernizations' like Hagen's. Fidelity to the composer's text was a basic requirement for any successful production, he declared.[41] Roth's own *Tamerlano* at Karlsruhe in 1924 was far from exemplary – the score was reworked throughout and the da capo arias truncated in the usual fashion – but he hewed closer to the original text and music when he revived the production at Leipzig the following year. Concern for authenticity spread in the late twenties and thirties, no doubt fostered by performances of Baroque chamber music on historical instruments. After Fritz Lehmann became musical director at Göttingen in 1934, fewer cuts and rearrangements were tolerated, the chorus and orchestra were placed almost on a level with the stage (as in an eighteenth-century theatre) and greater use was made of lavish costumes and painted backdrops in keeping with the Baroque style. Halle and other cities followed suit. When *Tamerlano* was revived in 1935 at the 456-seat Schlosstheater in Celle, the Baroque period was evoked not only in the sets and costumes but also in the stylized gestures of the singers. Dent reported that *Rodelinda* was performed in the eighteenth-century palace theatre in Ludwigsburg using 'genuine old scenery' and candlelight.[42]

Yet such historicizing productions continued to be the exception rather than the rule. Baroque oratorios, in particular, were frequently given outdoors in spectacular productions densely populated with dancers and extras – a heavy-handed but no doubt effective way of bringing Bach and Handel to the masses. Hanns Niedecken-Gebhard, one of the most successful stage directors of the time, showed a strong preference for choral movement and athletic displays derived from the contemporary dance idiom of Mary Wigman, Rudolf von Laban and Kurt Joos. Designers and directors availed themselves of the latest technology. Slide projections created striking scenic effects in a 1928 *Alcina* in Leipzig, and loudspeakers and a trautonium were used to reinforce the harpsichord at an outdoor performance of *Herakles* in Berlin in 1936. The trend toward monumentality and hero-worship was encouraged by the Nazis, but so were historically accurate sets and costumes. A 1938 *Rodelinda* in Halle was played against a copy of a Romanesque church, with costumes patterned after medieval miniatures – a far cry from the stark minimalism of the first Göttingen production. The emphasis on naturalistic décor occasionally got out of hand. In the 1935 Hamburg production of *Giulio Cesare*, Cleopatra's terrace – a Piranesi-like forest of heavy Neoclassical columns and architraves – reminded one critic 'more of a big bank lobby than of an African garden party'.[43]

Münster (where Niedecken-Gebhard served as Intendant) was the centre of Handel oratorio performances in Germany, as were Cambridge and Falmouth in England.[44] The Cambridge Operatic Society's revival of *Semele* in 1925 prompted William Barclay Squire to write: 'In the present state of operatic affairs in England, it is hardly to be wondered at that Handel's adopted country should have left it to Germany to take the lead in reviving his neglected operas.'[45] Still, Cambridge could take pride in a staging that was unusually elaborate for a university. Dent's description is graphic: 'Mr Beales of Corpus entered with next to nothing on, carrying a live fantail pigeon, and Mr Timberlake of Cat's, in a similar sort of costume, struggled with four champion borzois valued at £500 each!' To which menagerie was added, according to Percy Scholes, 'two goats that appeared to require a little more stage experience'.[46] Dent thought the production clumsy and disliked the black-and-white-checked capes worn by the chorus members, which made them look like 'dissipated parsons and nuns coming away from a night club'.[47] Dennis Arundell, the director, adopted Dent's novel method of abridging Handel's da capo arias by telescoping the three sections together and adjusting the harmonies as necessary. 'The advantage of it', Dent explained, 'is that it saves the whole of the music (apart from negligible cuts), avoids the loss of time spent on the *da capo*, and at the same time preserves the illusion of a *da capo* and makes the song end at the right place.'[48] Scholes thought it an excellent idea, since by decapitating the da capo 'progress to the next thing is not so long delayed as to become painful'.[49] Dent's surgical shortening was preferable to Hagen's wholesale excisions in that it preserved the outline of Handel's tonal scheme, but he was no less guilty than Hagen of distorting the proportions of Handel's arias in order to streamline the dramatic action.

Dent's attitude toward the da capo stemmed from his conviction (born of long experience) that modern singers had lost the art of ornamenting the repeats in Baroque arias. He was similarly inclined to compromise on the question of the castrato parts. Assigning them to men was unsatisfactory, since, as Barclay Squire observed, 'no modern tenor or baritone can cope with roulades written for singers like Senesino or Caffarelli'.[50] Dent tentatively advocated using female altos, as Handel did on occasion, though 'whether audiences would find this acceptable is another matter'.[51] When Dent produced Purcell's *Fairy Queen* at Cambridge in 1920, the baritone Clive Carey sang the lead role in falsetto, prompting *The Times* to remark that he looked and sounded 'every bit as absurd as the original "Mr Pate, in woman's habit"'.[52] The Baroque stage revival owes a good deal to Dent, not least his widely used edition of *Dido and Aeneas*, first produced at Münster in 1926. Another notable figure in England was the composer Rutland

Boughton, who produced several early stage works – including *Dido and Aeneas*, Locke's *Cupid and Death* and Blow's *Venus and Adonis* – at the Glastonbury Festival in the teens and twenties. 'It is clear that these 17th century pieces, which call so much more for fresh feeling and the grace of ingenuous youth rather than any grandeur of apparatus, will be irresistible in the Glastonbury of the future', opined the *Musical Times*.[53]

Londoners heard their first *Orfeo* in 1924 in a concert performance of the d'Indy edition at the French Institute. Monteverdi's opera naturally suggested itself for the maiden production of the Oxford University Opera Club the following year. At Dent's suggestion, J. A. Westrup, then a 21-year-old Balliol undergraduate, was commissioned to prepare a new performing edition based on materials in the Bodleian Library. Westrup modernized Monteverdi's scoring, using oboes and clarinets in place of cornetts and a piano-and-harmonium continuo. But unlike previous editors, he made virtually no cuts in the opera.[54] Frank Howes, in his review, regretted the absence of the plucked string sound which he considered 'a marked feature of Monteverdi's orchestration', but otherwise praised Westrup's work and that of R. L. Stuart, whose version of the libretto 'was decent English, not translationese'. Michael Martin Harvey's simple sets and choreography, he added, 'had the great virtue of signifying the emotion proper to every scene and situation'.[55]

Two years later Westrup and Stuart collaborated again on *L'Incoronazione di Poppea* at Oxford. *The Times* deemed the production 'simple and effective, some rich effects being produced by means of light against plain curtains', but pronounced Monteverdi's music 'primitive'.[56] Oxford essayed only one more Baroque opera before the war – *Castor et Pollux* in 1935 – but other organizations were taking up the cudgels on its behalf. Stuart translated and directed *Giulio Cesare* for the short-lived London Festival Opera Company in 1930. *The Times* made light of both the opera and the production. '"It seems that in this kingdom of Egypt murder is not infrequent", remarks Julius Caesar in a resonant recitative, and the audience not unnaturally guffaws. Two stage armies, consisting of two men apiece, kill each other to lively ballet music, and their antics are not exactly the right preparation for a magnificent scene in which Caesar mourns his fallen legions and steels himself for fresh encounters.'[57] Nevertheless, the paper editorially applauded the festival's audacious programme – a twin-bill of *Dido and Aeneas* and *Cupid and Death*, *Orfeo*, Mozart's *La Finta Giardiniera* and Weber's *Der Freischütz* – and lamented the poor attendance. 'Alas, that the congratulations of the first night should have been offered only by a few personal friends, a few of the more enterprising members of the Imperial League of Opera … and a few professional critics who tried to look as though they had paid for their seats and who actually in some cases did pay for their programmes!'[58] It is no wonder that professional opera companies in England shied away from Baroque works. A handful of amateur productions were mounted in the thirties – *Dido and Aeneas, Rinaldo, Serse, Rodelinda* and Scarlatti's *Trionfo d'Onore* – but they seem to have caused little stir.

Reporting on an operatic tour of Germany in the English periodical *The Sackbut* in 1929, the American critic Oscar Thompson challenged other countries to take up Handel's cause. 'Let us forget the artificial sopranos, quit quibbling over the necessity for substituting the voices of fully authenticated males for the now almost unimaginable sound of the notes that blossomed in the throats of Farinelli and Senesino, and rejoice – as this reviewer rejoiced when he heard *Caesar* four times in six days a year ago at Göttingen – in music that is of the finest, and altogether the *proudest*, that any composer has written for the lyric stage.'[59] Thompson's plea did not fall on deaf ears. The Handel Renaissance had in fact already reached America in the person of Werner Josten, a German-born composer who taught at Smith College in North-ampton, Massachusetts. Josten conducted the American premiere of *L'Incoronazione di Poppea* at the dedication of the college's new concert-lecture hall in 1926. Word of the venture spread quickly and the national press turned out in force for the following year's production of *Julius Caesar* (which, unlike the Monteverdi, was sung in English). Josten used Hagen's edition, fashioning a 'harpsichordized' piano for the continuo part and recruiting most of the singers locally. The reviews were glowing. Pitts Sanborn of the *New York Evening Telegram* called upon the big New York and Chicago opera companies to add Handel to their repertoire. H. T. Parker considered the singers' 'statuesque attitudes' undramatic, but Thompson suggested that Josten had not gone far enough. 'Conceivably, a highly stylized performance, in which the very opposite of realism was striven for, with an exaggeration of anachronisms and of the obtrusions of the manners of an alien age, might give such a work the necessary fillip.'[60]

Josten set his sights higher in 1928, importing a former Metropolitan Opera singer named Mabel Garrison to sing Romilda in *Serse* on a double-bill with Monteverdi's *Combattimento di Tancredi e Clorinda*. Sanborn disliked the décor ('like a cross between a toy shop and a Greenwich Village tea dive') but praised Smith College for creating 'for our American East its own little Bayreuth at Northampton, with Monteverdi and Handel as substitute for Wagner'. (Stravinsky's *Les Noces* was the companion piece when the *Combattimento* was repeated the following year at the Met under the auspices of the League of Composers.) The markedly cooler reaction to Josten's 1929 productions of *Orfeo* and Handel's cantata *Apollo e Dafne* may account for the year's hiatus that intervened before *Rodelinda* was presented in 1931.

Americans, it seemed, did not share the Germans' idolatry of Handel. 'People came to the opera in Handel's day only to be aurally titillated by the incredible vocal feats of the *castrati*', one critic wrote. 'It is because of the impossible soprano arias for *castrati* and the lifeless character of the subject matter that Handel's operas are no longer heard today.'[61]

Nevertheless, the United States soon developed a small but steadily growing audience for early opera. Artur Bodanzky's heavily reorchestrated version of *Dido and Aeneas* was frequently heard in New York and elsewhere in the twenties. Dent's comparatively restrained edition was staged at the Juilliard School in 1932 under the direction of Albert Stoessel and Alfredo Valenti. The same team took credit for student productions of *Giulio Cesare* in 1931, *Serse* in 1932 and *L'Incoronazione di Poppea* in 1933. Monteverdi's opera was seen at the Forty-Fourth Street Theater in 1937 in a professional production presented by the Salzburg Opera Guild. Olin Downes devoted a Sunday piece in the *New York Times* to Ernst Krenek's edition of *Poppea*, noting that it purported to be not a facsimile but a free 'interpretation' of the original.[62] He acknowledged that d'Indy had been more faithful to Monteverdi, but defended Krenek's liberties on the grounds that 'we could not have heard the opera last night as Monteverdi wrote it' because there were too many unknowns in the score. The performance, Downes wrote, 'was conspicuous for its simplicity, authority and expressiveness of interpretation'. And unlike the bewildered Met audience twenty-five years earlier, the listeners reportedly applauded and cheered vociferously all evening.[63]

It is a tribute to Monteverdi's genius that so many musicians over the years have tried their hands at adapting and arranging his three extant operas. One of the best-known versions of *Orfeo* is the one Carl Orff prepared for Mannheim in 1925. Orff made no pretence about having adapted, indeed rewritten, the work liberally. The original allegorical figures were eliminated, a narrator was introduced (delivering a text written by Orff's colleague Dorothée Günther), and scenes were reshuffled in a way that not even d'Indy or Hagen would have countenanced. Curt Sachs seconded Orff, on the rather dubious ground that since *Orfeo* had been written for a specific occasion in 1607, its values could not be said to be 'exclusively timeless and immortal'. Therefore, he concluded, 'to present Monteverdi's work in its original form to a modern audience in the theatre of to-day would be a graver injustice to the spirit of the work and of Monteverdi than a tactful revision with a due sense of artistic and historical responsibility'.[64] Similar arguments were adduced in support of the productions of *Orfeo* that two major Italian opera houses, Milan's La Scala and the Teatro dell'Opera in Rome, mounted in the mid-thirties. The editions used – by Respighi and Giacomo Benvenuti, respectively – were thoroughly reworked, if less blatantly than Orff's.

Respighi disarmingly defended his emendations (which included an off-stage chorus humming along, Puccini-style, during Orfeo's 'Possente spirto') by asserting that a new version of the opera 'can only be justified if it is a personal interpretation'. For his part, he had relied on his own 'musical sensitivity' to realize what Monteverdi had not 'expressly indicated' and to give the score 'symphonic treatment'.[65]

Monteverdi's third opera, *Il Ritorno d'Ulisse in patria*, finally reached the stage in Paris in 1925. The Petite Scène offered only snippets from the score, harmonized and orchestrated as usual by d'Indy, but André Tessier was sufficiently impressed to hail Monteverdi as 'the first verismo composer', every scene of whose operas represented 'a slice of life'. Tessier reserved special praise for the company's director, Xavier de Courville, who translated the libretto and designed the décor. 'What sort of theatre', he asked, 'would show such enthusiasm for a work of early music, even if it were decidedly beautiful and carried the name of an illustrious composer?'[66] The banner event of the Parisian early music season, however, was the Opéra's revival of *Le Triomphe de l'Amour*. 'At last Lully is taking back possession of the Opéra stage that he founded more than two and a half centuries ago', Henry Prunières declared.[67] Although less than half the work was performed, Prunières found the action readily intelligible and André Caplet's modern orchestration 'a continual tour de force'. Unfortunately the performance suffered from lethargic tempi, which Prunières attributed to 'the absurd stylistic prejudices that singers and instrumentalists are steeped in from their Conservatoire days'. When the Opéra staged the work anew in 1933, Prunières lauded the Baroque flavour of the décor and choreography, but railed against the 'mutilated' edition and 'indefensible orchestration' that were used. He refrained from mentioning the singers by name, 'because the word *execution* referring to them should be understood in the sense that one employs when speaking of criminals who are being sentenced'.[68] Prunières's principal objection – that the singers lacked a sense of Baroque style and constantly allowed the recitatives to bog down – had been voiced by reviewers ever since the first Schola Cantorum performances. It is not hard to understand why recitative was considered expendable in so many Baroque opera productions. Prunières reiterated his complaint in connection with the Opéra's 1935 production of *Castor et Pollux*, adding rather testily that performers would do well in the future to seek and heed the advice of competent musicologists.[69]

Both the artistic and geographical boundaries of the early opera revival expanded greatly in the interwar period. *Orfeo* was staged in Vienna, Lisbon, Budapest, Buenos Aires, Cairo and Leningrad. Florence's Boboli Gardens provided a verdant backdrop for *Poppea*. Amsterdam saw Lully's *Acis et*

Galatée; Buenos Aires, Rameau's *Castor et Pollux*; Algiers, *Dardanus*.
Telemann's *Der gedultige Socrates* and *Die ungleiche Heyrath*, Keiser's *Der
lächerliche Printz Jodelet* and Graun's *Montezuma* were revived in Germany,
while Fux's *Costanza e Fortezza* received airings in Prague and Northampton.
Serse and *Dido and Aeneas* were sung in Hungarian in Budapest, *Giulio Cesare*
in Polish in Poznań and *Acis and Galatea* in Danish in Copenhagen. *Le Jeu de
Robin et de Marion* was performed at Cape Town and broadcast by South
African radio. Various operatic progenitors – miracle and mystery plays,
farces, *sacre rappresentazioni, intermedi, masques* – reached the stage, together
with a steady stream of modern works in consciously archaizing idioms, such
as Rutland Boughton's *Bethlehem* and Federico Ghedini's *Le Notte Angeliche*.
Olimpiade, the highlight of the 1939 Settimana Musicale in Siena, was a
cornerstone of the post-war Vivaldi craze. During the war, the Nazis
promoted productions of Handel's operas and oratorios to keep nationalist
sentiment running high. At least once, however, the policy backfired:
Hellmuth Christian Wolff reports that a 1943 production of *Agrippina* was
'gratefully received' by the Halle audience as thinly veiled criticism of the
totalitarian régime.[70] An American observer perceived political overtones of
another sort in a staging of Bach's *St Matthew Passion* in New York. Jesus was
represented by shafts of yellow light engulfed in 'a bevy of hooded mimes,
who prowled about like Ku Klux Klansmen at a Konklave'.[71]

The post-war climate was more conducive to appraising Baroque opera on
its own terms. The significant productions of the past four decades can be
grouped into three broad categories: those which use the original work as a
pretext for lavish scenic display or creative embellishments by modern
composers and directors; those which attempt to strike a successful
compromise between Baroque and modern performance styles; and those
which purport to be more or less faithful facsimiles of Baroque productions.
A new concern for textual authenticity emerged in the early fifties. When
Benjamin Britten prepared his edition of *Dido and Aeneas* for the English
Opera Group, for example, he eschewed the kind of liberties taken by d'Indy,
Orff, Respighi and Krenek. Aside from an interpolated finale to Act II
(indicated in the original libretto but missing from the existing scores) and an
unmistakably personalized realization of the continuo part, Britten's Purcell
was essentially unretouched. Hindemith went a step farther in his version of
Orfeo, presented in Vienna in 1954. Not only did he follow Monteverdi's
instrumentation, borrowing period instruments from museums and private
collections, but the sets were copied from designs for another Baroque opera,
Cesti's *Pomo d'oro*. Nikolaus Harnoncourt, himself a distinguished conductor of the opera, recalled that Hindemith's production struck him like 'a
lightning flash'.[72] Even more influential, largely because it was recorded

almost immediately by Deutsche Grammophon, was August Wenzinger's 1955 *Orfeo* at Hitzacker in Lower Saxony, likewise using historical instruments.

While scholars were gradually coming around to the view that Baroque opera productions should take historical performance practices into account, no such consensus existed in the operatic world at large. Two major post-war productions – *The Fairy Queen* at Covent Garden and *Les Indes galantes* at the Paris Opéra – were treated as elaborate vehicles for spectacular stage effects rather than opportunites for exploring the works' original idioms. Neither Frederick Ashton in the Purcell nor the three choreographers (including Serge Lifar) who collaborated on the Rameau aimed at historical accuracy. Constant Lambert, who 'livened up' *The Fairy Queen* with thickened orchestration and interpolations from other Purcell works, disparaged the 'stately but monotonous dances of Purcell's period'.[73] An American observer described the Rameau production as 'the most fastuous spectacle ever offered in the present Opéra house . . . a kaleidoscope of exotic costumes and trick scenic effects that include a goddess floating on a cloud, ballet notables popping up through trapdoors behind disappearing gardens, perfume sprayed over the spectators to accompany a *divertissement* called "Les Fleurs," a shipwreck, a sweet-breathed Peruvian volcano erupting real fire, smoke, and incense, and an earthquake with falling temples.'[74] In some respects the production must have been an improvement over the Opéra's 1908 *Hippolyte et Aricie*, which Quittard had criticized for its 'deplorably conventional' staging and ballets that seemed 'utterly indifferent to the music'.[75] But in the context of the French Baroque *opéra–ballet*, with its intricate and highly artificial interweaving of choreography and dramatic action, it still fell far short of the ideal.

Choreography had long been a stumbling block in Baroque opera productions. The Paris Opéra made a stab at terpsichorean authenticity in its 1925 *Triomphe de l'Amour*: Prunières reported that Leo Staats's ballets 'were perfectly successful specimens of seventeenth-century theatrical dance', enjoyable both for their 'archaeological interest' and for 'the very agreeable impression' they made on the audience.[76] But the revival of early dance was still in its infancy – most of the important books on the subject, by Mabel Dolmetsch and others, began appearing only in the fifties[77] – and reviews often leave one wondering whether the choreographer was attempting a historical re-creation or merely imparting an 'old-style' flavour to the dancers' movements. In any case, the recent painstaking reconstructions of Baroque choreography by such scholars as Kay Lawrence, Catherine Turocy, Shirley Wynne, Belinda Quirey, Maria Drabecka and Karl-Heinz Taubert are a far cry from earlier choreographic exhumations, which tended to be either academic in nature or free interpretations of Baroque style. A far cry, too, from the static, monumental idiom of the early German Handel revivals. As the subtly inflected rhetoric of Baroque music was revealed in historically oriented performances, congruity demanded a similar approach to Baroque dance and theatrical gesture. The current trend toward historically accurate stagings of early operas, in which the singers' gestures are not simply 'stylized' in a generic way, but actually based, as musical performances long have been, on treatises and manuals of the period, has added yet another dimension to the search for authenticity.

In this, as in other respects, Handel's operas are reliable indicators of trends in Baroque opera production. Since the war, the two major German centres, Göttingen and Halle, have, by and large, represented opposing philosophies, the former being increasingly concerned with musical and textual authenticity, the latter with developing a modern tradition of Handel performance unfettered by adherence to historical principles. Since its inception in 1952, Halle's Handel Festival has devoted itself to bringing Baroque opera to the masses, in contrast to what a leading East German scholar terms 'the largely restrictive character' of the Göttingen productions.[78] Historicism clashed with the Marxist aesthetic governing the Halle productions; indeed, the writings of the musicologist Walther Siegmund-Schultze suggest that Hagen's spirit is alive and well in East Germany. Thus one learns that Handel's operas can be modernized without destroying their essential message, since 'they possess a timeless realism which does not require a "baroque" mask'. Siegmund-Schultze asserts that Handel was not writing about the aristocracy at all but about the proletariat, and that the madness of Caesar and Tamerlane 'is meant as social criticism, not as insanity'. Changes in the librettos are permissible as long as they enhance the 'psychological implications' of the drama. Indeed, in Siegmund-Schultze's view, 'anything is acceptable as long as it helps bring about the realistic presentation of Handel's music, promoting the contact between the music and the audience of today, without doing violence to the music'.

This unabashedly anti-historical attitude, while defensible on philosophical and aesthetic grounds, has increasingly fallen out of favour in recent years. In the fifties and sixties, the torch of the Handel Renaissance was passed from Germany to England, where the Handel Opera Society, founded in 1955 by Dent and the conductor Charles Farncombe, pointed the way to a more historically oriented style of production. Along with Anthony Lewis at the University of Birmingham, Alan and Frances Kitching's Unicorn Theatre at Abingdon, the English Bach Festival and Kent Opera, the Handel Opera Society has been responsible for bringing almost all of the composer's forty-odd operas to the stage in England in the past three decades. Post-war British productions have been distinguished by a growing concern for authenticity in all aspects of Baroque opera performance – scoring, disposition of voices, instrumentation, scenic design, choreography and staging – that makes most German Handel stagings seem old-fashioned.

Another advantage that England has enjoyed is an abundant supply of countertenors to replace the virtuoso castratos for whom the Baroque composers wrote some of their most brilliant roles. The renaissance of the countertenor voice in the forties and fifties was due almost entirely to one man: Alfred Deller. Male altos had been singing in English church choirs all along, but their occasional forays onto the operatic stage were not notably successful. Reviewing the London Festival Opera Company's *Giulio Cesare* in 1930, *The Times* complained that 'the male alto representative of Nirenius should not have been allowed on the stage at all. He merely emphasized the tendency to allow the opera to degenerate into absurdity.'[79] Deller's falsetto technique was so unorthodox that both Lincoln and Salisbury cathedrals rejected his applications to join their choirs; not until 1939 was he offered a position at Canterbury Cathedral. It was there that Michael Tippett and

8.0 CHORAL AND ORCHESTRAL CONCERT

BBC Symphony Orchestra
(Leader, Paul Beard)

Conductor, Sir Adrian Boult

Guest Conductor, Arthur Bliss

BBC Choral Society

BBC Chorus
(Chorus-Master, Leslie Woodgate)

Soloists : Isobel Baillie (soprano), Astra Desmond (contralto), Bradbridge White (tenor), Alfred Deller (counter-tenor), Charles Whitehead (counter-tenor), Harold Williams (baritone)

English music

Part 1

God Save The King

8.2 Festival Overture...............*Britten*
(Specially composed for the opening
of the Third Programme)
(First performance)

8.11 Music for the Royal Fireworks
Handel

8.32 Cantata: Come Ye Sons of Art
Purcell
Isobel Baillie, Alfred Deller, Charles Whitehead, and Harold Williams

Fig. 4   Radio Times *announcement of the Third Programme's inaugural broadcast on 29 September 1946*

Walter Goehr discovered him, resulting in an invitation to take part in a concert at Morley College in 1944. Two years later, Deller was featured on the inaugural broadcast of the BBC's Third Programme, taking part in a duet from Purcell's *Come, Ye Sons of Art*. Through his countless broadcasts and recordings, both alone and with the consort he founded in 1950, Deller did much to establish Purcell in the public mind as 'the British Orpheus'. Although he appeared on the opera stage only once – Britten wrote the part of Oberon in *A Midsummer Night's Dream* especially for him – Deller paved the way for James Bowman, Paul Esswood, René Jacobs, Drew Minter, Dominique Visse and a host of other operatic countertenors.

Many people agree with Dent that the female voice better approximates the power and brilliance of the extinct castratos, but countertenors have been an indispensable element in the revivals of Baroque, Renaissance and medieval dramatic works. The success of the New York Pro Musica's *Play of Daniel* in 1958 owed much to the American countertenor Russell Oberlin, for whom Greenberg fabricated the role of Balshazzar's Prince. Oberlin's voice, whose timbre resembled that of a high tenor rather than a falsetto, proved more palatable to many listeners than Deller's, and when Covent Garden invited him to play Oberon in a revival of *A Midsummer Night's Dream*, Deller was deeply offended. (Ironically, a 1965 production of *The Play of Daniel* in Adelaide, Australia, provided Deller with his only other acting role. 'He looked magnificent, until he moved,' a colleague recalled, 'and then it was all wrong.'[80]) Even so, Deller's impact on the early music field was unprecedented. Neither Yves Tinayre nor Hugues Cuénod, to name two of the outstanding early music singers of the pre-war period, achieved comparable stature. Tippett's remark that 'the centuries rolled back' when he heard Deller sing[81] is indicative of the fascination he exerted on many listeners. Yet it was not merely the atavistic quality of Deller's voice that captivated his admirers, but also his artistry. His free, expressive, overtly emotional approach to music was an important influence on performers like Gustav Leonhardt and the Kuijken brothers. Deller took the lead in reviving the art of vocal ornamentation, a field that scholars had been investigating since the late 1800s but which was largely ignored by performers until the 1950s. Only recently have historical techniques of vocal production become the subject of widespread interest, a trend which promises to have a significant impact on performances of Baroque opera and other dramatic works.

Of all the issues the Baroque opera revival has raised, none has proved more contentious than the question of establishing authoritative editions and preparing them for performance. Scholar–performers like Anthony Lewis, Newell Jenkins, Nikolaus Harnoncourt and Alan Curtis have rewritten the ground-rules of the debate. The freely modernized performing edition has fallen from grace; nowadays everyone pays at least lip-service to the ideal of presenting early operas in a form as close as possible to the original (though the *Urtext* concept is hardly less problematic in Baroque opera than in standard-repertory works like *Carmen*, *Boris Godunov*, *Don Carlos* and *Lulu*). Nonetheless, a substantial body of opinion holds that some editorial licence is either necessary or at least permissible within the framework of an authentic Baroque opera production. The British conductor Raymond Leppard maintains that the Baroque masters resembled Broadway composers in their working habits, constantly tinkering with their scores to make them fit specific performers and circumstances. In his editions of the Monteverdi and Cavalli operas, Leppard opts for a hybrid orchestra of old and modern instruments, while making whatever cuts, alterations and transpositions he deems necessary to put the operas on stage. 'It is foolish – and finally impossible – to adopt a prissily "pure" attitude to these works', Leppard contends. 'It is equally foolish to resent or reject the element of compromise which must play a part in their modern-day performance.' In this view, the paramount need to re-create a viable performing tradition for early opera takes precedence over what Leppard calls 'the arid, inhibiting cut and thrust of academicism'.[82]

Leppard's combativeness has predictably made him something of an apostate in the eyes of many musicologists and critics, but the popular success of his empirical approach to Baroque opera is indisputable. The modern revival of Cavalli's operas stems almost exclusively from his performances at Glyndebourne in the sixties and seventies. By tailoring the music for singers like Janet Baker and Hugues Cuénod, and by striving for superbly synchronized ensemble work, Leppard has shown that Baroque opera can survive as something more than a hot-house flower in the twentieth-century climate. Some commentators gladly set aside their reservations about Leppard's productions in their enthusiasm for what Robert Donington calls 'the glorious and essential authenticity of the evening's work as a whole'.[83] On the other hand, Winton Dean, reviewing a recent revival of Leppard's *Incoronazione di Poppea* at Glyndebourne, flatly dismissed it as being 'as outdated as Hagen's rehash of Handel's operas in the 1920s'.[84] Andrew Porter praises Leppard for restoring Monteverdi and Cavalli to the world's stages but questions his scissors-and-paste treatment of the scores. 'Most charges against Mr. Leppard's editions can be defended on practical grounds', Porter writes. 'They should nevertheless continue to be brought. Gluck–Wagner, Mozart–Strauss, and Handel–Prout were once similarly defended. Only by bearing this in mind can the limits of the possible be progressively raised.'[85]

A contrasting but no less controversial approach to Baroque opera is illustrated by the Monteverdi cycle that the Zurich Opera mounted in the 1970s. Conducted by Harnoncourt (who also edited the scores) and staged by Jean-Pierre Ponnelle, the productions were widely praised for the spontaneity and polish of the singing and orchestral playing, but criticized for their obtrusive histrionics. (At one point in *Ulisse*, for instance, Irus jumped into the pit and cried on the conductor's shoulder.) Porter denounced Ponnelle's trendy, free-wheeling stagings as 'comic-strip perversions of operatic masterpieces',[86] but audiences registered their approval vociferously and his approach was at least partly vindicated when the operas were later shown on television. The Zurich Monteverdi productions are by no means the most extreme instance of directorial licence in recent years. Peter Sellars, the *enfant terrible* of the American theatre in the 1980s, devised an outrageously updated version of *Giulio Cesare* in which the action was transferred to a Middle Eastern resort hotel, with Caesar transformed into a modern politico and Cleopatra portrayed as a sex kitten who delivered 'V'adoro pupille' as she was lowered onto the stage by a construction crane. 'Opera for the TV generation', harrumphed one critic.[87] It is doubtful that either Sellars or Ponnelle would construe that as an insult.

At the opposite end of the spectrum are Nicholas McGegan's productions of Handel operas, in which every element – staging, costumes, sets, choreography, singing, playing and even lighting – has been carefully reconstructed on the basis of historical evidence. McGegan's is a minority approach, better suited to festival conditions than to the tight schedules and limited resources of the average opera company. Period reconstructions have been tried elsewhere, however, notably by Lina Lalandi's English Bach Festival and by Concert Royal in the United States, and there is today an unmistakable drift toward authenticity in Baroque stagecraft as well as musical practice. Porter, among others, has welcomed this trend, though he does not go as far as McGegan in advocating historical verisimilitude. 'On the purely musical side,' he writes in a recent symposium on Vivaldi's operas, 'we have all heard now how authentic performing practice (as close as we can get to it) on the right instruments makes anything else – however accomplished it may be on its own terms – seem no more than second best. The same sort of thinking now needs to be applied to *all* aspects of an operatic presentation. Whenever it has been applied with knowledge, imagination, and skill, its results have been totally convincing.'[88]

The extent to which the historicist view becomes the new orthodoxy in Baroque opera production will depend on many factors, not least the receptiveness of the operatic establishment to the ideas of historically minded musicians like McGegan, Harnoncourt, Curtis, Jean-Claude

Malgoire, Michel Corboz, John Eliot Gardiner, Gustav Leonhardt, Sigiswald Kuijken, Ton Koopman, Roger Norrington and Andrew Parrott. As Ernst Neufeldt remarked three-quarters of a century ago, 'we are still in the period of experimentation'.[89] Late-twentieth-century musical culture embraces a wide variety of approaches to early opera. The current fashion for authentic productions is not likely to staunch the flow of such radical departures from tradition as Luciano Berio's *Orfeo* for the 1984 Florence Maggio Musicale, incorporating a rock group, electronic tape and a Hell's Angels-type motorcycle gang that spirited Euridice back to the underworld, or Hans Werner Henze's *Ritorno d'Ulisse* at the 1985 Salzburg Festival, featuring an even more bizarre assortment of modern instruments and a gigantic armillary sphere enclosing minimalist sets. Perhaps the only essential difference between these productions and earlier attempts to modernize Baroque opera is that we see them for what they are and no longer accept them as substitutes for the originals. The steadily growing list of composers adopted by the revivalists – Monteverdi, Handel, Cavalli, Vivaldi, Scarlatti, Caldara, Keiser, Lully, Rameau, Steffani, Arne, Telemann, Purcell, Pergolesi, Gluck and many more – has so far ensured that there is no dearth of material to engage the talents of enterprising singers, scholars, conductors, stage directors, designers and choreographers. The future may well record that we have barely scratched the surface of this inexhaustibly rich repertoire.

22 The Paris Opéra's landmark revival of Rameau's Hippolyte et Aricie in 1908 was lavishly staged but, according to contemporary critics, dramatically inert. 23 Heinrich Heckroth's severe constructivist sets for Radamisto at the 1927 Göttingen Festival illustrate the modernizing tendencies of Germany's 'Handel Renaissance'.

24 Monteverdi's Orfeo was played in front of a monumental Renaissance façade at the Hamburg State Theatre in 1942. The score and libretto were freely adapted by Carl Orff, who telescoped the original five acts into three and added a narrator. 25 Nicholas McGegan's 1983 production of Handel's Orlando in St Louis attempted to re-create Baroque stagecraft in toto, from simulated candlelight to the singers' carefully choreographed movements. The American countertenor Drew Minter sang the title role.

26 (RIGHT) Handel's Serse at Smith College in Massachusetts in 1928, one of a series of Baroque opera revivals conducted by Werner Josten. A critic described the fanciful décor as resembling 'a cross between a toy shop and a Greenwich Village tea dive'. The cast included Mabel Garrison as Romilda and Charles Kullman as Xerxes.

27 (LEFT) Richard Lewis and Saramae Endich in the 1964 Glyndebourne Festival production of Monteverdi's Incoronazione di Poppea. The editor–conductor Raymond Leppard, an outspoken foe of the early music purists, argues that the score of a Baroque opera is no more definitive or sacrosanct than that of a modern Broadway musical.

28 (RIGHT) Conductor Nikolaus Harnoncourt and director Jean-Pierre Ponnelle collaborated on the Zurich Opera's opulent Monteverdi cycle in the 1970s. The exuberant (and un-Baroque) naturalism of Ponnelle's staging contrasted sharply with Harnoncourt's historicist approach. Shown here is a tableau from the 1985 revival of Orfeo, with Philippe Huttenlocher in the title role.

29 (LEFT) Historicism was cast to the winds in the 1985 Opera Factory/London Sinfonietta production of Cavalli's La Calisto. Mercury glided across the stage on roller skates and the traditional allegorical figures – Nature, Eternity and Destiny – were transformed into preening beauty queens.

30 (ABOVE LEFT) *Ralph Kirkpatrick was the first American harpsichordist to win international recognition. An authority on Scarlatti and Bach, he advocated the use of eighteenth-century fingerings.*
31 (ABOVE) *Alfred Deller's refined artistry brought the countertenor voice back to prominence after the Second World War. The composer Michael Tippett remarked that 'the centuries rolled back' when he first heard Deller sing.* 32 (BELOW LEFT) *Thurston Dart exerted an enormous influence on England's post-war early music life. A distinguished musicologist and keyboard virtuoso, he represented the new breed of scholar–performers who came to the fore in the 1950s and 1960s.*

33 (OPPOSITE TOP) *The Munich-based Studio der frühen Musik, founded in the early 1960s by the American Thomas Binkley (far right), applied techniques derived from Middle Eastern folk music to the medieval repertoire.* 34 (OPPOSITE BOTTOM) *David Munrow (second from left) made a deep imprint on England's early music movement in his meteoric career. The Early Music Consort of London, which he led from 1967 until his death in 1976, set new standards of instrumental virtuosity. Also shown are Christopher Hogwood, James Tyler, Oliver Brookes and James Bowman.*

35 (TOP LEFT) *An American early music enthusiast named Leo Traynor (shown at far right taking part in a broadcast in 1951) persuaded the Japanese government to mandate the study of the recorder in primary schools after the Second World War.*

36 (CENTRE LEFT) *The Dutch harpsichordist and conductor Gustav Leonhardt has been one of the most influential early musicians of the post-war period. His empathy with the old masters is demonstrated not only by his musical performances but also by his portrayal of J. S. Bach in Jean-Marie Straub's film* The Chronicle of Anna Magdalena Bach. 37 (BOTTOM LEFT) *The American musicologist Joshua Rifkin excited controversy in the 1980s with his scaled-down version of Bach's B minor Mass, using one voice to a part. Rifkin's reductivist approach offers a radical alternative to the traditional big-choir performances, such as those of the Bethlehem Bach Choir (ill. 18).*

40 (OPPOSITE) *Hortus Musicus, based in Tallinn, Estonia, is one of dozens of early music ensembles that have sprung up in Eastern Europe and the Soviet Union, particularly in the past two decades. The group's director, Andres Mustonen (far right), says that lack of instruction in state music schools and a shortage of good instruments have hampered the revival in his country.*

38 (LEFT) *The Dutch recorder virtuoso Frans Brüggen has prompted other players to revise their ideas about Baroque phrasing, tone production and ornamentation. Recently Brüggen has distinguished himself as a conductor with the period-instrument Orchestra of the Eighteenth Century.*

39 (RIGHT) *The harpsichordist Ton Koopman exemplifies the combination of strict historicism and interpretative freedom that characterizes the Dutch early music school. As conductor of the Amsterdam Baroque Orchestra, he, like Brüggen, has lately ventured into the Classical repertoire.*

41 *The expanding borders of the early music movement are mirrored in the proliferation of specialist magazines around the world. Pictured in this montage are* Flûte à bec & instruments anciens *(France),* Concerto *(West Germany),* Musick *(Canada),* Tijdschrift voor oude muziek *(Holland),* Musica antiqua *(Belgium),* The American Recorder *(United States),* Consort *(Japan),* Zpravodaj společnosti pro starou hudbu *(Czechoslovakia) and* Early Music *(England).*

8

THE EARLY MUSIC SUBCULTURE

Thurston Dart, Noah Greenberg and the Post-War Rapprochement of Scholars and Performers · David Munrow and Gustav Leonhardt Contrasted · Their Continuing Influence · The Amateur Factor in the Recent Early Music 'Boom' · Early Music in Japan, Eastern Europe, the Soviet Union, Scandinavia and Elsewhere · Steadily Rising Performance Standards · Early Music and the Post-War Avant-Garde.

FROM THE VANTAGE POINT of the late 1980s, the Second World War can be seen as the great watershed in the early music movement. The emergence of Amsterdam, The Hague, London, Vienna and New York as major centres of activity in the 1950s marked the beginning of a new era. The ravages of the preceding decades had taken a heavy toll on musical life in Germany and France. No longer did they dominate the revival, artistically and intellectually, as they had since the time of Kiesewetter, Mendelssohn, Fétis and Choron. An infusion of fresh talent and ideas, emanating increasingly from the Schola Cantorum Basiliensis and the United States, revitalized early music performance in the fifties and sixties. It is hardly surprising that this process should have been fuelled by a reaction against Dolmetsch, Landowska, Wenzinger, Cape and other leading figures of the old guard.

Thurston Dart's ambivalent assessment of Dolmetsch's career (see page 42) typified the outlook of the post-war generation. While they admired Dolmetsch's headstrong independence and intellectual integrity, they regarded the amateur culture he stood for as a relic of the past. In their eyes, Dart was clearly the man of the future. Pre-eminent both as a musicologist and as a player of early keyboard instruments, he represented the new breed of performing scholars – and scholarly performers – who came to the fore in the fifties and sixties. Musicians like Denis Stevens, Anthony Lewis, Karl Haas, Charles Mackerras, Newell Jenkins, Charles Farncombe, Karl Richter, Claudio Scimone, Raymond Leppard and Karl Münchinger brought a historical dimension to their performances of pre-Classical music which had often previously been lacking. Dart's influence was especially strong in Britain, where the tradition of amateur scholarship and music-making was deeply ingrained. His stimulating and highly readable book *The Interpretation of Music*, first published in 1954, heralded the new philosophy of historical performance that transformed the early music movement in the post-war period.

A maverick in his performing as well as in his academic career, Dart galvanized Britain's early music community much as Noah Greenberg did on the other side of the Atlantic. His provocative, contentious, almost reckless approach to music, both inside and outside the classroom, left a lasting impression on everyone who came into his orbit. One of his students at Cambridge in the fifties has written that Dart 'soon had us playing Landini in what were then unheard-of realizations, singing nasal medieval songs, attempting to play viols . . . and generally having a whale of a time with what we had all thought (if we had thought about it at all) dull, pedant's music'.[1] Nothing could be less dull or pedantic than the robustly imaginative performances of Baroque and Renaissance music that can be heard on Dart's many solo recordings, as well as those he made with the Boyd Neel Orchestra, the Academy of St Martin-in-the-Fields, and his own Jacobean Ensemble and Philomusica Orchestra.

Dart readily acknowledged his debt to the conductors Arnold Goldsbrough and Boris Ord, who did much to raise the standards of vocal and instrumental early music performance in England in the first half of the century. But it was the Belgian musicologist Charles van den Borren for whom he felt the deepest sympathy and respect. Cape's Pro Musica Antiqua had given Van den Borren what he described as 'my practical apprenticeship in a field where before my head was my only guide'.[2] But in contrast to the mannerly, low-keyed performances of the Pro Musica Antiqua, Dart's exuded a spirit of élan and derring-do. No more than Greenberg did he allow musicological strictures to inhibit his spontaneity in performance. Nevertheless, both men had the highest regard for musicological discipline. Writing to Edward Lowinsky – who, like Gustave Reese, served as an invaluable sounding-board for his ideas – Greenberg spelled out a key component of his artistic credo: 'The responsiblity of re-establishing a tradition about which very little is known, is a great one. I feel that those of us who attempt this *must* seek the advice and critical comments of the scholars they identify with.'[3]

Greenberg's fruitful collaboration with Lowinsky and Reese set an important precedent. Performers and musicologists had long eyed one another warily, if not with outright hostility. Those who ventured into the no-man's land separating the two camps, as Dolmetsch did, risked getting caught in the ideological crossfire. Reporting from the battlefront on a visit to the 1933 Haslemere Festival, the Belgian musicologist Paul Collaer wrote that an *impasse* had been reached: 'On one side sit the musicologists with their knowledge of a silent, written-down music. On the other side are the instrumentalists, unable to put their skill at the service of early music because they lack guidance in the study of the necessary instruments.'[4] Dolmetsch and Dart were almost unique in possessing the ability – and the inclination – to excel both as scholars and as practical musicians. Many, if not most, of their peers continued to hold with Alfred Deller that 'musicology and the performance of music are two worlds best kept apart from one another'.[5] Yet just as Robert Donington felt moved to declare, in his compendious survey of early performance practice, that 'an unmusical musicologist is not acceptable in this line of work',[6] so early musicians gradually came to accept musicologists as allies in their search for stylish and perceptive interpretations.

As far as the English-speaking world was concerned, the launching of the London-based *Early Music* magazine in 1973 formally ratified this belated rapprochement. Sumptuously designed and bearing the prestigious imprint of Oxford University Press, the new journal set out to forge 'a link between the finest scholarship of our day and the amateur and professional listener and performer'. That such a publication could survive and indeed flourish was an indication of how far the early music movement had come in the four decades since the Schola Cantorum Basiliensis had issued a similar manifesto. John M. Thomson, the founding editor of *Early Music*, noted that 'a journal such as this would have been impossible' as long as interest in early music was confined to a specialized minority.[7] By 1973, however, early music in England and many other countries had become a prominent feature of the musical landscape, a vibrant and rapidly growing subculture with its own institutions and organs of communication, its own jargon and catch-phrases, its own celebrities and gurus.

Two exceptionally gifted performers stand out as key figures in the post-war early music scene. One can scarcely imagine two more disparate personalities than David Munrow, early music's youthful 'pied piper' (to borrow the title of his enormously popular BBC radio series), and Gustav Leonhardt, the aristocratic purveyor of Bach and Couperin. Yet each in his own way exercised a seminal influence on the younger generation of early musicians. In Munrow's case, this influence derived partly from his uncanny skills as a programme-maker and partly from his supreme versatility. Never before in modern times had an early musician played historical wind instruments like the shawm, recorder and crumhorn with such verve and virtuosity. The Early Music Consort of London, which Munrow founded in 1967, provided a glittering showcase for his multi-faceted artistry. Everything he turned his hand to, be it a medieval *basse danse* or a Baroque recorder concerto, bore the stamp of his exuberant, extraverted personality. Though he lacked the time (and, one suspects, the temperament) to pursue scholarly research in a systematic fashion, Munrow did write an important study of medieval and Renaissance instruments, accompanied by his group's recorded illustrations.[8]

Munrow's suicide in 1976, at the age of thirty-three, deprived early music of its most charismatic and widely acclaimed practitioner since Greenberg. Indeed, his penchant for showmanship – and the often controversial inventiveness he displayed in doctoring up old music – marked him out as the American's natural successor. Anthony Lewis's glowing tribute to Munrow might well have been inspired by Greenberg: 'Gone was the unease that beset so many previous performances of earlier music – the starved tone, the flaccid rhythms, the listless phrasing – this was replaced by confidence and mastery that enabled the music to break through the veil of insecurity that had previously surrounded it.'[9] This is not to slight such outstanding British groups as the Deller Consort, the Julian Bream Consort and Musica Reservata (whose innovative performances in the sixties and seventies, under Michael Morrow and John Beckett, revealed the earthy vitality of medieval secular music). But no other ensemble captured the imagination of musicians and lay listeners alike quite as strongly as the Early Music Consort. Munrow was *sui generis*, unprecedented and irreplaceable.

The Dutch harpsichordist Gustav Leonhardt, Munrow's senior by fourteen years, occupies an analogous position in the Baroque music revival. His playing is often described as austere and uncompromising, and indeed there is more than a trace of Calvinist sobriety in his demeanour, on stage as well as off. But the daring, incisive, unconventional persona that Leonhardt projects through his music gives the lie to this Apollonian image. Unlike Munrow, Leonhardt professes to be totally uninterested in making music accessible or entertaining. Instead of reaching out to audiences, he draws them into the music with performances of surpassing subtlety and intensity. The results can be just as dazzling as Munrow's performances, for Leonhardt, too, is a consummate virtuoso. But whereas Munrow's warmly communicative artistry demonstrated the timelessness and modernity of early music, Leonhardt's playing has a slightly hermetic, other-worldy quality that evokes the master clavecinists of the seventeenth and eighteenth centuries.

This aura is enhanced by the character of the instruments Leonhardt plays. The start of his career coincided with the post-war revolution in harpsichord design, and he was one of the first major artists to align himself squarely behind the historical instruments of the German maker Martin Skowroneck and the Boston school of Hubbard and Dowd. Leonhardt shows the same meticulous concern for historical accuracy in his treatment of musical texts as in his choice of harpsichords; his eagerness to strip away encrusted performance traditions epitomizes the modern *Urtext* mentality. 'Nowadays', he once told an interviewer, 'it's no problem getting hold of a facsimile edition of early music. What else is there to add? When you've read what the composer has written, you don't really need anything else.'[10] This is a gross oversimplification, of course: only Leonhardt's encyclopaedic knowledge of Baroque music and performance practice justifies such a disarming prescription. Yet it is easy to understand why legions of young musicians, groping for a key to unlock the secrets of the past, have found Leonhardt's serene certitude so inspiring.

Leonhardt and Munrow loom so large in the recent history of the revival that few early musicians can have escaped their influence. The roster of Leonhardt's protégés and colleagues contains most of the big names in Baroque performance: Frans Brüggen, Jaap Schröder, Nikolaus Harnoncourt, Anner Bylsma, Ton Koopman, Alan Curtis, the Kuijken brothers and many more. Ensembles like Jean-Claude Malgoire's La Grande Ecurie et la Chambre du Roy and Reinhard Goebel's Musica Antiqua of Cologne have capitalized on his pioneering work. Munrow's legacy is equally impressive. Alumni of the Early Music Consort include the countertenor James Bowman, the lutenist James Tyler of the London Early Music Group (the would-be successor to Munrow's consort) and the peripatetic harpsichordist–conductor Christopher Hogwood of the Academy of Ancient Music. The Consort of Musicke, which Anthony Rooley founded with Tyler in 1969, has brought Munrow's convictions to bear on the late Renaissance and early Baroque repertoires. A dozen years after his death, Munrow's spirit is still very much alive in England, even among younger musicians who had little or no direct contact with him.

It would, of course, be rash to imply that *only* Munrow and Leonhardt have left lasting marks on the early music scene in the past two or three decades. Harnoncourt's prolific Concentus Musicus of Vienna, for instance, is second to none in the continuing exploration of the Baroque repertoire, although, unlike Leonhardt, Harnoncourt has rarely been on the cutting edge of the movement. Thomas Binkley's Munich-based Studio der frühen Musik revolutionized the interpretation of medieval monophonic music in the sixties and seventies by applying improvisatory techniques derived from Middle Eastern folk music. Binkley's easily imitated style inspired many early musicians to concoct what Joel Cohen calls 'weird *salades composées* of Bernard de Ventadorn and Ravi Shankar'.[11] Vienna's lowbrow Clemencic Consort, the off-beat French ensemble Les Menestriers, Michel Piguet's Ricercare and Jordi Savall's Hesperion XX, to say nothing of older groups like Konrad Ruhland's Musica Antiqua of Munich and Kees Otten's Syntagma Musicum of Amsterdam, all merit more than the passing mention they can be given here. Nor should one overlook the spectacular flowering of vocal ensembles in the post-war period – the Clerkes of Oxenford, Pro Cantione Antiqua, the Monteverdi Choir, the Ensemble Clément Janequin, the Prague Madrigal Singers, Collegium Vocale of Ghent, Concerto Vocale, the Hilliard Ensemble, Western Wind, the Tallis Scholars, Gothic Voices and so on – which has challenged the instrumentalists' long-standing hegemony in the field.

The true magnitude of the early music 'boom' becomes still more apparent when one considers that professional music-making is only the tip of the iceberg: as in the nineteenth century, the recent groundswell of interest in early music is largely the result of amateur activity. As we have seen, the renaissance of the recorder between the wars transformed early music from an esoteric art form into a popular pastime. Societies of recorder and viol players sprang up around the world, promoting the idea of amateur music-making and heightening the movement's visibility. The introduction of recorders in schools, most notably in Carl Orff's *Schulwerk* programme, and the mass-production of inexpensive wood and plastic instruments brought early music into everyday life. Recorder players flocked to study with teachers like Edgar Hunt and Walter Bergmann in England, Waldemar Woehl and Gustav Scheck in Germany, Johannes Collette and Kees Otten in Holland, Hans Ulrich Staeps in Austria, Mario Duschenes in Canada and Erich Katz in America.[12] The recorder orchestra, the creation of a German schoolteacher name Rudolf Barthel, offered further opportunities for ensemble-playing. Dolmetsch's dream of installing a recorder consort, a chest of viols and a clavichord or harpsichord in every home may have been utopian, but without its army of amateur acolytes, early music would never have rid itself of the stigma of élitism so quickly.

Nowhere has the amateur factor been more decisive than in Japan. Thanks largely to a resident American enthusiast named Leo Traynor, study of the recorder was made compulsory in Japanese primary schools in the late 1940s. The recorder's resemblance to the indigenous *shakuhachi*, or folk flute, undoubtedly contributed to its speedy and widespread acceptance. Masses of schoolchildren playing recorders in disciplined unison soon became a common sight in the land of Suzuki, and by the late sixties a fully-fledged early music movement was afoot, with European performers beating a path to the Far East and Japanese students training in European conservatories. Many of Japan's early musicians, like their European counterparts, were opting out of a mainstream musical culture that they found narrow and inflexible. The founding of the Medieval Choir of Tokyo in 1953 led to the establishment of numerous ensembles specializing in early music of various periods. Several Japanese music schools have instituted courses in early music. This increasingly diverse scene is chronicled in the magazine *Consort*, a distinctively Japanese version of *Early Music* providing a lively mixture of news and commentary, profiles of performers and instrument-makers, how-to articles and even poetry.[13]

Early music, as Japan's experience has proved, possesses a remarkable power to cut across national and cultural boundaries. Even before the Second World War, the revival had gained footholds far beyond its birthplaces in England, Germany and France. Choral directors like Gustav Petterson in Finland, Mogens Wöldike in Denmark and Wacław Gieburowski in Poland consistently championed pre-Classical music in the twenties and thirties, while the concerts sponsored by the Music History Museum in Stockholm and Prague's Pro Musica Antiqua (a viol-and-harpsichord consort formed in 1928) attest to the growing audience for early instrumental music. Geographically speaking, though, the period of major expansion in the early music movement commenced in the late fifties and early sixties, notably in Poland, Hungary and Czechoslovakia, each of which had a significant corpus of indigenous early music ripe for revival.

As though making up for lost time, Eastern Europe has lately produced a bumper crop of early music ensembles. The Camerata Hungarica, Warsaw's Fistulatores et Tubicinatores Varsovienses, Ars Cameralis in Prague, the Ensemble Universitas Studiorum Zagrebiensis and dozens more have been performing and recording pre-Classical music with increasing proficiency. Bydgoszca in Poland, Szombathely in Hungary and Zadar in Yugoslavia have emerged as regional early music centres, the Eastern European counterparts of York, Amsterdam and Bruges. A growing traffic of early musicians plying between Eastern and Western Europe has borne fruit not only in collaborative projects like Nicholas McGegan's recent recordings with Hungary's Capella Savaria but also in a marked improvement in the standards of execution attained by Eastern European performers.[14]

This improvement is all the more impressive because several factors have inhibited the growth of an early music movement in Eastern Europe: Marxism's wariness of 'regressive' tendencies, particularly in the form of early religious music; poor communication with Western musicians and scholars; and, most crucially perhaps, the difficulty of obtaining historical instruments and scores. When the New York Pro Musica toured the Soviet Union in the mid-sixties, they encountered early music enthusiasts everywhere they went, but official recognition was nil. Andrei Volkonsky, a composer who founded the early music ensemble Madrigal in Moscow and later emigrated to the West, told one of the visiting Americans that he had been the first person in forty years to check the works of Machaut out of the Moscow Conservatory library.[15] An American musicologist who spent a year in the Soviet Union more recently recalls that Soviet early musicians were virtually cut off from outside contacts, making it difficult for a native early music movement to take root.

Times have changed, or so it would appear. The leading Estonian ensemble Hortus Musicus now plays some fifty concerts a year in the Soviet Union and another forty abroad, a schedule that many Western early music groups might envy. Andres Mustonen, who directs the Tallinn-based group, compares the level of interest in early music in the Soviet Union today to that in the West twenty years ago. But he points out that the expansion of the revival is still hampered by a chronic shortage of historical instruments, most of which have to be imported from East Germany or the West, and by the unavailability of instruction in Soviet music schools. The latter factor helps explain why Hortus Musicus and other early music groups in Eastern bloc countries have tended to model their performances on those of Western ensembles like the New York Pro Musica and the Early Music Consort of London (whose recordings have always been obtainable to those who knew where to look). The scarcity of reliable, up-to-date information makes it difficult for an outsider to assess the situation in other East European countries. Recent reports, however, suggest that Yugoslavia and East Germany are rapidly catching up with Hungary, Czechoslovakia and Poland. The East Germans naturally consider Bach, Handel and Telemann part of their national heritage, and outstanding groups like the Capella Fidicina and the Capella Lipsiensis have become familiar to Western audiences through recordings.[16]

Elsewhere in Europe, post-war trends have been much the same. Vienna's rise to prominence in the 1950s stemmed largely from the musicologist Josef Mertin, who counted Harnoncourt, René Clemencic and Eduard Melkus among his pupils at the Akademie für Musik. As the home of Leonhardt (who taught at the academy in the early fifties), the Concentus Musicus, the Clemencic Consort, Melkus's Capella Academica and the Wiener Blockflötenensemble, Vienna staked its claim to being a capital of the early music world. West Germany, too, has made a bid to recoup its erstwhile glory. In recent years Munich and Cologne have once again become important centres for performance and study, while the admirable magazine Concerto surveys the early music scene from a central European perspective. At the same time the revival has been migrating northward to places like Helsinki, the Norwegian cities of Oslo and Trondheim, and Stockholm and Drottningholm in Sweden. While Finland's Sonores Antiqui, Norway's Ringve Kammerensemble and Sweden's Musica Holmiae have yet to become household names outside Scandinavia, they have definitely put northern Europe on the early music map. Steady if less spectacular gains have been registered in France, Switzerland, Canada, Belgium, Spain, Italy and

Denmark, and early music beachheads have been established as far afield as Buenos Aires, Rio de Janeiro, Santiago, Vancouver, Toronto, Sydney and Wellington.[17]

In sum, early music has become as cosmopolitan as the rest of the musical world. Many ensembles draw their personnel from an international pool of early musicians, the best of whom commute from city to city or even from continent to continent, like modern troubadours. Some, like the directors of two prominent 'German' ensembles of recent years, become more or less permanent expatriates. Thomas Binkley of the Studio der frühen Musik and Ben Bagby of Sequentia are not the only Americans who have followed in Cape's footsteps; many others – the lutenists James Tyler and Hopkinson Smith, the harpsichordists William Christie and Alan Curtis, the wind players Bruce Haynes and Don Smithers, the singers Judith Nelson and Jantina Noorman – have been lured abroad by opportunities for performing, studying, teaching and recording. Conversely, a growing number of European early musicians are seeking greener pastures across the Atlantic. As performers like Hogwood, McGegan and Schröder develop closer ties with the United States, the American early music scene is becoming increasingly internationalized and activity has begun to percolate away from New York and Boston to Washington, Oberlin (Ohio), Ann Arbor, Chicago, San Francisco and other regional centres.

If the revival has expanded dramatically in geographical terms, the qualitative improvement in performance standards has been no less remarkable. It used to be said, not altogether unjustly, that early music groups were filled with performers who had failed to make the grade in the mainstream musical world. This is patently untrue of musicians like Landowska, Leonhardt, Harnoncourt, Brüggen and Munrow, whose virtuosity and musicianship command universal respect. An influx of talented young instrumentalists and singers, many of them conservatory graduates disenchanted with traditional musical careers, has brought a new level of professionalism to early music. The small but growing number of international early music competitions is a further indication of this trend. Prestigious events like America's Bodky Competition and Belgium's Musica Antiqua Competition regularly attract contestants from around the world, a sign that early musicians, once quick to scorn such badges of worldly success, are no longer averse to following the conventional path to recognition.

Ironically, while this elevation of standards is generally welcomed, one often hears complaints that early musicians are becoming *too* professional in their outlook, that young performers are sacrificing idealism on the altar of commercial success and cultivating technical facility at the expense of well-rounded musicianship. This complaint is not unique to early music, of course; it is virtually a cliché of performance criticism that today's young virtuosos can run rings around their elders but that their performances often lack depth and originality. What gives this charge special gravity is that early musicians have long prided themselves on being different from other musicians – more adventurous, readier to question received opinions, less narrowly preoccupied with career-building. But the forces that have transformed musical life in recent decades – recordings, jet travel, high-powered publicity, superstar fees and the rest – have inevitably left their mark on early music as well. To expect early musicians to remain 'pure' and impervious to such enticements is simply unrealistic.

Whether this is, on balance, a desirable state of affairs is another matter. Professionalism *per se* is surely no bad thing, especially if it induces mainstream musicians to take their colleagues in early music more seriously. And while technical proficiency may be appraised too highly today, it is well to remember that it was grossly undervalued on the early music market a few years ago. A more disturbing development spotted by some observers is the tendency of up-and-coming musicians to mimic successful performers like Leonhardt, Munrow and Binkley instead of cultivating their own ideas and personalities. To the extent that the early music movement thrives on individualism and rebellion, facile imitation unquestionably poses a serious threat to its continuing vitality. On the other hand, it is difficult to see how a viable early music tradition can ever be established if all performers are expected to start from scratch. Young musicians have always emulated their idols; the better ones outgrow this phase and achieve mastery in their own right. This is no less true in early music than in mainstream music. In any case, a musical culture that has produced such superlative and highly individualistic artists as Paul O'Dette, Sigiswald Kuijken, Jordi Savall and Trevor Pinnock is in no imminent danger of stagnation.

The 'new virtuosity' (to borrow a term more commonly associated with contemporary music) of today's early musicians has had a significant impact in the creative as well as the re-creative spheres. In Chapter 4 we considered a few of the modern compositions for old instruments inspired by Landowska, Kirkpatrick and other early musicians. The prevailing Neoclassicism of the interwar period was displaced in the fifties and sixties by experiments with radically new sonorities and instrumental techniques. A number of early musicians – notably the harpsichordists Antoinette Vischer and Elisabeth Chojnacka and the recorder players Frans Brüggen and Michael Vetter – became closely associated with avant-garde music for their instruments. Largely as a result of the stimulus they supplied, most composers have long since ceased to treat the harpsichord and recorder as 'historical' instruments. They have been incorporated into the modern instrumentarium and their

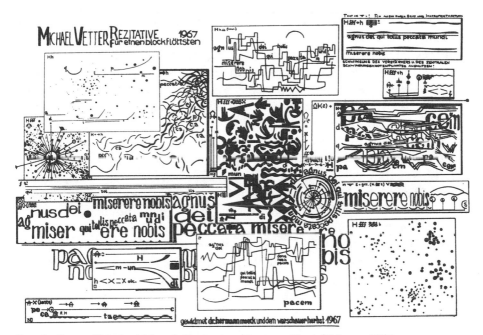

Fig. 5   Score of Michael Vetter's Rezitative für einen Blockflötisten, 1967

sounds, once perceived as quaint and archaic, by now seem scarcely less contemporary than those of the vibraphone and synthesizer.

A few examples will suffice to illustrate the wide-ranging treatments of the recorder and harpsichord by composers in the post-war era. Luciano Berio's *Gesti* for solo recorder makes use of flutter-tonguing and vocalizing, not as extraneous special effects but as integral elements of the composition. In Karlheinz Stockhausen's *Spiral*, Vetter simultaneously played an amplified recorder and a short-wave radio, whose sounds were 'imitated, transformed and transcended' (in the composer's words) by means of sophisticated electronic apparatus that sent the music swirling around the audience's heads. John Cage's *HPSCHD*, one of Vischer's many commissions, calls for an equally elaborate array of tape machines and amplifiers. Computer-realized mixtures of music by various composers, early and modern, are combined with projections and colourful lighting effects in a typically free-wheeling Cagean *son et lumière* extravaganza.

Chojnacka pioneered the use of tone-clusters and sounds produced by plucking and striking the harpsichord strings, a vocabulary that Iannis Xenakis has employed to memorable effect in his *Komboi*. György Ligeti's *Continuum* consists of a sequence of oscillating chords, played so rapidly that the individual notes merge into a characteristically dense, unarticulated mass

171

of sound. If the harpsichord lends itself to Ligeti's neo-Impressionistic language, it is equally well suited to the crystalline, highly organized music of Elliott Carter and Milton Babbitt. Each of these composers has explored the intrinsic properties of the harpsichord, albeit paradoxically often in ways that mask its traditional character. The fact that virtually all twentieth-century harpsichord music has been written for modern instruments suggests that composers are more interested in its sonority than in its historical associations. Carter's Double Concerto for harpsichord and piano, for instance, exploits the registrations and dynamic range of a Challis harpsichord; strictly speaking, to play it on a Hubbard or Skowroneck instrument would be as inauthentic as playing Froberger on a 'Landowska' Pleyel.

Carter's ahistorical approach to the harpsichord exemplifies the 'systematic alienation of conventional instrumental sound' that Mauricio Kagel aspired to in his *Musik für Renaissance-Instrumente*.[18] Kagel deploys a large battery of early instruments: crumhorns, shawms, Renaissance trombones, cornett, percussion, lute, theorbo, viole da braccia, gambas, regal and a positive organ that has been 'denatured' by inserting tubes of various shapes and materials into the pipes. The music constitutes a virtual catalogue of 'extended' instrumental techniques: tone-bending, multiphonics, glissandos, vocal effects and so forth. Moreover, Kagel invites the performers to invent sonorities of their own, using tone colours as an embellishment 'in a way similar to the performance practice of much Renaissance and Baroque music'. In thus grafting the improvisatory procedures of pre-Classical music onto the Schoenbergian *Klangfarben* idiom, Kagel created an eerie, unsettling, phantasmagorical work which, in his own words, 'contains neither predictions, pointers to the future, nor a comforting return to the past'.

All of this is very far removed indeed from the *leichte Spielmusik* of the twenties and thirties (though many composers, it must be said, continue to write for early instruments in a more conventional vein that lies well within the grasp of amateur players). Contemporary composers have diversified their techniques of recycling the past as an ever wider range of early music becomes available in scores and recordings. While the Neoclassicists found inspiration in the clarity of form and texture that characterized Baroque music, composers of the post-war avant-garde have been increasingly drawn to music of earlier eras. Peter Maxwell Davies, perhaps the best-known representative of this group, has confessed to feeling a 'certain nostalgia for the medieval period, where life had a very deep level of meaning and symbolism, without being in the least self-conscious'.[19] Davies's involvement with composers like Dunstable, Taverner and Byrd was in reaction to what he perceived as the *laissez-faire* attitudes emanating from Darmstadt, the citadel of Modernism in the fifties and sixties.

'My interest in Dunstable and company', he explains, 'was my answer to the way total serialism was making a lot of processes of musical choice unconscious. They were becoming mechanical .... I saw many more possibilities in the careful thinking through of a musical problem ....'[20] Davies's preoccupation with the internal structures and techniques of early music, rather than its superficial sound, explains why his scores do not as a rule call for historical instruments. (An exception is his opera *Taverner*, which features a stage-band part written for Munrow's Early Music Consort.) He prefers instead to set up a dialogue between past and present, typically by presenting a piece of old music in a more or less straightforward transcription for modern instruments as a prelude to subjecting it to increasingly extravagant and even grotesque distortions. In his *Missa super l'Homme Armé*, the purity of the familiar medieval tune is subverted by the fractured wailing of an eighteenth-century-style chamber organ, while the stately dances in the *Fantasia and Two Pavanes after Henry Purcell* are ingeniously transformed into boisterous foxtrots. Davies makes it clear that these none-too-scrupulous arrangements are his way of thumbing his nose at the puritans in the early music movement:

> I have long been fascinated by Purcell's music, but utterly bored by well-meaning 'authentic' performances, which possibly get every double-dotted rhythm right but convey no sense of Purcell's intensity of feeling, sense of fun or sheer outrageousness. I feel the profoundest respect for the 'great' composers of the past, but have no feeling of slavish reverence towards them whatsoever – after all, they were living, real people, not priests .... Musical purity in these matters is about as interesting as moral purity. I am sure many people will consider my Purcell realizations wholly immoral.[21]

That Davies chooses to call his flagrant distortions of Purcell's music 'realizations' reveals as much about contemporary attitudes toward early music as it does about his own compositional processes. Nothing, it would seem, is out of bounds to historically sophisticated composers in the second half of the twentieth century. They cloak early music in modern sonorities, as in Charles Wuorinen's *Bearbeitungen aus dem Glogauer Liederbuch* and Davies's *Renaissance Scottish Dances*. They transform and twist it out of shape, as in Lukas Foss's *Baroque Variations* and Hans Werner Henze's *Vitalino raddoppiato* (based on the Vitali Chaconne). They lace their music with allusions to the past, as in Bernd Alois Zimmermann's *Musique pour les soupers du Roi Ubu*, and delight in the aural dislocations caused by juxtaposing old and new musical idioms in a kind of Postmodernist collage. In his opera

Eros and Psyche, for instance, the American composer Conrad Cummings combines a modern pit orchestra with an off-stage quartet of musicians playing eighteenth-century instruments tuned fractionally lower to Baroque pitch. What Cummings calls the 'rubbing of historical shoulders'[22] as the two ensembles collide and clash is an experience common to today's period-hopping performer.

As they dust off the hocket, canon, cantus firmus, isorhythm and other time-honoured compositional devices, contemporary composers are reaffirming the sense of intimacy with the past that has nourished the early music movement since the eighteenth century. The line between 'old' and 'new' has become so blurred that one early musician (who also performs a good deal of contemporary music) can quip that 'Perotin was the first minimalist composer'.[23] United in rejecting the status quo, early music and the avant-garde have mounted a two-pronged attack on established musical values and institutions. As the musicologist Laurence Dreyfus has written, 'Schoenberg's Chamber Symphony of 1906 and Leonhardt's Bach in 1977 wreak similar havoc'.[24] Just as Schoenberg's atonality undermined the harmonic system that had governed Western music for three centuries, so the ideas formulated by Leonhardt and his colleagues have challenged the way music is performed and listened to today. The revolutionary implications of Leonhardt's Bach can be subsumed under a single heading: authenticity.

9

PLAYING BACH 'HIS WAY'

The Pursuit of 'Authenticity' · Work-Fidelity and Growing Interest in Historical Performance Practices · Importance of Style and Sonority in Music · 'Subjective' and 'Objective' Modes of Interpretation · Adorno vs. Hindemith · Instrumental Fetishism and the Neglect of Historical Singing Styles · Reactions Against Musicological 'Positivism' · Taste and Imagination as Components of Authenticity.

AUTHENTICITY IS, of course, the nub, the central issue, the very *raison d'être* of the early music movement. In a sense, the history of the movement is the history of the search for authenticity – or, more accurately, the history of changing concepts of authenticity – in the performance of early music. A distinction must now be drawn between the early music revival, as that umbrella phrase has been rather loosely used so far in this book, and what has come to be called the historical performance movement. Clearly, many of the musicians associated with the revival of early music and instruments have had little or no interest in historical modes of performance. Only recently has the attitude expressed in Landowska's famous remark 'You play Bach *your* way, I'll play Bach *his* way' gained general acceptance among early musicians.

Landowska herself was hardly an authenticist, but her oft-quoted aphorism, whether genuine or apocryphal, puts the issue in a nutshell. To play Bach *his* way – to enter, through a kind of spiritual transmigration, the mind of a composer of another era – has long been the underlying premise of the historical performance movement. Yet the gulf that divides us even from music of comparatively recent vintage enjoins caution: few of today's early musicians would couch their goals in such unequivocal language as Landowska used. One prominent artist describes her ambition more cautiously as performing a piece in such a way that the composer would recognize it 'at worst, without bewilderment, and at best, with pleasure'.[1] This seems a workable definition of authenticity for the 1980s, one that will serve as a starting point for a consideration of this crucial but elusive concept.

Problems arise immediately on the semantic level. While it is generally agreed that authenticity of some sort is the ultimate goal of historical performance, no clear consensus exists as to what the word means. Constant use and abuse have eroded whatever firm sense it may once have conveyed. As the musicologist Joseph Kerman writes, the epithet 'authentic' has 'acquired the same cult value when applied to music as "natural" or "organic" when applied to food'.[2] In short, 'authentic' has become one of those noxious buzzwords that one would willingly dispense with if a satisfactory alternative could be found. Unfortunately, none of the substitutes on offer quite fills the bill. The current favourites, 'historically aware' or 'historically informed' performance, though cumbersome, are at least reasonably accurate as far as they go. Yet the words 'authentic' and 'authenticity' crop up so often in discussions of early music performance that they can hardly be ignored. Nor need they be expunged from the critical lexicon, provided one bears in mind their inherent limitations and misleading overtones.

The concept of authenticity has it origins in the doctrine of *Werktreue*, or work-fidelity, a term coined by German musicologists to denote adherence to accurate and reliable musical texts. So the minimum requirement for an authentic performance is simply that: getting the notes right. This is seldom as straightforward as it sounds. In general, the farther one goes back in time, the less precise musical notation becomes and the harder it is to determine what notes are to be played, let alone how they should be interpreted. Performances of medieval and Renaissance music are necessarily based to a large extent on speculation. It is not surprising, then, that many performers and scholars have withdrawn to the comparatively firm ground of the more familiar Baroque and Classical repertoires – a trend that record companies and concert promoters are only too happy to encourage.

Establishing an accurate musical text is, moreover, only the first step. The musical notation must then be translated into sound. This is where textual criticism leaves off and performance practice takes over. *Aufführungspraxis*, to use its original German name, deals with details of interpretation that composers thought too vague – or too obvious – to write down. These include such basic elements as tone colour, instrumentation, phrasing and ornamentation. The systematic study of such matters is a fairly recent phenomenon in the English-speaking world, but the Germans have been at it for a long time. The 1954 edition of *Grove's Dictionary of Music and Musicians* has no entry on the subject, while the great German encyclopaedia *Die Musik in Geschichte und Gegenwart* contains a lengthy article, based almost exclusively on German scholarship. However, the *New Grove* commissioned an illuminating essay from the American musicologist (and one-time director of the University of Chicago collegium ensemble) Howard Mayer Brown, which reflects the importance currently attached to historical performance.

Brown writes that 'the means and style of performance imagined by the composer are so indissolubly bound up with the whole musical fabric that he has set down, that the communication and impact of the composition are seriously impaired if the sounds he imagined are not at least kept in mind when preparing modern performances'. In other words, style and sonority are intrinsic elements of a composer's creation, as indispensable to its proper understanding as the notes themselves. Over the past three-quarters of a century, as the trickle of books and articles on performance practice swelled into a stream and finally a torrent, what Denis Stevens calls the 'do-it-yourself musicology kit'[3] has become part of every early musician's stock-in-trade. The prototype of the genre is Arnold Dolmetsch's *The Interpretation of the Music of the XVIIth and XVIIIth Centuries*, which blended scholarship and practical prescriptions in a handy *vade-mecum* to the Baroque repertoire.

Although the book was highly praised, Dolmetsch's broadly humanistic approach to historical performance soon fell victim to changing fashions in musicology. Where he talked abstractly about feeling and expression in early music, later writers preferred to lay down concrete rules of interpretation. The conflict between these two schools of thought is at least as old as the early music revival itself. The idea of work-fidelity arose in reaction to the spread of Romanticized performing editions in the nineteenth century. Mendelssohn represented what the musicologist Frederick Dorian described as the 'objective' school: he conscientiously attempted to ascertain what Bach actually wrote, although he reserved the right to interpret it in his own fashion. This scrupulousness contrasts with Fétis's high-handed arrangements of pre-Classical music (not to mention his notorious 'corrections' of the Beethoven symphonies). The vogue for work-fidelity in turn provoked a strong reaction. Nietzsche, one of the chief spokesmen for the opposition, argued cogently that the old masters needed to be up-dated for modern audiences. The very idea of performing old music historically struck him as misbegotten, since 'the really historical performance would talk to ghosts'.[4]

This 'subjective' viewpoint stressed the performer's paramount role in realizing the composer's conception. Indeed, critics in Nietzsche's day and for many years thereafter routinely complained not that performances of early music were overly Romanticized but that they were not Romantic (that is, expressive) enough. Thus Jules Ecorcheville criticized the Schola Cantorum for ironing out the rhythmic and dynamic nuances implicit in Bach's music in a misguided effort to perform it *tout droit*. Modern performers, he charged, approached early music in a spirit of 'false modesty'.[5] Dolmetsch revealed an essentially nineteenth-century sensibility when he wrote of the necessity of 'understanding what the Old Masters *felt* about their own music ... what was the *Spirit of their Art*'. He vehemently rejected the idea 'that expression is a modern thing, and that the old music requires nothing beyond mechanical precision'.[6] Landowska put it more bluntly: 'The idea of objectivity is utopian. Can the music of any composer maintain its integrity after passing through the living complex – sanguine or phlegmatic – of this or that interpreter? Can an interpreter restrict himself to remaining in the shadow of the author? What a commonplace! What a joke!'[7]

For a performer to subdue his or her personality in deference to the composer struck Landowska, as it would have struck almost any musician of her generation, as tantamount to abdicating responsibility. To early musicians of a later day, on the other hand, Landowska's intuitive concept of authenticity looked suspiciously like old wine in new bottles. Yet here, too, our frame of reference is continually shifting. The critic who, in 1930, paired Landowska and Toscanini as 'objective' performers, viewed the harpsichordist from a different perspective than we do today. 'She does not interpret', wrote Boris de Schloezer; 'she contents herself with playing what is written as it is written. Each note receives precisely the treatment indicated by the black signs traced on the music paper.'[8] Landowska herself would surely have bristled at the suggestion that she played music 'com'è scritto', Toscanini-fashion. For despite her repeated protestations that she aspired only to serve composers, her performances were anything but self-effacing.

Nevertheless, the Stravinskian aversion to 'interpretation' impressed itself deeply on the early music movement in the first half of the century. Having turned their backs on virtuosity and exhibitionism, many early musicians went on to banish all traces of Romantic expression from their performances, elevating reticence to the level of an aesthetic principle. Safford Cape, for example, asserted that although the performer should not be 'cold or mechanical', he should take care to keep his 'emotivity' in the background.[9] This philosophy was enunciated in its purest form in a programme note that Erwin Bodky wrote for the Cambridge Society for Early Music in the early 1950s:

> Early Music was a highly aristocratic art and restraint governed even the display of emotion as well as the exhibition of technical virtuosity. This deprives concerts of Early Music of the atmosphere of electricity which, when present, is one of the finest experiences of the modern concert hall. Who seeks but this may stay away from our concert series. We want to take this opportunity, however, to thank our artists for the voluntary restraint in the display of their artistic capabilities which they exercise when recreating with us the atmosphere of equanimity, tranquillity and noble entertainment which is the characteristic feature of Early Music.[10]

This is the sort of thinking that gave authenticity a bad name and made the epithet 'scholarly', when applied to musical performances, synonymous with dull and unimaginative. Like many nineteenth-century early musicians, Bodky believed that the old masters should be cultivated in a spirit of reverence and self-abnegation. His attitude epitomized the 'impotent nostalgia' that hostile critics like Theodor Adorno saw as endemic to the early music movement. In a famous essay entitled 'Bach Defended Against His Devotees', Adorno accused the historicists of turning Bach into 'a composer for organ festivals in well preserved Baroque towns .... At times one can hardly avoid the suspicion that the sole concern of today's Bach devotees is to see that no inauthentic dynamics, modifications of tempo, oversize choirs and orchestras creep in; they seem to wait with potential fury lest any more humane impulse become audible in the rendition.' Adorno rejected the concept of *Werktreue*, asserting that the only valid way to revive early music was to reinterpret it in contemporary language, as Schoenberg and Webern had done. The purists missed the point: performance presupposed interpretation, and interpretation was by definition subjective.[11]

Writing as he did in 1951, Adorno naturally singled out Hindemith for censure as the ringleader of the objectivist conspiracy. The *Neue Sachlichkeit* that Hindemith represented did indeed bear a superficial resemblance to the purism preached by Stravinsky and his followers. But Hindemith's views on historical performance were considerably subtler than Adorno would have one believe. 'All the traits that made the music of the past lovable to its contemporary performers and listeners', he wrote in *A Composer's World*, 'were inextricably associated with the kind of sound then known and appreciated. If we replace this sound by the sounds typical of our modern instruments and their treatment we are counterfeiting the musical message the original sound was supposed to transmit. Consequently, all music ought to be performed with the means of production that were in use when the composer gave it to his contemporaries.' This sounds like a ringing endorsement of historicist orthodoxy. Yet a few pages on, Hindemith pinpoints the contradiction embedded in the historical performance ideal: 'Our spirit of life is not identical with that of our ancestors, and therefore their music, even if restored with utter technical perfection, can never have for us precisely the same meaning it had for them. We cannot tear down the barricade that separates the present world from things and deeds past; the symbol and its prototype cannot be made to coincide absolutely.'[12]

Hindemith's very choice of vocabulary – 'spirit', 'symbol', 'prototype' – betrays an underlying sympathy with the subjectivist school. In fact, he and Adorno saw very nearly eye to eye on the futility of historical reconstructions. But the reasoning that led them to this conclusion reflects their diametrically opposed concepts of authenticity – indeed, of the fundamental nature of music. For Adorno, music was an abstract Platonic concept of which no performance could offer more than an imperfect glimpse. 'The musical score is not identical to the work', he wrote; 'devotion to the text means the constant effort to grasp that which it hides.'[13] The meaning or essence of a piece of music existed independently of its sound; therefore historical performances, by stressing the superficial components of sonority and style, actually made it harder for modern listeners to apprehend the 'intrinsic substance' of Bach's music. For Hindemith, on the other hand, the sound of the music was inseparable from its substance. It was therefore incumbent on the performer to reproduce the sonorities envisioned by the composer as faithfully as possible. To do otherwise would be to distort and possibly even falsify the essential meaning of the music.

Hindemith's view of authenticity gained adherents in the post-war period as reproductions of early instruments and techniques of playing them became increasingly sophisticated. Even musicologists, traditionally preoccupied with textual authenticity, were beginning to change their tune. At an international congress in 1938, Paul Collaer voiced the hope that it would be 'just as possible to render an old composition in its original sonority as it is to show a Memlinc or a Giotto that has not been arranged to suit today's taste'.[14] The comparison with the visual arts was apt: the early music revival did, in effect, constitute a kind of music history museum in which works were displayed, as far as practicable, in their original condition. Some of Collaer's colleagues, though, took exception to his analogy. Hans Redlich's condemnation of 'musealer Klangmaterialismus' – which he defined as 'the tendency of some modern arrangers of old music to restore it according to the letter rather than to the spirit, by using obsolete and historical instruments'[15] – reflects the vigorous resistance to the historical performance creed that existed within the scholarly community.

Bach's music serves as a touchstone of the contrasting attitudes to authenticity represented by Redlich and Adorno on the one hand, and on the other by Collaer and Hindemith. We have seen how habitually nineteenth- and early-twentieth-century musicians invoked the composer's 'spirit' to validate Romanticized performances which would be frowned on today. Yet within this interpretative framework, the spectrum of Bach performances ranged to both extremes, whether one chooses to label them subjective and objective, Romantic and historicist, or something else. A pronounced shift in the spectrum occurred sometime after the Second World War. When Adrian Boult and Walter Emery argued that the 'obsolete' instruments in the St Matthew Passion – recorders, oboi d'amore and viola da gamba – could be replaced by modern instruments 'with so little loss of effect that they are hardly worth considering',[16] they were simply expressing the prevailing view in 1949. Had they been writing a few years later, they could hardly have failed to take note of the inroads the historical performance movement was making even among mainstream performers of Bach's music.

Glenn Gould's 1955 recording of the Goldberg Variations was a harbinger of things to come: Gould firmly suppressed all traces of Romantic pianism in his playing; even the engineering of his recording seems calculated to make the piano sound brighter, clearer – more like a harpsichord, in fact.[17] This implicit recognition that the sound and the spirit of Bach's music were indivisible had far-reaching consequences. Other recordings of the period – Helmut Walcha's of the Bach organ works, Hermann Scherchen's of the oratorios, Karl Münchinger's of the Brandenburgs – attest to a heightened sensitivity to Baroque style and sonorities, a sensitivity that would soon bear fruit in the more radical historicism of Gustav Leonhardt and Nikolaus Harnoncourt. The monumental Bach cantata series that they embarked on in 1972 offers a convincing alternative to the more traditional performances of conductors like Karl Richter, Helmuth Rilling and Robert Shaw. Joshua Rifkin's scaled-down version of the B minor Mass, in which the choruses are performed by the soloists with one voice to a part, represents a still more uncompromising application of historicist principles. In taking such an extreme position, Rifkin laid himself open to the charge that he was obeying the letter of the music (at least as he interpreted it) but violating its spirit.

Is Rifkin's Bach the product of inspired scholarship or a musical *reductio ad absurdum*, a classic example of 'performance malpractice'? The American musicologist Robert Marshall, one of Rifkin's most formidable critics, takes the latter view, arguing that there is no justification, historical or aesthetic, for such a reductivist treatment of Bach's choruses. Marshall accuses Rifkin of perpetrating

> an anemic Mass, deprived of its full resources of carefully contrasted and balanced colors, textures, and densities, in which (at least in a live performance) the handful of singers become increasingly exhausted from their ordeal, mercilessly obliged as they are to sing every single note and instinctively attempting to compensate for the absent ripienists [singers who take part only in the choruses] by trying (inevitably in vain) to project the power and grandeur residing in and demanded by these mighty choruses. The result is an eccentric travesty.[18]

Significantly, despite the wealth of historical evidence they adduce to support their contentions, neither Marshall nor Rifkin relies exclusively on documentation to make his point. Both rest their cases on the subjectivist argument that Bach's music *sounds* better when performed according to their specifications. Marshall once described authenticity in another context as 'primarily a matter not of facts but of discretion' and suggested that performers, when confronted with incomplete or contradictory evidence, must base their decisions on some other (and presumably higher) authority.[19] This implicit appeal to the spirit of the music – what another observer calls 'musical' as opposed to 'historical' authenticity[20] – brings the debate onto familiar territory. For authenticity in this sense is simply a function of intuition or feeling. And so we have come full circle, back to the concept of authenticity as Dolmetsch and Landowska understood it, a concept rooted less in objective rules and evidence than in the performer's subjective musical responses.

It is easy to see why so many discussions of authenticity turn on the question of period instruments, for this is one area in which historical evidence is both plentiful and reasonably unambiguous. Dolmetsch set the parameters of the debate when he declared that 'the study of the Music of any period should . . . be based upon that of the instruments of the same period'.[21] This is a defensible view (although it led Dolmetsch to the indefensible conclusion that vocal practice invariably imitated instrumental practice instead of the other way round), but it can easily be carried too far. Within a year of Dolmetsch's death, the musicologist Manfred Bukofzer warned that 'the quarrel about instruments has led the revival of old music into a blind alley'; such 'mechanical details' of performance should not be allowed to overshadow stylistic considerations. 'Bach may well be played on a harpsichord, with viols and recorders, but if the harpsichord is played in the style of Liszt, and the viols are bowed with the technique of Spohr and Rode the result will not be convincing. The use of correct instruments does not in itself ensure a correct, that is, musically good, performance.'[22] A few years earlier, Redlich had written in a similar vein that 'the belief that the employment of ancient instruments alone ensures a historically faithful reading of old compositions shows an exaggerated appraisal of the purely *material* side of old music. Unless the method of performance is supported by an equally faithful interpretation of the notation, the attempt at restoration is bound to remain ill-balanced and one-sided.'[23]

This argument has been echoed, in various guises, by many writers, including Robert Donington, who puts the issue into perspective in his recent book on Baroque performance practice: 'The instruments matter very largely because they are one aspect of the style. The right instruments will not play for the wrong musicians. A fine performance on modern instruments may actually be more authentic than a weak performance on baroque instruments; for fine musicianship is also an aspect of authenticity.'[24] The success of instrumentally dominated ensembles like the Concentus Musicus and the Academy of Ancient Music has given rise to a widespread belief that historical instruments are the key to authentic performances. This is simply not true, any more than the reverse argument that it is impossible to play pre-Romantic music stylishly on modern instruments. What can be said is that, as a general rule, old instruments lend themselves more readily to producing the sounds that composers of earlier periods had in mind. The generic style that used to be applied indiscriminately to music of all eras is rightly frowned on today. Yet, once again, it is impossible to make hard and fast rules. Inasmuch as pre-Classical composers often wrote with no specific instruments in mind, it ill behoves modern performers to be dogmatic. Moreover, a strong case can be made that a stylish performance of, say, an overture by Lully is more dependent on the sonorities of period instruments than a performance of a Bach orchestral suite. Bach's music is intrinsically more abstract than Lully's, less tied to a specific sound-world and set of instrumental techniques.

Still, the growing refinement of historical instrument reproductions in recent decades has given fresh impetus to discussions of authenticity. Specialist musicians demanded instruments tailored to particular repertoires: a reproduction of an eighteenth-century French harpsichord for Couperin, Renaissance recorders for Elizabethan consort music, and so forth. As a result, instrument-makers like Frank Hubbard and Friedrich von Heune in the United States, Hugh Gough and Christopher Monk in Britain, and Martin Skowroneck and Otto Steinkopf in Germany have wielded enormous influence in the historical performance movement. As Renaissance bands and Baroque orchestras multiplied, with record sleeves advertising the use of 'original instruments' (as if modern reproductions were in any sense 'original'), historical instruments have acquired a kind of mystique. Indeed, one sometimes gets the impression that the instruments are the principal attraction in concerts and recordings of early music, relegating the performers – and even the music itself – to a supporting role.

The fact that the early music revival has long been led by instrumentalists explains why early vocal technique has only recently begun to be explored in the same depth as instrumental practice. The more or less unbroken performance tradition of Renaissance and Baroque choral music fostered the illusion that styles of singing had not changed substantially over the centuries. Singers, besides, have no tangible artifacts to tell them how their predecessors may have sounded in the pre-recording era. Alfred Deller relied more on intuition than on scholarship in challenging the plush, homogeneous vocal sound that audiences in the late forties and fifties were accustomed to hearing from early music singers. England's Musica Reservata flouted convention more boldly in the sixties by cultivating a pinched, nasal, vibrato-less tone that resembled nothing so much as a raucous shawm. How much this style of vocal production has to do with historical practice is open to question. It is, however, unquestionably *different*, and this seems to have been sufficient justification for Michael Morrow, who told John M. Thomson that his primary goal as director of Musica Reservata was to avoid emulating the BBC Singers and the 'mish-mash of University Choral Society sounds'.[25]

This repudiation of the traditional, all-purpose vocal style defines the modern school of early music, as represented by the likes of Deller, Jantina Noorman, Andrea von Ramm, Emma Kirkby, Nigel Rogers, Montserrat Figueras, Kurt Equiluz and Julianne Baird. Kirkby's pure, penetrating, choirboy-like soprano epitomizes what many listeners think of as the authentic 'early music sound'. In reality, of course, this sound is largely, if not exclusively, a product of late-twentieth-century musical taste. It may be that the qualities associated with contemporary vocalism were also prized in the pre-Classical period; much of the available evidence suggests that this is indeed the case, particularly with respect to vibrato (which singers in the nineteenth and early twentieth centuries tended to apply more indiscriminately than their predecessors). But the evidence also suggests that the variation in vocal styles and production was as great in the pre-Classical period as it is today. To call Kirkby's singing authentic – and thus, by implication, to dismiss other kinds of singing as inauthentic – is unwarranted on either historical or aesthetic grounds. In the end, it is as much a question of taste as of authenticity, and it is surely no coincidence that the quest for authenticity in the performance of early music has reached its zenith in an era characterized by its craving for the 'original-state' product in so many areas of activity: stripped wood, organic farming, unadulterated food, to name a few.

It may, therefore, be that the tendency towards historically aware performance owes as much, if not more, to contemporary trends and fashions as to musicological rectitude. Yet as Richard Taruskin has pointed out, many musicians shy away from making aesthetic judgments and take refuge behind 'a smokescreen of musicological rationalization'.[26] The howls of protest elicited recently by Joseph Kerman's trenchant analysis of the historical performance movement[27] suggest that his indictment of 'positivistic' musicology touched a raw nerve. But the 'musicological fundamentalism'[28] that characterized so much thinking about early music in the past has been largely discredited. Donald J. Grout's *bon mot* that 'Historical Musicology, like Original Sin, has given everybody a bad conscience'[29] no longer seems as relevant as it did in the positivistic climate of the 1950s. Experience has taught us that musicology does not have answers to all or perhaps even most of the questions the historical performance movement has raised. More and more early musicians are coming to the conclusion that taste, in Howard Mayer Brown's well chosen words, 'is the other side of the coin on which authenticity is stamped'.[30]

If this eminently sensible proposition is still not fully accepted in some circles, it may be because 'taste', to many musicians in the late twentieth century, is a concept only slightly less nebulous than 'authenticity'. Hans Keller, an astute critic of contemporary musical culture, argued that preoccupation with authenticity was symptomatic of 'the progressive artistic insecurity of our age', since 'the less you know instinctively what's good, both in creation and interpretation, the more frantically you depend on extraneous, historical, "scientific" evidence'.[31] The pianist Peter Hill offers a similar analysis in a provocative examination of authenticity in contemporary music:

> The 'hands-off' attitude of the specialized musician has its roots, I suspect, in a deep-seated loss of confidence, so that we rely increasingly on rules and evidence as a means of evading responsibility for artistic judgements. It is this quality of confidence which is so striking to modern ears in 'pre-authentic' playing, as in the Bach performances of Casals or Hamilton Harty, for example: a bedrock of convictions on which their particular 'authenticity' resides.[32]

Early musicians have begun to realize, albeit somewhat belatedly, how much they may have lost by isolating themselves from mainstream traditions. In their approach to vibrato and rubato, for example, some performers of the 'old school' may even have been in closer touch with pre-Classical performance practice than today's early musicians. The latter are indisputably more historically aware than their forebears, but it is easy to forget that they, too, are inescapably creatures of their time. One need not go as far as Taruskin in arguing that 'historical' performance is not really historical at all in order to recognize that today's early musicians have no monopoly on historical insight. Ironically, the early music movement, having rejected the notion of 'progress' in composition, has too often fallen into the trap of applying that yardstick to performance. The danger is not only that early musicians thereby discount the achievements of 'pre-authentic' performers, but that they rashly view performance practice as a scientific discipline, and thus delude themselves into believing that they can find the answers they are looking for simply by amassing more and more data.

Paradoxically, the more we learn about the way early music was performed when it was new, the more we realize remains to be discovered. Historical musicology, like modern science, has taught us that there may be no such thing as definitive answers. The great scholarly controversies of recent years – over *notes inégales*, 'musica ficta', historical temperaments, the use of instruments in early *a cappella* music and the rest – have led not to new certitudes but to more questions. This, in turn, has prompted the philosophers of the early music movement to revise their thinking about authenticity. Taruskin, speaking from a background as both musicologist and performer, argues that 'research alone has never given, and is never likely to give . . . enough information to achieve that wholeness of conception and that sureness of style – in a word, that fearlessness – any authentic, which is to say authoritative, performance must embody'. Echoing Nietzsche's words, Taruskin asserts that historical reconstructions of early music 'can only evoke the pastness of the past'. If authenticity is to mean more than 'time-travel nostalgia', performers must be willing to make 'imaginative leaps' to bridge the gaps in their imperfect knowledge of historical performance practice.[33]

Some musicians welcome Taruskin's plea for 'vividly imagined' performances of early music as a timely challenge to the objectivist approach; to others, it smacks uncomfortably of performers 'knitting their own Middle Ages' (to use Thurston Dart's memorable phrase). For that matter, it can hardly be denied that the chances are slight of producing an 'authentic' performance of a medieval piece, even one that the composer would recognize 'without bewilderment'. The historical evidence is simply too scanty and inconclusive. Performers of medieval music have no choice but to venture where cautious musicologists fear to tread. Some of the most compelling renditions of medieval music, from the Studio der frühen Musik's exotic, improvisatory performances of the *Carmina Burana* to Esther Lamandier's incantatory solo recitations of troubadour lyrics, have been unabashedly conjectural. Both imagination and scholarship play a part, too, in the mannered inflections and *messa di voce* swellings of the Dutch school of Baroque performance. That this style is now widely accepted as authentic is a tribute to the conviction and intelligence that musicians like Leonhardt, Brüggen and the Kuijkens bring to their performances.

The 'new, undogmatic spirit' that Kerman perceives in today's historical performance movement[34] is thus, on one level, an acknowledgment of the unavoidable limitations of historical research as a guide to performance. In rebelling against codified rules, whether of mainstream tradition or of the *Aufführungspraxis* manuals, early musicians are making a bid to recover the autonomy that Landowska described when she confessed that she no longer cared about 'the rules of interpretation. What I do is comparable to the style of a dancer like Argentina or to the improvisations of a good jazz band. What

I seek is a seemingly improvisatory manner which does not let the listener foresee what is coming.'[35] This improvisatory manner, the sensation that music flowed not from her fingertips but from her soul, set Landowska's playing apart from the relentlessly predictable Baroque performances of the sewing-machine school, just as it distinguishes the most inspired and original of today's early musicians.

To be sure, there is always a danger that historical performance will stifle rather than nurture spontaneity and individuality. Paul Henry Lang cautions: 'To the extent that the study of performance practice by scholars has opened new insights into what is vaguely called old music, it has indeed been a most welcome spur to fruitful activity both in education and in practice; but to the extent that the new discipline attempts to structure and regiment the whole experience of musicians concerned with pre-romantic music, it may actually be impeding the revival of old music.'[36] But any style, whether historical or contemporary, structures and regiments performers in the sense that it prescribes guidelines. Only in the twentieth century has the performer's role been so circumscribed as to leave little scope for subjective interpretation. Composers in earlier eras allowed performers more latitude, but always within a clearly defined stylistic frame. So, while blinkered reliance on textbook rules can indeed inhibit and ultimately thwart the search for authenticity, historical performance can, at its best, have a liberating effect on musicians schooled in the mainstream tradition.

'The most central virtue of historical performance practice is that it can offer performers a freedom of choice, a multiplicity of "right" ways to play ...', the critic Will Crutchfield has written. 'In contrast to the enervating, dully anarchic international melting pot, it offers the chance to create for oneself an interpretive process of discipline and integrity, and to develop individual freedom within a coherent style.'[37] It should hardly need pointing out that the process of nurturing and developing this individual freedom takes time. Re-establishing a viable performing tradition for pre-Classical music is not something that can be accomplished in one or two generations. The interpretative licence that Landowska took for granted no longer comes naturally to younger musicians. Now that performers are tentatively reasserting that freedom, they are doing so within the context of an enhanced sense of historical awareness and responsibility. In other words, freedom is encouraged not because it is the performer's accustomed prerogative, but because the contemporary concept of authenticity demands it.

Even if one accepts Michael Morrow's contention that any historical performance is bound to be 'a more or less successful counterfeit',[38] it is nonetheless possible to make early music sound fresh and convincing to modern ears. The idea that we can divine 'the composer's intentions' looks more and more like hubris. As Taruskin points out, even as meticulous a composer as Stravinsky interpreted his own music in so many different ways that it is often impossible to say exactly what his intentions were.[39] Some performers go one step farther and ask why respecting the composer's wishes should be the beginning and end of authenticity. 'Are we getting over-anxious, over-orthodox, over-purist, more afraid of things unusual than the composer himself?', wonders the Czech harpsichordist Zuzana Růžičková.[40] A frank confession of ignorance or agnosticism, rather than unfounded dogmatism, would appear to be the most sensible and productive guideline for the historical performer in the late twentieth century.

Authenticity, in the final analysis, is a chimera – something that exists primarily in the eyes (or ears) of the beholder. Like most metaphysical concepts, it is far easier to describe than to define. Such meaning as it possesses derives as much from subjective perceptions as from objective reality. Perhaps authenticity, like perfection or happiness, is best conceived as an ideal to be pursued rather than as a goal to be attained; or, as Kerman suggests, not as an end in itself but as a means to 'the ever-better interpretation of music'.[41] Putnam Aldrich once wrote that authenticity lies 'at the end of a trip along roads from which the signposts have been largely removed'.[42] And, he might have added, the journey is such that the performer has no way of knowing when – or if – he has reached his destination.

Is authenticity then a valid concept or simply a marketing device, useful for distinguishing yet another performance of Vivaldi's *Four Seasons* or Bach's *Christmas Oratorio* from all the rest? If, as Laurence Dreyfus proposes, authenticity is best viewed 'as an evolving and necessarily incomplete paradigm rather than as a set of documented index cards set atop inferences culled from freshman logic texts',[43] then clearly it can never serve as a foolproof criterion for historical performance. It is far easier to say what is *not* authentic than what is. Authenticity, in other words, sets the parameters within which a variety of historically plausible performances can take place. For interpretation, the play of the performer's skill and personality on the composer's creation, is the lifeblood of old and new music alike. It may not be reasonable to expect that Bach would recognize his music in a modern performance. And perhaps this is irrelevant after all. Landowska, try as she might to play Bach *his* way, merely succeeded in playing it *her* way. That, too, is a kind of authenticity.

10

BEETHOVEN, BRAHMS
AND BEYOND?

*Classical and Romantic Music on Period Instruments · The Fortepiano
Revival · Historicist Productions of Mozart and Rossini Operas · The
Proliferation of Baroque Orchestras · The Confluence of Early and
Mainstream Music · Its Impact on Concert Programming, Musical
Education, the Recording Industry, Etc. · Historical Performance: the
Dominant Musical Ideology of Our Time.*

ONE OF THE MOST highly acclaimed recording projects of the 1980s was the
Academy of Ancient Music's complete traversal of the Mozart
symphonies on period instruments. Jointly directed by Jaap Schröder and
Christopher Hogwood, in collaboration with the American musicologist
Neal Zaslaw, this ambitious series firmly set the early music revival on a new
course. Indeed, the very phrase 'early music revival' has become something
of an anachronism as the historical performance movement surges forward
into the late eighteenth and nineteenth centuries. Most people, after all,
would not recognize Mozart's music as 'early', and works that have been
central to the orchestral repertoire for the better part of a century can hardly
be said to need reviving.

Not only Mozart's symphonies but those of Haydn, Beethoven, Schubert
and Mendelssohn as well can now be heard in accomplished performances on
period instruments. A vast new frontier has opened up for historically
minded performers and their patrons in the recording industry. In England
alone, no fewer than three Beethoven symphony cycles have been under-
taken by Hogwood's ensemble, Roger Norrington's London Classical
Players and the conductorless Hanover Band. L'Estro Armonico, an early-
instrument orchestra led by the violinist Derek Solomons, is working
through the Haydn symphonies under the expert guidance of H. C. Robbins
Landon. Frans Brüggen, Nikolaus Harnoncourt, Jean-Claude Malgoire,
Sigiswald Kuijken and other Continental 'early music' conductors are
delving into the Classical and early Romantic orchestral repertoires. Record-
buyers can choose from among competing period-instrument versions of the
Mozart and Beethoven piano concertos played by Malcolm Bilson, Jörg
Demus, Paul Badura-Skoda and Steven Lubin. The fortepiano, as Joseph

Kerman points out, has replaced the harpsichord as the symbol of the historical performance movement in the 1980s.[1]

In fact, the fortepiano renaissance dates back at least to the turn of the century, when Dolmetsch, Landowska and a few others began performing publicly on early pianos. Around 1906 a 'Fortepiano' society was founded in Munich to present eighteenth-century music on appropriate instruments.[2] None of these early efforts, however, seems to have met with much success. Typical of the reactions they elicited was that of the German critic who remarked that the harpsichord at least sounded *different* from the piano, whereas the fortepiano merely sounded worse.[3] Such prejudice against the fortepiano is partly explained by the inferior condition of the instruments, most of which were museum pieces hardly fit to be played. Paul and Eva Badura-Skoda, in their 1957 book on Mozart interpretation, asserted that the scarcity of well-preserved historical instruments and reproductions rendered the revival of the fortepiano 'impracticable' at that time (a verdict they subsequently reversed).[4] Ralph Kirkpatrick pronounced the fortepiano 'a revelation' when he first heard one in 1931, but later had second thoughts about the direction the historical performance movement was taking. 'The next thing you know', he grumbled prophetically, 'they'll be doing *Winterreise* with a counter-tenor and a rattletrap piano.'[5]

Yet no one who has heard Schubert's songs accompanied on a good Viennese-style fortepiano, or Beethoven's sonatas played on an early-nineteenth-century Broadwood, can deny that historical instruments bring out qualities in the music that are obscured or lost altogether in performances on a modern concert grand. In the hands of a skilful player, the fortepiano's crisp articulation, evenness of registers and overtone-rich sound seem as 'right' for the music of Mozart and Schubert as the harpsichord's brittle brilliance does for Bach and Couperin. The marked improvement in fortepiano reproductions in recent decades has convinced many sceptics. There is a world of difference between the Challis fortepiano that Kirkpatrick owned, finely crafted as it was, and the historical models of leading contemporary makers like Derek Adlam and Philip Belt. Bilson has attributed his conversion to the experience of playing a Belt fortepiano, an experience which also led him to question the conventional wisdom that a performance by a great artist on the 'wrong' instrument is necessarily preferable to hearing a mediocre artist playing the 'right' (that is, historical) instrument.[6]

Bilson's well-publicized espousal of the historical performance cause has been repeated many times by players of other instruments. For instance, the revival of the basset clarinet by performers like Antony Pày and Hans Deinzer has progressed to the point where it seems likely that performances of the Mozart concerto on a modern clarinet (which lacks the four lowest notes of its ancestor) will soon be considered unacceptable. Haydn's baryton trios, Schubert's sonata for the arpeggione and other works can once again be heard on the instruments for which they were written. Historical performers have turned their attention to the pre-Boehm flute, natural horn, serpent, ophicleide and other obsolete instruments of the Classical and Romantic periods. Such ensembles as the Music Party, the Collegium Aureum and the Esterhazy, Salomon and Smithson quartets, along with pianists like Richard Burnett and Melvyn Tan, have subjected everything from Mozart to Brahms to the period-instrument treatment.

The chronological advance of historical performance is beginning to impinge on the operatic world. Over the past decade, Sweden's well preserved Drottningholm Court Theatre has provided an authentic eighteenth-century setting for period-style productions of the Mozart operas led by Arnold Östman. Ton Koopman's Amsterdam Baroque Orchestra entered the field with a well-received production and recording of *Die Zauberflöte*, followed closely by Deutsche Grammophon's announcement of a major series of Mozart operas to be recorded in the 1990s under the baton of the British early music specialist John Eliot Gardiner. Harnoncourt and Ponnelle have been duplicating the success of their aforementioned Monteverdi productions with a popular Mozart cycle in quasi-historical style at the Zurich Opera. Gabriele Ferro's period-instrument performances of Rossini operas with the Cappella Coloniensis have carried the historicist approach into the bel canto repertoire, seemingly presaging a wholesale reappraisal of the nineteenth-century operatic canon.

Naturally enough, many mainstream musicians view this relentless encroachment on their territory with a mixture of alarm and indignation. Must they stand by and watch as one citadel after another of the standard repertoire falls to the historicist onslaught? Will modern-instrument performances of Mozart and Beethoven become as intellectually unfashionable as those of Monteverdi and Bach? Granted, Mozart and Beethoven seem unlikely to vanish from orchestra programmes in the foreseeable future, but large swathes of the Baroque and early Classical repertoires have already been effectively ceded to specialist ensembles. Compact disc releases of popular Baroque pieces like the Brandenburg Concertos and *Messiah* are heavily weighted in favour of period-instrument recordings. For those disposed to view it in this light, Hogwood's appointment in 1986 as artistic director of Boston's venerable Handel and Haydn Society provided further proof that, as one critic puts it, 'the historicists are in the ascendant'.[7]

Whether one regards these developments as blessing or bane, historical – or at any rate historically informed – performance has unquestionably become the dominant musical ideology of our time. Even a cursory survey of concert programmes, conservatory course announcements, publishers' and record company catalogues and the musical press leaves no doubt of the extent to which historical performance permeates contemporary musical life. Performers and critics habitually invoke the magic formula of 'respecting the composer's intentions'. Books and articles about performance practice continue to stream off the presses. More and more modern-instrument players are emulating the sound of early instruments or adopting (however superficially) a plausible period style when they perform Baroque and Classical music. Orchestras regularly import early music experts to participate in performances of works like the St Matthew Passion. The days are long past when orchestras blithely deployed eighty or ninety players in a Haydn or Mozart symphony; conductors like Neville Marriner and Michael Tilson Thomas have habituated concert-goers to a leaner, crisper sound in the Classical repertoire. Each composer has now been assigned his own historical niche and corresponding performance style. Even the Bach transcriptions of Stokowski and Busoni are scrupulously revived as period pieces. In other words, the concept of authenticity has grown to embrace approaches previously considered out of bounds to early music purists.

The thrust toward historical authenticity is not about to make symphony orchestras obsolete, but it has spurred some of them to change with the times. A few years ago the musicologist Robert Winter dismissed as idle fantasy the idea of hearing the Philadelphia Orchestra play Schubert on gut strings;[8] today performances of the Schubert symphonies on period instruments are commonplace (though not, so far, by the Philadelphia Orchestra). Sergiu Luca, who plays both the modern and the Baroque violin, has even called upon orchestras to purchase sets of historical instruments for their players to use in early music performances.[9] The Boyd Neel Orchestra (at Thurston Dart's behest) did use Baroque-style 'Corelli' bows when they played Bach and Handel, but, not surprisingly, major orchestras are not queuing up to implement Luca's intriguing suggestion. More and more conductors are, however, striving to stay abreast of the latest scholarship and make their performances more in keeping with the style and character of the Baroque and Classical periods. 'It is difficult to believe', a prominent critic writes, 'that the comfortable, conservative world of the modern symphony orchestra and opera house ... can ever be quite the same again.'[10]

The Baroque orchestras that have proliferated around the world in recent years, from San Francisco to Budapest and from Toronto to Rio de Janeiro, pose a serious challenge to the orchestral status quo. The old-guard modern-instrument chamber orchestras – the I Musicis, Academies of St Martin-in-the-Fields, Camerata Berns – can no longer claim to be in the forefront of the

Baroque revival. Their place has been taken by the specialized period-instrument orchestras, ranging in size from fewer than a dozen players to as many as forty or fifty. The organizational structures of these ensembles are equally diverse: some are built around a single charismatic performer, while others, such as England's Orchestra of the Age of Enlightenment, are self-governing to greater or lesser degrees. Leonhardt, Hogwood, Pinnock and Koopman have joined the ranks of itinerant guest conductors. Brüggen's Orchestra of the Eighteenth Century draws players from throughout Europe, England and the United States, who come together twice a year for intensive periods of rehearsal and performing. Few Baroque orchestras are in a position to offer their members anything like full-time employment, but as opportunities for performing with period-instrument ensembles become more plentiful, early musicians are discovering that they can earn a livelihood by playing part-time with a number of ensembles – a situation most of them would have found unimaginable only a few years ago.

The familiar image of the early musician as an eccentric counterculture figure eking out a living on the fringes of the musical world is increasingly out-of-date. Prosperous ensembles like the Academy of Ancient Music and the Amsterdam Baroque Orchestra have administrative staffs to handle concert promotion, the engaging of guest artists, scheduling tours, fund-raising and other functions. As traditional funding sources dry up, early musicians are honing their skills in soliciting underwriting from businesses, private philanthropists and public agencies. For all but a few early music groups, touring – increasingly under the auspices of major artists agencies in America and Europe – has become a significant or even vital source of income. Like the young Dolmetsch and Landowska, today's early musicians spend much of their time on the road, performing, teaching, attending seminars and conferences, and shuttling between cities like York, Boston, Utrecht and Vancouver on the burgeoning early music festival circuit. Societies catering to specialist constituencies, from serpent players to early music singers, have mushroomed in recent years. A related phenomenon is the growth of professional organizations like Early Music America and England's Early Music Centre, which serve as conduits for information about activities in the field, coordinate touring networks, and lobby for recognition and support.[11]

Early music, in short, has become increasingly institutionalized within the musical mainstream, a development which many observers regard as a mixed blessing. It is an open question whether a movement that grew up outside – indeed, in opposition to – established musical institutions can adapt to these new conditions without becoming hidebound and resistant to change. The pressures on performers to curb their adventurousness are all too apparent. Recording contracts, for instance, have given early musicians the security to perform works that might turn audiences away at the box-office, thus helping to insulate artistic decisions from commercial concerns. But the recent slump in the classical recording industry has steadily tipped the balance in favour of more marketable repertoire. Hence the never-ending stream of recordings of such early music chestnuts as the Bach orchestral suites and Vivaldi's *Four Seasons*. Hence, too, the current spate of period-instrument recordings of Mozart and Beethoven, a trend which reflects the industry's eagerness to capitalize on the historical performance movement's latest discoveries. Recent recordings pairing celebrities from the early- and mainstream-music worlds – Hogwood and Joan Sutherland, Jacobs and Teresa Berganza, Harnoncourt and Dietrich Fischer-Dieskau – bespeak a determination on the part of performers and record companies alike to reach beyond the traditional early music audience, for financial as well as artistic motives.

The confluence of the two musical cultures has, however, generated some indisputably salutary by-products. One area of mainstream music that has benefited most from the historicist influence is concert programming. To the extent that the historical performance movement has circumscribed the repertoire available to non-specialist performers, its influence is justifiably decried by those who believe in a multiplicity of approaches to musical interpretation. On the other hand, historical performance has been a positive force in mainstream music by promoting better rounded and more coherent programming. As we have seen, the historical concerts of the nineteenth century prefigured today's 'theme' concerts, in which a specific genre, period or composer's work is explored in depth. Those rambling, potpourri programmes that once distinguished the early music world are much rarer nowadays. The omnivorous eclecticism that inspired them has gradually yielded to what Hogwood calls a 'healthy didacticism'[12] which decrees that music of every period can best be appreciated in its proper historical context.

In essence, this is what the historical performance movement is all about: placing music in an appropriate context. Kerman's suggestion that 'contextual' be adopted as a substitute for that refractory adjective 'authentic' has much to recommend it. But there is a danger here, as well: at times it seems the musical archaeologists have done their work too diligently. The uncritical zeal of the amateur performer, coupled with the *Kleinmeister* syndrome that afflicts many non-performing musicologists, has brought to light vast quantities of inferior music that would better have been left buried. Still, the trade-off seems worth the price: audiences have early musicians to thank for recovering the music of Dunstable, Ockeghem, Morales, Zelenka, Sigismondo d'India, Michael Haydn, C. P. E. Bach and countless 'minor' masters of genuine stature and individuality. Likewise, the welcome reappearance of composers like Spohr, Hummel, Alkan and Clementi on concert programmes has brought the achievements of the great nineteenth-century masters into sharper focus.

In the long run, the historical performance movement's most significant impact may well be in the area of musical education. Most music schools in Western Europe and the United States have added courses in performance practice and tuition on historical instruments to their curricula in recent years. Institutions like the Schola Cantorum Basiliensis, the Royal Conservatory of the Hague and the Oberlin College Conservatory in the United States offer comprehensive early music programmes addressed to both scholars and performers.[13] In addition, dozens of summer courses are held each year; for instance, the ambitious series of festivals, interdisciplinary academies and performance practice institutes sponsored since 1973 by the Aston Magna Foundation has had a major impact on the study and performance of Baroque music in the United States. Historical performance and its sister discipline, ethnomusicology, are the big growth-areas in music education. As the second and third generations of early musicians assume positions in conservatories and university music departments, conventional musical training is undergoing a transformation just as profound in its implications as the changes the historical performance movement has brought about on the concert stage and in the recording studio.

Early musicians in this increasingly competitive environment are learning what professionals in other fields have long understood: that specialized knowledge and abilities can be valuable assets. Hogwood predicts that the symphony orchestra will evolve from a general-purpose ensemble into one that takes 'specialist approaches to its Baroque, Classical, Romantic, and Modern performances'. The American critic John Rockwell predicts that the New York Philharmonic will one day comprise several instrumental groupings – 'an authentic Baroque ensemble, a larger group for the Classical scores of Haydn and Mozart, and period orchestral ensembles for early and late Beethoven, Berlioz, Schubert, Liszt and Brahms'.[14] If these forecasts are accurate, there will clearly be a continuing need for conductors and instrumentalists versed in historical performing techniques. But how can early musicians best take advantage of this golden opportunity? Should they emulate the generalists like Dolmetsch and Munrow who ranged widely over a large area of early music? Or should they, like Landowska and Leonhardt, concentrate intensively on a narrower spectrum of music until it becomes, in effect, second nature to them? Proponents of the latter view argue that specialization, in this sense, is not restrictive but broadening: a means of achieving fluency in languages that most musicians no longer speak.

This effort would seem to become easier, or at least less problematic, as the historical performance movement sweeps through the nineteenth century and nudges the twentieth. This music, after all, is written in our own language. But this in itself presents considerable problems. As Kerman writes, 'the historical task with music after 1800 is one of revising a tradition that is already there, rather than of reconstructing one that has been forgotten'.[15] It is this revisionist spirit that animates recent attempts to uncover the 'authentic' Mozart, Beethoven, Schubert, Weber, Schumann, Chopin, Berlioz, Brahms, Franck, Elgar, Wagner – even Rachmaninoff and Gershwin. Hogwood's interpretatively streamlined performances of the Beethoven symphonies, illustrating the low conductorial profile that many scholars consider appropriate in early-nineteenth-century music, has rekindled the debate about expressivity in a new context. Indeed, historical performances of Classical and Romantic music raise a whole new set of questions concerning interpretative freedom, the role of the conductor, metronome markings, orchestral seating plans, the use of rubato and so on. These questions are only beginning to receive the attention that has long been lavished on performance practices of the pre-Classical period. Robert Winter's call for 'a few dozen Arnold Dolmetsches applying their imagination and zeal to nineteenth-century problems'[16] remains as valid today as it was a decade ago.

If the trends we have touched on in this chapter are apparent to any attentive observer, it is by no means equally clear where all of this activity is leading. It is frequently assumed that the early music movement will loose its momentum as it reaches into the twentieth century – after all, 'period' instruments in Stravinsky or Sibelius are virtually indistinguishable from modern ones. In fact, the doctrine of historical performance has no natural chronological boundary, since it connotes not a fixed body of music but a philosophy of making music. Yet there can be little doubt that the early music movement – as a discrete, recognizable entity – will sooner or later run its course. In a sense, historical performance will have attained its goal when it ceases to call attention to itself and becomes one of many modes of musical interpretation available to performers in the late twentieth or early twenty-first century. The evidence suggests that the process is already under way: as Hogwood, Harnoncourt, Pinnock, Gardiner and other early musicians become familiar figures on the podiums of modern orchestras, and as music schools turn out more and more versatile performers capable of moving with ease between instruments and musical styles of various periods, the line between 'historical' and 'mainstream' performance is rapidly fading. The merging of the two cultures seems close at hand. 'Success will come', writes Paul Henry Lang, 'when we are able to forgo the restrictive category "old music" and make it an integral part of our musical experience.'[17] This is a prospect that excites many musicians, whether or not they count themselves part of the historical performance movement.

A graph of the early music revival's trajectory, in the eventful century since Arnold Dolmetsch launched his one-man crusade, would take the form of a steadily rising curve. More than one observer, however, has suggested that the movement has already passed its peak. 'A spark is missing', one critic lamented in a recent issue of the *Musical Times*. 'All are recalling those heady days back in the mid 70s, when early music was a new ball we all wanted to get our hands on. Now, somehow, it has lost its shine and everyone is looking for a beneficent umpire to conjure up a replacement and put a little more life back into the game.'[18] This is fair comment: much of the novelty and exhilaration of the old days has inevitably worn off as early music takes its place within the newly redefined mainstream. But the implication that the early music movement is on the decline flies in the face of the evidence. On the contrary, all the signs point to the conclusion that the revival is moving from strength to strength. Its vitality and influence have never been greater. The discoveries of the past century and more are being tested, absorbed and disseminated. There is plenty of life in the game yet. This book is offered not as a post-mortem but as an interim report.

NOTES

The titles of several periodicals are abbreviated as follows:

EM: *Early Music* (London, 1973–)
MQ: *The Musical Quarterly* (New York, 1915–)
MT: *The Musical Times* (London, 1844–)
NZ: *Neue Zeitschrift für Musik* (Leipzig, Regensburg and Mainz, 1834–)
RM(1): *La Revue musicale* (Paris, 1901–12)
RM(2): *La Revue musicale* (Paris, 1920–)

INTRODUCTION

1 Percy Lovell, '"Ancient" Music in Eighteenth-Century England', *Music and Letters* 60 (1979), 402.
2 Andreas Holschneider, 'Über alte Musik', *Musica* (Kassel) 34 (1980), 345. Unless otherwise credited, all translations are by the author.
3 Joseph Kerman, *Contemplating Music: Challenges to Musicology* (Cambridge, Mass., 1985); *Musicology* (London, 1985), 210.
4 Friedrich Blume, *Two Centuries of Bach*, trans. Stanley Godman (London and New York, 1950), 60.

CHAPTER 1
'THE MUSICAL POMPEII'

1 Donald Mintz, 'Some Aspects of the Revival of Bach', *MQ* 40 (1954), 209.
2 Letter to Goethe quoted in Martin Geck, *Die Wiederentdeckung der Matthäuspassion im 19. Jahrhundert* (Regensburg, 1967), 16. Mendelssohn joined the Singakademie choir in 1820, at the age of eleven; see also Georg Schünemann, *Die Singakademie zu Berlin 1791–1941* (Regensburg, 1941), 43f.
3 Eduard Devrient, *My Recollections of Felix Mendelssohn-Bartholdy*, trans. Natalia Macfarren (London, 1869), 46.
4 Paul Steinitz, *Bach's Passions* (London, 1979), 108.
5 The meetings of these societies were as much social as musical occasions, often being held in public houses. See Thomas Day, 'Old Music in

England, 1790–1820', *Revue Belge de musicologie* 26–27 (1972–73), 25–37; Lovell, op. cit. (Preface, note 1); and J. G. Crawford, 'The Madrigal Society', *Proceedings of the Royal Musical Association* 82 (1955–56), 33–46.
6 F. G. Edwards, 'Bach's Music in England', *MT* 37 (1896), 652–57. See also Eliza Wesley, ed., *Letters of Samuel Wesley to Mr Jacobs* (London, 1875), and James Lightwood, *Samuel Wesley, Musician; The Story of His Life* (London, 1937).
7 Inspired by England's nascent early music revival, Kiesewetter referred to his concerts (in English) as the Academy of Ancient Music; see Rudolf Flotzinger and Gernot Gruber, eds., *Musikgeschichte Österreichs* (Graz, 1979), 259. Herfrid Kier gives a full account in 'Kiesewetters historische Hauskonzerte', *Kirchenmusikalisches Jahrbuch* 52 (1968), 95–119.
8 Day, op. cit., 30. See also Ernst Savelsberg, 'Anton Friedrich Justus Thibaut und der Heidelberger Singkreis', in *Musicae Sacrae Ministerium* (Cologne, 1962), 17–39.
9 See Martin Geck, 'Bachs Matthäuspassion als Symbol des Fortschritts', *NZ* 129 (1968), 164–65.
10 Mendelssohn's score of the *St Matthew* is at the Bodleian Library, Oxford (MS M. Deneke Mendelssohn c. 68). The composer's grandmother had it copied from a manuscript in Zelter's possession and gave it to him for Christmas in 1823.
11 'I cannot rescore the work, nor can I point out any alterations, as it has always been a rule for me to leave these works absolutely as they were written, and as I have often quarrelled with those who did not.' Thus Mendelssohn in 1847 to William Bartholomew, apparently in response to an enquiry about performing the *St Matthew* in England. The letter was published in *MT* 33 (1892), 36.
12 Harold C. Schonberg, *The Great Pianists* (New York, 1963; London, 1964), 130.
13 Vincent Novello's description of Choron is in Nerina Medici and Rosemary Hughes, eds., *A Mozart Pilgrimage* (London, 1955), 240–41. François-Joseph Fétis supplies further particulars in the entry on Choron in his *Biographie universelle des musiciens* (Paris, 1883). His remark about

Choron's choice of repertoire is quoted in Gabriel Vauthier, 'L'Ecole de Choron', RM(1) 8 (1908), 669.

14 Vauthier, op. cit., 668 n. 2.

15 F. Danjou, 'Concert de Musique Vocale Religieuse et Classique', Revue et gazette musicale 12 (25 May 1845), 170–71.

16 James Haar, 'Music of the Renaissance as Viewed by the Romantics', in Anne Dhu Shapiro, ed., Music and Context: Essays for John M. Ward (Cambridge, Mass., 1985), 132.

17 C. Saint-Saëns, On the Execution of Music, and Principally of Ancient Music [lecture delivered at the 1915 Panama–Pacific International Exposition in San Francisco] (San Francisco, 1915), 3–4.

18 A. W. Pugin, An Earnest Appeal for the Revival of the Ancient Plain Song (London, 1850). The Helmore quote is in Peter Hardwick, 'The Revival of Interest in Old English Music in Victorian England, and the Impact of This Revival on Music Composed into the Twentieth Century' (Diss., U. of Washington, 1973). See also Bernarr Rainbow, The Choral Revival in the Anglican Church (London and New York, 1970).

19 Paléographie musicale, First Series, vol. 11 (Solesmes, 1912), 9.

20 L. E. Gauthier, Eloge d'Alexandre Choron (Paris and Caen, 1845), 63.

21 Robert Wangermée, 'Les Premiers Concerts Historiques à Paris', in Mélanges Ernest Closson (Brussels, 1948), 188.

22 Julien Tiersot, 'Victor Hugo musicien', RM(2) September–October 1935, 185. Hugo sent Fétis a book of his poems; in return he asked for the music of two pieces Fétis had performed, which the poet wanted to use in a play he was writing.

23 Aristide Farrenc, Les Concerts historiques de M. Fétis à Paris (Paris, n.d.). Auguste Tolbecque, the instrument-maker and gambist, said that Fétis had difficulty finding musicians capable of playing the old instruments and so resorted to the expedient of modernizing them; see his Notice historique sur les instruments à cordes et à archet (Paris, 1898), 15f. Presumably this was also true of the instruments Fétis sent to London in 1845 for the concerts of early music given in the presence of Queen Victoria and Prince Albert, at one of which the double bass virtuoso Domenico Dragonetti played a 'violone'; see the report in the Revue et gazette musicale 12 (20 April 1845), 128.

24 Jean-Baptiste Weckerlin cites chapter and verse of Fétis's deceptions in Musiciana (Paris, 1877), 55–66, and Nouveau musiciana (Paris,

1890), 67f. On the library scandal, see François Lesure, 'L'Affaire Fétis', Revue Belge de musicologie 28–30 (1974–76), 214–21.

25 Wilibald Gurlitt, 'Franz-Joseph Fétis und seine Rolle in der Geschichte der Musikwissenschaft', in Musikgeschichte und Gegenwart, vol. 2 (Wiesbaden, 1966), 137.

26 Robert Wangermée, François-Joseph Fétis: musicologue et compositeur (Brussels, 1951), 270.

27 See Willi Kahl, 'Das Nürnberger historische Konzert von 1643 und sein Geschichtsbild', Archiv für Musikwissenschaft 14 (1957), 281ff.

28 On Kiesewetter and Molitor, see Herfrid Kier, 'Musikalisches Historismus im vormärzlichen Wien', in Walter Wiora, ed., Die Ausbreitung des Historismus über die Musik (Regensburg, 1969), 66–69.

29 The programmes of Mendelssohn's historical concerts are given in Alfred Dörffel, Geschichte der Gewandhausconcerte zu Leipzig von 25. November 1781 bis 25. November 1881 (Leipzig, 1884), 91, 98 and 115f. See also Susanna Grossmann-Vendrey, Felix Mendelssohn-Bartholdy und die Musik der Vergangenheit (Regensburg, 1969), 159–72.

30 F.-J. Fétis, 'Concerts historiques de la musique de piano donnés à Londres par M. Moscheles', Revue et gazette musicale 5 (11 February 1838), 62–64.

31 See Joshua Berrett's introduction to Louis Spohr: Three Symphonies, in Barry S. Brook, ed., The Symphony, 1720–1840, Series C, vol. 9 (London and New York, 1980), xxiv–xxvii. For more on Spohr's interest in early music, in particular his revival of the St Matthew Passion in Cassel in 1832, see Herfried Homburg, 'Louis Spohr und die Bach-Renaissance', Bach-Jahrbuch 47 (1960), 65–82.

32 Ignatz [sic] Moscheles, Recent Music and Musicians, edited by Charlotte Moscheles, adapted from the original German by A. D. Coleridge (New York, 1873), 245.

33 Frank Ll. Harrison, Mantle Hood and Claude V. Palisca, Musicology (Princeton, 1963), 41.

34 See Martin Ruhnke, 'Moritz Hauptmann und die Wiederbelebung der Musik J. S. Bachs', in Anna Amalie Abert and Wilhelm Pfannkuch, eds., Festschrift Friedrich Blume zum 70. Geburtstag (Basle, 1963).

35 On Brahms's interest in early music, both as composer and as conductor, see Virginia Hancock, 'Brahms's Performances of Early Choral Music', 19th Century Music 8 (1984), 125–41; the same author's Brahms's Choral Compositions and

His Library of Early Music (Ann Arbor, Mich., 1983); and Karl Geiringer, 'Brahms as a Musicologist', *MQ* 69 (1983), 463–70.

36 The programmes of Bohn and Riedel illustrate the scope of the revival in the second half of the nineteenth century; see Emil Bohn, *Hundert historische Concerte, 1881–1905* (Breslau, 1905) and Albert Gohler, ed., *Der Riedel-Verein zu Leipzig* (Leipzig, 1904).

37 M. D. Calvocoressi, 'Bourgault-Ducoudray: A Memory', *Monthly Musical Record* 53 (1923), 37 38. Friedrich Chrysander, 'Über die altindische Opfermusik', *Vierteljahrsschrift für Musikwissenschaft* 1 (1885), 21–34. Many performers and scholars, from Fétis and Chrysander to Eta Harich-Schneider and Frank Ll. Harrison, have devoted themselves to both pre-Classical and non Western music.

38 Friedrich Blume, 'Bach in the Romantic Era', *MQ* 50 (1964), 305.

39 Anton Rubinstein, *A Conversation on Music*, trans. Mrs John P. Morgan, (New York, 1892), 123f. In the 1885–86 season, Rubinstein gave a highly publicized series of historical recitals in Russia and Europe.

40 'The Bach Festival at Eisenach', *Monthly Musical Record* 14 (1884), 248–49. A fuller report appeared in *NZ* 45 (1884), 452.

41 Ernest Closson, *Gevaert* (Brussels, 1929).

42 *Le Guide musical* 25 (25 December 1879).

CHAPTER 2
'THE APOSTLE OF
RETROGRESSION'

1 Richard Terry, 'A Forgotten Composer', in *On Music's Borders* (London, 1927), 40–41. Eugene Goossens directed the Handel Society from 1921 to 1925; the Crystal Palace Handel Festival was suspended the following year.

2 J. A. Fuller Maitland, *A Door-Keeper of Music* (London, 1929), 220–21.

3 G. B. Shaw, *Music in London 1890–94* (London, 1932), vol. 2, 100. Repr. in *Shaw's Music* (London and New York, 1981).

4 Paul Steinitz, *Bach's Passions* (London, 1979), 114–15. In an unsigned programme note for the 1858 performance, George Grove wrote: 'The treatment of these solemn scenes may seem somewhat too dramatic; but it is hoped that the few excisions which have been made, and which are identical with those which Mendelssohn found necessary when the work was performed under his guidance, will have removed every-thing objectionable to English taste or feeling.' (British Library MS 7898. o. 12.) A detailed comparison of the editions used by Mendelssohn, Bennett and Vaughan Williams is given in R. Sterndale Bennett, 'Three Abridged Versions of Bach's St Matthew Passion', *Music and Letters* 37 (1956), 336–39.

5 'The Bach Choir', *MT* 26 (1885), 203. The choir gave the first British performance of the B minor Mass in 1876; see H. E. Wortham, 'The Bach Choir: A Brief Retrospect', *The Sackbut* 6 (1925–26), 305–09.

6 'Historic Concerts at the Inventions Exhibition', *MT* 26 (1885), 477–79.

7 Fuller Maitland, op, cit., 107. Shaw, op. cit., vol. 3, 253.

8 *Fantasies of Three Parts Composed for Viols by Orlando Gibbons*, ed. Edward F. Rimbault (London: Musical Antiquarian Society, 1843), 10.

9 Margaret Campbell, *Dolmetsch: The Man and His Work* (London and Seattle, 1975), 41.

10 Mabel Dolmetsch, *Personal Recollections of Arnold Dolmetsch* (London, 1958), 163.

11 Shaw, op. cit., vol. 3, 258.

12 Arthur Symons, 'On an Air of Rameau', in *Poems*, vol. 2 (London, 1924), 78.

13 Shaw, op. cit., vol. 2, 224.

14 Robert Donington, *The Work and Ideas of Arnold Dolmetsch* (Haslemere, 1932), 8.

15 See Lilian M. Ruff, 'James Joyce and Arnold Dolmetsch', *The James Joyce Quarterly* 6 (1969), 224–30.

16 Letter to Dolmetsch, 26 January 1906, in *Bernard Shaw: Collected Letters 1898–1910*, ed. Dan H. Laurence (New York and London, 1972), 602.

17 Mabel Dolmetsch, op. cit., 17–18.

18 Arthur Symons, 'A Reflection at a Dolmetsch Concert', in *Plays, Acting and Music* (London, 1909), 271.

19 John Runciman in the *Saturday Review*, 2 April 1898, 461–62.

20 'Some Old-Time Music', in *The Year's Music 1896* (London, 1896), 24.

21 Shaw, op. cit., vol. 3, 148.

22 See Stanley Godman, 'Francis William Galpin: Music Maker', *Galpin Society Journal* 12 (1959), 8–16.

23 Frederick Niecks, 'Historical Concerts', *The Monthly Musical Record* 12 (1882), 217 and 244.

24 Percy Young, *George Grove: A Biography* (London, 1980), 248.

25 See *English Music [1604 to 1904]; Being the lectures given at the Music Loan Exhibition of the*

Worshipful Co. of Musicians held at Fishmongers Hall, London Bridge, June–July 1904 (London and New York, 1906).

26 Edward Dannreuther, *Musical Ornamentation* (London, 1893), vol. 1, vii.

27 Campbell, op. cit., 95.

28 Ibid., 261.

29 Anselm Hughes, *Septuagesima* (London, 1959), 56.

30 Arnold Dolmetsch, *The Interpretation of the Music of the XVIIth and XVIIIth Centuries* (London, 1915; repr. Seattle, 1969), 468.

31 John Runciman in the *Saturday Review*, 2 April 1898, 461–62.

32 Thurston Dart, 'The Achievement of Arnold Dolmetsch', *The Listener* 59 (1959), 400.

33 George Moore, *Evelyn Inness* (London, 1898). James Joyce, *Ulysses* (Paris, 1924), 615. Dolmetsch is mentioned in Ezra Pound's Cantos 80, 81 and 99. In a 1917 essay entitled 'Vers Libre and Arnold Dolmetsch', Pound wrote that 'poetry must be read as music and not as oratory'. Dolmetsch's study of rhythm and tempo in old music fascinated the poet; see R. Murray Schafer, ed., *Ezra Pound and Music* (London, 1978).

34 William Rothenstein, *Men and Memories 1872–1900* (New York and London, 1931), 212f.

35 Gabriele d'Annunzio, undated letter to Dolmetsch (Dolmetsch Archives, Haslemere). Dolmetsch declined the invitation and Ildebrando Pizzetti eventually wrote the music for the play.

36 Mabel Dolmetsch, op. cit., 39. Dolmetsch's career in America is discussed in Chapter 5.

37 According to Margaret Campbell (op. cit., 138), Dolmetsch claimed to have 'revived the classical method of singing' as early as 1901. In Paris he served briefly as director of the Chanterie de la Renaissance, a choir founded by the musicologist Henry Expert, but vocal music was never his forte, as Shaw noted in a review of 7 February 1894: 'The singers, with their heads full of modern "effects", shew but a feeble sense of the accuracy of intonation and tenderness of expression required by the pure vocal harmonies of the old school.' Shaw's complaint was echoed forty years later by Percy Scholes. 'At the one concert of your last [Haslemere] Festival the choral standard was not (to me as a Yorkshireman) anything like high enough', he wrote to Dolmetsch on 6 January 1934 (Dolmetsch Archives, Haslemere).

38 Fuller Maitland, op. cit., 221.

39 Beecham sang bass on the Oriana Madrigal Society's first concert and later wrote programme notes for the group. See 'Mr Beecham, Musicologist' in Humphrey Procter-Gregg, ed., *Beecham Remembered* (London, 1976), 159–70. Kennedy Scott, who later co-founded the Bach Cantata Club, conducted the society's last concert in 1961.

40 Edmund H. Fellowes, *Memoirs of an Amateur Musician* (London, 1946), 120. See also Edward J. Dent, 'Edmund Horace Fellowes', *The Score* 6 (1952), 52–54.

41 See Mary Berry, 'Gregorian Chant', *EM* 7 (1979), 203.

42 *The Plainsong and Mediaeval Music Society: Annual Report, 31 October 1892* (London, 1892). The report states that the choir 'has commenced its practices at the Chapter House of St Paul's Cathedral, under the superintendence of Mr C. F. Abdy Williams'. The choir is mentioned again in the following year's report, but not in 1894. On the society's later activities, see Anselm Hughes, *Septuagesima* (London, 1959).

43 John Runciman, 'William Byrde, His Mass', *The Saturday Review*, 2 December 1899, 703–04.

44 Hilda Andrews, *Westminster Retrospect* (London, 1948), 171. Imogen Holst discusses her father's performances of Palestrina, Bach, Lassus, Weelkes and other old masters in *Gustav Holst* (London, 1969).

45 See Steuart Wilson, 'The English Singers', *Recorded Sound* 2 (1965), 375–81.

46 *MT* 64 (1923), 545.

47 See Elizabeth Roche, 'The Elizabethan Competitive Festivals, 1923–6', *EM* 11 (1983), 519–22.

48 Vaughan Williams directed the Bach Choir from 1920 to 1926. Though sympathetic to the trend toward small-scale Bach performances, as a practical matter he felt that large choirs and orchestras were better suited to London's concert halls; see Ursula Vaughan Williams, *R.V.W.: A Biography of Ralph Vaughan Williams* (London and New York, 1964), 427ff.

49 *MT* 68 (1927), 357. The Bach Cantata Club comprised some 30 singers – about one tenth the size of the Bach Choir. Chamber-sized performances of Baroque choral works were not unprecedented in England. In 1906, A. H. Mann conducted a performance of Handel's *Messiah* in Cambridge using a choir of 24 voices and a slightly larger orchestra; see the review in *MT* 47 (1906), 608–09.

50 *MT* 70 (1929), 807.

51 See W. A. Marshall, 'Sixty Years of the Haslemere Festival', *Dolmetsch Foundation Bulletin* 41 (1984).

52 W. B. Yeats, letter to Dolmetsch, 21 November 1934 (Dolmetsch Archives, Haslemere). This intriguing initiative apparently came to naught.
53 Campbell, op. cit., 270.
54 Ralph Kirkpatrick, 'On Playing the Clavichord', EM 9 (1981), 294. Percy Grainger, 'Arnold Dolmetsch: Musical Confucius', MQ 19 (1933), 195.
55 Ernest Newman, 'Arnold Dolmetsch', The Sunday Times, 17 March 1940, 3.
56 Basil Maine, 'The Cool Music of Haslemere', in Reflected Music (London, 1930), 69–70.
57 Grainger, op. cit., 194.
58 Kirkpatrick, op. cit., 295.
59 Elizabeth Goble, 'Keyboard Lessons with Arnold Dolmetsch', EM 5 (1977), 89.
60 Thurston Dart, 'The Achievement of Arnold Dolmetsch, The Listener 59 (1959), 400–02.
61 Grainger, letter to Dolmetsch (Dolmetsch Archives, Haslemere).
62 Grainger, op. cit. See also Gustave Reese, 'Percy Grainger and Early Music', Studies in Music (U. of Western Australia) 10 (1976), 13–14; and Lewis Foreman, ed., The Percy Grainger Companion (London, 1981). In 1936 Grainger addressed the Plainsong and Mediaeval Music Society on 'The Old Music from the Standpoint of a Modern Composer'. Unfortunately, no copy of this talk has survived.
63 Mabel Dolmetsch, Personal Recollections of Arnold Dolmetsch (London, 1958), 22.
64 Mabel Dolmetsch touches on her husband's interest in early dance in Dances of England and France from 1450 to 1600 (London, 1949), xi. Several early musicians actively took part in the British folk dance revival. Violet Gordon Woodhouse, the English Singers and the Oriana Madrigal Society were guest artists at Cecil Sharp's festivals in Hammersmith in the early 1920s; see Maud Karpeles, Cecil Sharp: His Life and Work (London, 1967), 180.
65 Newman, 'Arnold Dolmetsch', The Sunday Times, 17 March 1940, 3.
66 Dart, op. cit., 400–02.
67 Arnold Dolmetsch, The Interpretation of the Music of the XVIIth and XVIIIth Centuries (London, 1915; repr. Seattle, 1969), 471.

CHAPTER 3
FROM SCHOLA TO SCHOLA

1 Julien Tiersot, 'Promenades Musicales à l'Exposition', Le Ménestrel 53 (9 June 1889), 179–80. The 1889 Paris Exposition stimulated the Art Nouveau movement in France, which, like England's Arts and Crafts movement, had close ties with the early music revival; see Albert van der Linden, 'Aspects de la fin du XIXe siècle: la musique ancienne aux concerts de la "Libre Esthétique"', Bulletin de la classe des beaux-arts, Académie Royale de Belgique, 52/4–5 (1970), 123–36.
2 Le Guide musicale 34 (16 February 1888), 53.
3 Edmund van der Straeten, 'Société des Instruments Anciens', London Musical Courier, 1 July 1897, 10. Van der Straeten gives brief biographies of Delsart and other early gambists in his History of the Violoncello, the Viol da Gamba, Their Precursors and Collateral Instruments (London, 1915; repr. 1971). See also John Rutledge, 'Towards a History of the Viol in the 19th Century', EM 12 (1984), 328–36, and Ruth Daniells, 'Viols in the Twentieth Century', The Consort 20 (1963), 203–10.
4 Margaret Campbell, Dolmetsch: The Man and His Work (London and Seattle, 1975), 135.
5 This and many other details of the Chanteurs' early history are found in René de Castéra, Dix années d'action musicale religieuse (Paris, 1902).
6 Paul Dukas, Les Ecrits de Paul Dukas sur la musique (Paris, 1948), vol. 1, 146.
7 Georges Servieres, 'Charles Bordes', S.I.M. Revue musicale mensuelle, December 1909, 987–95.
8 Romain Rolland, Musicians of Today, trans. Mary Blaiklock (London, 1915), 288. Laurence Davies discusses Franck's influence on Bordes and d'Indy in César Franck and His Circle (London and Boston, 1970), 142–59 and 284–318.
9 Rolland, op. cit., 293.
10 In her autobiography, La Chanson de ma vie (Paris, 1927), Yvette Guilbert states that she became interested in early French songs around 1900. Reviewing her concert with the Chanteurs de St Gervais in 1905, Louis Laloy praised the singer's 'variety of tone' and 'inimitable sense of fun' (Le Mercure musicale, 15 January 1906, 80–81). Guilbert later included a selection of medieval and Renaissance lyrics in her anthology La Chanson de France.
11 Le Temps, 11 June 1902; reprinted in full in appendix to Castéra, op. cit., 13–15.
12 Camille Mauclair, cited in Ursula Eckhart-Bäcker, Frankreichs Musik zwischen Romantik und Moderne (Regensburg, 1969), 229.
13 Rolland, op. cit., 318–19.
14 This and the following quote are taken from Claude Debussy, Debussy on Music, ed. François

Lesure and trans. Richard Langham Smith (London and New York, 1977).

15 Paul Dukas used the phrase 'hypnose wagnérienne' in 'Charles Bordes', RM(2) August 1924, 99. The Debussy anecdote is in Louis Laloy, La Musique retrouvée, 1902–27 (Paris, 1928), 83. Constant Zakone in RM(1) 3 (1903), 307–09.

16 Bordes's article was reprinted as a pamphlet, De l'opportunité de créer en France un théâtre d'application pour la reconstitution des anciens opéras français des XVIIe et XVIIIe siècles (Paris, 1906). The Schola's operatic society, La Petite Scène, was founded sometime before 1914 and revived after the First World War under the direction of d'Indy and Xavier de Courville. Cf. Chapter 7, notes 20 and 66.

17 Romain Rolland in RM(1) 2 (1902), 55.

18 André Pirro. 'Charles Bordes et les cantates de J. S. Bach', in Charles Bordes (1863–1909): In memoriam. Publié par ses amis de la Schola. Special number of the Tribune de St Gervais 15 (1909), 18.

19 Jules Ecorcheville, 'La Schola Cantorum et le style de Bach', Le Mercure musicale et bulletin français de la S.I.M., 15 April 1907, 399–406.

20 The Société Bach was founded by Gustave Bret in 1904, the Société Haendel by Eugène Borel and Félix Raugel four years later; see André Marty, 'La Société Bach', S.I.M. Revue musicale, 15 March 1912, 57–61.

21 See Eugène de Bricqueville, La Couperin: Un orchestre d'anciens instruments à Versailles (Versailles, 1905). A catalogue of Bricqueville's collection, published ten years earlier, lists 125 instruments, all purportedly in playable condition.

22 Jules Ecorcheville, 'La Musique ancienne au concert en 1909', Le Bulletin français de la S.I.M., 15 November 1908, 1192.

23 Tolstoy letter to Henri Casadesus, reproduced in Régina Patorni-Casadesus, Ma famille Casadesus: Souvenirs d'une claveciniste (Paris, 1962), 111.

24 Alfredo Casella, Music in My Time, trans. Spencer Norton (Norman, Okla., 1955), 72.

25 Denise Restout, ed., Landowska on Music (New York, 1964), 10.

26 Albert Schweitzer, Jean Sebastien Bach (Paris, 1905); trans. Ernest Newman (London, 1923), 353.

27 See Timothy Bainbridge, 'Wanda Landowska and Her Repertoire', EM 3 (1975), 39–41.

28 See Richard Buchmayer, 'Cembalo oder Pianoforte?', Bach-Jahrbuch 5 (1908), 64–93; Karl

Nef, 'Bachs Verhältnis zur Klaviermusik', ibid. 6 (1909), 12–26; J. Joaquín Nin, 'A propos du Festival Bach à Eisenach', S.I.M. Revue musicale mensuelle, 15 December 1911, 100–02; and Wanda Landowska, 'Piano ou clavecin?', ibid., 15 March 1912, 72.

29 See, for example, the review of the festival in NZ 72 (1911), 527.

30 Restout, op. cit., 11.

31 Ibid., 356.

32 Virgil Thomson in the New York Herald Tribune, 22 February 1942.

33 See Momo Aldrich, 'Reminiscences of St Leu', Diapason 70 (July 1979), 3f.

34 'Conversation with Harpsichordist Alice Ehlers', The Harpsichord 6 (1973), 4ff. Landowska's relationship with Ehlers was strained; for a more favourable view of her as a teacher, see Irma Rogell, 'Ralph Kirkpatrick and Wanda Landowska', Music Journal 42 (1985), 9–13. See also 'Conversation with Denise Restout', The Harpsichord 7 (1974), 6ff.

35 Léon Kochnitzky in RM(2), July 1934, 133–35.

36 Restout, op. cit., 350–51.

37 Eta Harich-Schneider, The Harpsichord (St Louis, 1954), 7.

38 Hugo Leichtentritt, 'Aufführungen älterer Musik in Berlin', Zeitschrift der internationalen Musikgesellschaft 7 (1905–06), 368–71.

39 Leichtentritt, ibid. 8 (1906–07), 357–58, and Edgar Istel, ibid. 7 (1905–06), 106–07.

40 See Christian Döbereiner, Zur Renaissance alter Musik (Tutzing, 1950) and 50 Jahre alte Musik in München (Munich, 1955).

41 See Paul Grümmer, Begegnungen (Munich, 1963), 80.

42 See August Wenzinger, Hans Eberhard Hoesch und die Kabeler Kammermusik (Hagen, 1985).

43 Shelagh Godwin, 'The F. T. Arnold Correspondence', The Consort 33 (1977), 244.

44 See Marjorie Bram, 'An Interview with August Wenzinger', The Journal of the Viola da Gamba Society of America 12 (1975), 78–83; and Dieter Gutknecht, 'Der Gesamtüberblicht fehlt!' [interview with Wenzinger], Concerto 3 (June 1986), 18–27.

45 See Rudolf Steglich, 'Hugo Riemann als Wiedererwecker älterer Musik', Zeitschrift für Musikwissenschaft 1 (1918–19), 611.

46 See Friedrich Ludwig, 'Musik des Mittelalters in der Badischen Kunsthalle, Karlsruhe, 24–26 Sept. 1922', Zeitschrift für Musikwissenschaft 5 (1922–23), 434–60; and Heinrich

Besseler, 'Musik des Mittelalters in der Hamburger Musikhalle, 1–8 April 1924', ibid. 7 (1924–25), 42–54.

47 Arnold Dolmetsch, *The Interpretation of the Music of the XVIIth and XVIIIth Centuries* (London, 1915; repr. Seattle, 1969), 437.

48 For Schweitzer's views on organ design, see Charles R. Joy, *Music in the Life of Albert Schweitzer* (New York, 1951), 136ff.

49 H. H. Eggebrecht, *Die Orgelbewegung* (Stuttgart, 1967), 21.

50 Wilibald Gurlitt, 'The Praetorius Organ in Freiburg', *The American–German Review* 22 (April–May 1956), 7–9.

51 See Hilmar Höckner, *Die Musik in der deutschen Jugendbewegung* (Wolfenbüttel, 1927) and Hans A. Martens, 'Die Blockflöte in heutiger Zeit', *NZ* 92 (1931), 26–28.

52 See, for example, Erwin Walter, 'Arnold Dolmetsch über Verfall und Wiederbelebung der Hausmusik', *NZ* 91 (1930), 102–04; and Emil Brauer, 'Arnold Dolmetsch', *Der Blockflötenspiegel* 1 (1931).

53 One of the best-known German early music societies was Die Sackpfeife in Düsseldorf; see Hermann Moeck, 'The Twentieth-Century Renaissance of the Recorder in Germany', *The American Recorder* 23 (1982), 61–67.

54 See Karl Vötterle, *Haus unterm Stern* (Kassel, 1969).

55 See Joshua Rifkin, 'Whatever Happened to Heinrich Schütz?', *Opus* 1/6 (1985), 10–14f.; and Kurt Gudewill, 'Heinrich Schütz und die Gegenwart', in Adam Adrio et al., *Bekenntnis zu Heinrich Schütz* (Kassel, 1954), 65–78.

56 Alfred Einstein, 'Das Heinrich-Schütz-Fest in Berlin', *Zeitschrift für Musikwissenschaft* 13 (1930–31), 217–18.

57 See Theodor Kroyer, 'Karl Straube und die historische Renaissance', *NZ* 91 (1930), 897–99.

58 *MT* 74 (1933), 810.

59 This and the following quotes are taken from Bernard Gagnepain, 'Safford Cape et le "Miracle" Pro Musica Antiqua', *Revue Belge de musicologie* 34–35 (1980–81), 204–19.

60 For example, the Austrian musicologist Rudolf von Ficker arranged a selection of 'Gothic' choral music for a historical concert in the Burgkapelle at the 1927 Beethoven festival in Vienna. The performances, according to one report, 'transported the fascinated listeners into the remote land of medieval mysticism'; see *Die Musik* 19 (1927), 616.

61 A. L. Flay, 'Pro Musica Antiqua', *MT* 88 (1947), 17–18.

62 See Jean Jenkins, 'Geneviève Thibault, Madame H. de Chambure: An Appreciation' and Fiona McAlpine, 'Paris: A Survey', both in *EM* 4 (1976); and G. Thibault, 'A la Société de Musique d'Autrefois', in Denise Mayer and Pierre Souvtchinsky, eds., *Roger Désormière et son temps* (Monaco, 1966).

63 Société de Musique d'Autrefois brochure (n.d.). I am indebted to Mme Thibault's successor at the Paris Conservatoire, Josiane Bran-Ricci, for calling this to my attention.

64 Léonie Rosenstiel, *Nadia Boulanger* (New York and London, 1982), 279. However, Boulanger played the harpsichord when she recorded a second set of Monteverdi madrigals in the early fifties.

65 Raymond Petit in *RM*(2), June 1934, 64.

66 This and the following quotations are taken from Wulf Arlt, 'Zur Idee und zur Geschichte eines "Lehr- und Forschungsinstituts für alte Musik" in den Jahren 1933 bis 1970', in Peter Reidemeister and Veronika Gutman, eds., *Alte Musik: Praxis und Reflexion* (Winterthur, 1983). See also Arlt's 'Musicology and the Practice of Music: Thoughts from the Work of the Schola Cantorum Basiliensis', *Current Musicology* 14 (1972), 88–94.

67 Thirty-six years later, for the 1972 Olympics in Munich, Orff arranged the medieval canon 'Sumer is icumen in' for choir and a mixed ensemble of early and modern instruments.

CHAPTER 4
'BACK TO BACH'

1 'Kreisler's "Classics"', *The New York Times*, 3 March 1935. This and the following quotations are taken from Louis P. Lochner, *Fritz Kreisler* (New York, 1950), 295ff.

2 Jean-Baptiste Weckerlin, *Nouveau musiciana* (Paris, 1900), 67.

3 Jacques Barzun, *Berlioz and the Romantic Century* (Boston, 1950; London, 1951), vol. 2, 90.

4 Kreisler in the *New York Times*, 18 February 1935, 19.

5 Lochner, op. cit., 303.

6 Einstein gives his reasoning in *Essays on Music* (New York, 1956), 233–36. Régina Patorni-Casadesus tells the Saint-Saëns anecdote in *Ma famille Casadesus: Souvenirs d'une claveciniste* (Paris, 1962), 73. For more on the Casadesus brothers' forgeries, see Walter Lebermann, 'Apokryph, Plagiat, Korruptel oder Falsifikat?', *Die Musikforschung* 20 (1967), 413–25.

7 Thomas Beecham, *A Mingled Chime* (New

York, 1943; London, 1944; repr. 1976 as *The Lyric Stage*), 315f.

8 See Barry S. Brook, 'Pergolesi: Vindication After 200 Years', *MT* 127 (1986), 141–45; and Frank Walker, 'Two Centuries of Pergolesi Forgeries and Misattributions', *Music and Letters* 30 (1949), 297–320.

9 Lochner, op. cit., 299.

10 Igor Stravinsky and Robert Craft, *Expositions and Developments* (London and New York, 1962), 113. The version of the *Pulcinella* episode that Stravinsky told Craft differs in several respects from the account given in his autobiography *Chroniques de ma vie* (Paris, 1935; Eng. trans. London, 1936), where he expresses unqualified admiration for Pergolesi.

11 Stravinsky and Craft, *Expositions and Developments*, 112–13.

12 *Stravinsky in Conversation with Robert Craft* (London, 1962), 35.

13 In the mid-1960s, Stravinsky was impressed by tapes Greenberg had made in Russia of polyphonic singing in the mountain villages near Tiflis; see 'Stravinsky on the Musical Scene and Other Matters', *New York Review of Books*, 12 May 1966, 19. Stravinsky's earlier encounters with Cape are noted in Bernard Gagnepain, 'Safford Cape et le "Miracle" Pro Musica Antiqua', *Revue Belge de musicologie* 34–35 (1980–81), 204–19.

14 This and the following quotation are taken from Ferruccio Busoni, *The Essence of Music*, trans. Rosamund Ley (London, 1957), 20.

15 Antony Beaumont, *Busoni the Composer* (London and Bloomington, Ind., 1985), 163.

16 Edward J. Dent, *Ferruccio Busoni* (London, 1933), 259–60.

17 Andreas Holschneider, 'Bach-Rezeption und Bach-Interpretation im 20. Jahrhundert', *Musica* (Kassel) 30 (1976), 11.

18 Alan Lessem, 'Schoenberg, Stravinsky, and Neo-Classicism: The Issues Reexamined', *MQ* 68 (1982), 527–42.

19 Schoenberg to Casals, 20 February 1933, in *Arnold Schoenberg Letters*, ed. Erwin Stein, trans. Eithne Wilkins and Ernest Kaiser (London, 1964), 171–72.

20 Igor Stravinsky and Robert Craft, *Memories and Commentaries* (London and Garden City, N.J., 1960), 116f.

21 Willi Reich, 'Paul Hindemith', *MQ* 17 (1931), 490.

22 Carl Engel, 'Harking Back and Looking Forward', *MQ* 14 (1928), 13.

23 See, for example, Adolf Aber, 'Old Forms in New Music', *The Sackbut* 7 (1926–27), 248–50.

24 Alfredo Casella, *Music in My Time*, trans. Spencer Norton (Norman, Okla., 1955), 226. Igor Stravinsky, *The Poetics of Music* (Cambridge, Mass., 1942), 57. Gian Francesco Malipiero, 'Claudio Monteverdi of Cremona', *MQ* 18 (1932), 396.

25 Paul Dukas, *Les Ecrits de Paul Dukas sur la musique* (Paris, 1948), 24.

26 Pierre Lalo in *Le Temps*, 16 November 1920.

27 Georges Jean-Aubry, *French Music of Today*, trans. Edwin Evans (London, 1919), 33.

28 Denise Restout, ed., *Landowska on Music* (New York, 1964), 347–48. Henri Hell, *Francis Poulenc, musicien français* (Paris, 1958), 56. Claude Rostand, sleeve note to Angel 35993.

29 Michael Steinberg, 'Some Observations on the Harpsichord in Twentieth Century Music', *Perspectives of New Music* 1 (1963), 189–94.

30 Christopher Palmer, *Herbert Howells* (London, 1978), 71.

31 R. Murray Shafer, ed., *Ezra Pound and Music* (London, 1978), 46.

32 Helmut Wirth, 'Hans Pfitzner', *The New Grove Dictionary of Music and Musicians*, vol. 14, 613.

33 See Karen Forsythe, *Ariadne auf Naxos by Hugo von Hofmannsthal and Richard Strauss* (London, 1982), 15–53; and Norman del Mar, *Richard Strauss*, vol. 3 (London and Philadelphia, 1969), 86ff. and 274ff. The *Capriccio* suite was arranged for the harpsichordist Isolde Ahlgrimm.

34 Igor Stravinsky and Robert Craft, *Memories and Commentaries* (London and Garden City, N.J., 1960), 123.

35 Friedrich Blume et al., *Protestant Church Music* (New York, 1974; London, 1975), 408.

36 See Arthur Hutchings, 'Vaughan Williams and the Tudor Tradition', *The Listener* 45 (1951), 276.

37 Michael Tippett, *Music of the Angels*, ed. Meirion Bowen (London, 1980), 75. On Britten's interest in early music, see George Malcolm, 'The Purcell Realizations', in Donald Mitchell and Hans Keller, eds., *Benjamin Britten: A Commentary on His Work from a Group of Specialists* (London, 1952), 74ff.

38 *MT* 42 (1921), 431.

39 Constant Lambert, *Music Ho!* (London, 1934; repr. New York, 1967), 69 and 75.

40 Ernst Krenek, *Music Here and Now*, trans. Barthold Fles (New York, 1939), 68ff. Paul Dukas, 'Charles Bordes', *RM(2)*, August 1924, 99. Virgil Thomson, *The State of Music* (New

York, 1962), 95.

41 Olin Downes interview with Varèse, *The New York Times*, 25 July 1948, sect. X, 5.

42 Krenek, op. cit., 75.

43 Casella, op. cit., 172ff.

44 Krenek, op. cit., 68f.

45 Krenek, *Horizons Circled* (Berkeley, Cal., 1974), 29.

46 Krenek, *Johannes Ockeghem* (New York, 1953), 80ff.

47 'To make it accessible at long last, by trying through my orchestration to express my view of it, was the ultimate object of my bold undertaking', Webern wrote to Hermann Scherchen; see Hans Moldenhauer, *Anton von Webern* (New York and London, 1978), 444.

48 Ferruccio Busoni, *The Essence of Music*, trans. Rosamund Ley (London, 1957), 87.

49 Paul Hindemith, *A Composer's World* (Cambridge, Mass., 1952), 140 and 142.

50 Donald Mitchell discusses Bach's influence on Mahler in *Gustav Mahler: The Wunderhorn Years* (London, 1975; Boulder, Colo., 1976), 345ff.

51 NZ 91 (1930), 738.

52 See 'Un Nouvel instrument: l'orphéal', *S.I.M. Revue musicale*, 15 February 1913, 70; and Gustave Lyon, 'Un Nouvel instrument; la harpe-luth', ibid., 1 July 1907, 360–62. The harp-lute is not to be confused with the guitar-like instrument of the eighteenth century.

53 Schweitzer made a spirited defence of the 'Bach' bow in 'A New Bow for Unaccompanied Violin Music,' *MT* 74 (1933), 792–95. The controversy flared up again when Telmányi recorded the Bach sonatas and partitas in the mid-1950s; see his 'Some Problems in Bach's Unaccompanied Violin Music', *MT* 96 (1955), 14–18. See also the rebuttals by Denis Stevens ('Another View of the Bach Bow', ibid., p.98) and Sol Babitz ('The Vega Bach Bow', ibid., pp.251–53). Allan Kozinn recapitulates the arguments in 'Bach's Solo Violin Works', *Opus* 2/5 (1986), 27ff.

54 This and the following quotation are taken from Oliver Daniel, *Stokowski: A Counterpoint of View* (New York, 1982), 442f. Daniel addresses the vexed question of Stokowski's authorship of the Bach transcriptions. He concludes that Lucien Caillet, a clarinettist in the Philadelphia Orchestra, executed the orchestrations in consultation with the conductor until 1938.

55 Sam Franko, *Chords and Discords* (New York, 1938), 105.

56 David Ewen, *The Man with The Baton* (Freeport, N.Y., 1968), 179. For a discussion of Toscanini's literalism in the context of the *Neue Sachlichkeit*, see Joseph Horowitz, *Understanding Toscanini* (New York and London, 1987), 334–41.

57 Ernest Ansermet, *Ecrits sur la musique* (Neuchâtel, 1971), 74. Margaret Campbell reviews his correspondence with Dolmetsch in 'To Dot or Double-Dot? The Eternal Question', *The Consort* 31 (1975), 142–47.

58 Putnam Aldrich, 'Wanda Landowska's *Musique Ancienne*', *Notes* 27 (1971), 461–68.

59 Wilhelm Furtwängler, *Concerning Music*, trans. L. J. Lawrence (Westport, Conn., 1977), 70–71.

60 Reprinted in Furtwängler's *Ton und Wort: Aufsätze und Vorträge 1918 bis 1954* (Wiesbaden, 1954).

61 See *Alte und Neue Musik: 50 Jahre Basler Kammerorchester* (Zurich, 1977).

62 Carl Dolmetsch interview with author, 29 January 1986. According to Margaret Campbell, Segovia visited Haslemere in 1924 and asked Dolmetsch to make him a guitar, but Dolmetsch declined.

CHAPTER 5
OLD MUSIC IN THE NEW WORLD

1 See Judith T. Steinberg, 'Old Folks Concerts and the Revival of New England Psalmody', *MQ* 59 (1973), 602–19.

2 N. Lindsay Norton, 'A Plea for Pure Church Music', *MQ* 4 (1918), 196–208.

3 *Dwight's Journal of Music*, 2 March 1853. This and the following quotations are taken from H. Earle Johnson, ed., *First Performances in America to 1900* (Detroit, 1979).

4 MT 42 (1901), 464.

5 *Zeitschrift der internationalen Musikgesellschaft* 2 (1900–01), 394–98.

6 Charles D. Isaacson, 'Something "Bigger" Than the Bethlehem Bach Festivals', *MQ* 7 (1921), 118–29.

7 *The New York Times*, 24 May 1901, 8.

8 Ibid., 25 May 1901, 8.

9 Isaacson, loc. cit.

10 Raymond Walter, *The Bethlehem Bach Choir* (Boston and New York, 1918), 71.

11 Later directors of the Bethlehem Bach Festival include Ifor Jones, Alfred Mann, William Reese and, currently, Greg Funfgeld.

12 George Martin, *The Damrosch Dynasty* (Boston, 1983), 230f.

13 *Musical America*, 23 December 1905, 4.

14 Richard Aldrich, 'The Closing of a Chapter', *The New York Times*, 5 December 1920. See also *The Musical Art Society of New York: A Brief History* (New York, 1913).

15 Jane Maslin, ed., *Reminiscences of Morris Steinert* (New York and London, 1900), 196. See also Steinert's *The M. Steinert Collection of Keyed and Stringed Instruments* (New York, 1893).

16 Charles Edward Russell, *The American Orchestra and Theodore Thomas* (New York and Garden City, N.J., 1927), 133.

17 Rose Fay Thomas, *Memoirs of Theodore Thomas* (New York, 1911), 200f.

18 This and the following quotations are taken from Sam Franko, *Chords and Discords* (New York, 1938).

19 Richard Aldrich, *Concert Life in New York 1902–23* (New York, 1941), 55.

20 *The New York Tribune*, 28 November 1907.

21 Aldrich, op. cit., 19.

22 Ibid., 76.

23 Arthur Whiting, 'The Lesson of the Clavichord', *The New Music Review* 8 (1909), 69–72 and 138–42. The articles were subsequently reprinted as a pamphlet.

24 *Musical America*, 21 December 1907. *The New York Sun*, 13 December 1907.

25 *Musical America*, 10 February 1906.

26 Ibid., 17 February 1906.

27 Ibid., 17 December 1910.

28 See William E. Smith, 'Ancient Instruments Society Holds National Festival', *Musical America*, 25 April 1937, 30; and *The American Society of Ancient Instruments* (Philadelphia, 1983). The society's honorary patrons have included Stokowski, Toscanini, Henri Casadesus, Pablo Casals and John Frederick Wolle; it is still active.

29 See Paul Boepple, 'Renaissance Music', *The New York Times*, 25 January 1942. See also the reviews of the Dessoff Choirs' performance of *L'Amfiparnaso* in *Musical America*, 15 February 1933, 27; and 25 March 1933, 24.

30 Paul Rosenfeld, 'Palestrina on Twenty-Second Street', in *Musical Chronicle [1917–1923]* (New York, 1923), 43.

31 *The New York Times*, 31 March 1947. See also Chou-Wen Chung, 'Varèse: A Sketch of the Man and His Music', MQ 52 (1965), 151–76.

32 *The New York Times*, 10 December 1923.

33 Ibid., 15 March 1925.

34 See Ralph Kirkpatrick, 'On Playing the Clavichord', *EM* 9 (1981), 293–305.

35 See 'Portrait of a Builder: John Challis', *The Harpsichord* 2/3 (1969), 14–23.

36 See 'Conversation with Builder–Harpsi-

chordist Claude Jean Chiasson', *The Harpsichord* 5/3 (1972), 4ff.; 'Portrait of a Builder: Frank Hubbard', ibid. 5/1 (1972), 5–15; and F. Hubbard, 'Reconstructing the Harpsichord', in Howard Schott, ed., *The Historical Harpsichord*, vol. 1 (New York, 1974), 6–23.

37 For differing assessments of the American Recorder Society's impact, see the short essays by Suzanne Bloch, Thomas Binkley and others in 'Reflections on the Early Music Scene', *The American Recorder* 26 (February 1985), 4–11.

38 For a first-hand account of this episode, see 'Conversation with Harpsichordist Denise Restout', *The Harpsichord* 7/1 (1974), 6–23.

39 *The New York Herald Tribune*, 22 February 1942. The following quotation appears in the same review.

40 See Léonie Rosenstiel, *Nadia Boulanger: A Life in Music* (New York, 1982), 285ff.

41 Robert Hodesh, 'Smith College Gives Four Day Music Festival', *Musical America*, 25 May 1941, 42.

42 Helen S. Slosberg, Mary V. Ullman and Isabel K. Whiting, eds., *Erwin Bodky: A Memorial Tribute* (Waltham, Mass., 1969) gives the programmes and recordings of the Cambridge Society for Early Music.

43 Cited in Howard Boatwright, 'Hindemith's Performances of Old Music', *Hindemith-Jahrbuch* 3 (1973), 39–62.

44 Eckhart Richter, 'Paul Hindemith as Director of the Yale Collegium Musicum', *College Music Symposium* 18 (1978), 30. Cf. Hindemith's views on historical performance in Chapter 9.

45 Ibid., 38.

46 Nathan Broder in *High Fidelity* 8 (October 1958), 66.

47 Alan Rich in the *New York Herald Tribune*, 10 December 1963.

CHAPTER 6
'TO OPEN WIDE THE WINDOWS'

1 Noah Greenberg, 'Early Music Performance Today', in Jan LaRue, ed., *Aspects of Medieval and Renaissance Music* (New York, 1966), 315.

2 Philip M. Dowd, 'Charles Bordes and the Schola Cantorum of Paris' (Diss., Catholic U. of America, 1969), 124–25.

3 Mary Berry, 'Gregorian Chant', *EM* 7 (1979), 197.

4 These recordings were recently reissued on Discant Dis 1 and 2.

5 Mabel Dolmetsch, *Personal Recollections of*

Arnold Dolmetsch (London, 1958), 31.
6   *The Gramophone* 15 (1937–38), 280.
7   Violet Gordon Woodhouse, 'The Harpsichord and the Gramophone', *The Gramophone* 1 (1923–24), 36–37.
8   See John Gwynne, 'Violet Gordon Woodhouse', *Recorded Sound* 41 (1971), 721–29.
9   Margaret Campbell, *Dolmetsch: The Man and His Work* (London and Seattle, 1975), 210.
10   *The Gramophone* 11 (1933–34), 10.
11   Ibid. 16 (1938–39), 67.
12   P. H. R., 'Dolmetsch Recordings', *The American Music Lover*, 4 September 1938.
13   See Steuart Wilson, 'The English Singers', *Recorded Sound* 20 (1965), 375–81.
14   *The Gramophone* 6 (1928–29), 436.
15   R. D. Darrell, ed., *The Gramophone Shop Encyclopedia of Recorded Music* (New York, 1936), iv.
16   Landowska's recording on harpsichord of Bach's A minor English Suite was included in the Fischer set.
17   *The Gramophone* 13 (1934–35), 228. The album featured Nancy Evans as Dido, Kennedy Scott's A Cappella Singers and the Boyd Neel String Orchestra, conducted by Clarence Raybould.
18   René Dumesnil, *Dix siècles de musique: l'Anthologie Sonore* (Paris, 1943).
19   *The Gramophone Shop Encyclopedia of Recorded Music*, 3rd ed. (New York, 1948), 608.
20   *The Gramophone* 13 (1934–35), 465.
21   David Hall, *The Record Book* (New York, 1940), 243.
22   *MT* 66 (1925), 622–33.
23   Ibid. 69 (1928), 716.
24   Ernst Latzko, 'Probleme des musikalischen Rundfunks', *Zeitschrift für Musikwissenschaft* 14 (1931–32), 352–56; and Richard Baum, 'Grenzen musikalischer Rundfunksendung', ibid., 471–74.
25   *NZ* 91 (1930), 240.
26   Straube and the Thomanerchor broadcast virtually all the Bach cantatas between 1931 and 1938. In May 1931 the *Neue Zeitschrift für Musik* reported 3,509,509 radio listeners in Germany.
27   *RM*(2), April 1932, 317–19.
28   Ibid., May 1932, 393.
29   Ibid., July 1930.
30   Cited in 'Broadcasting', *The New Grove Dictionary of Music and Musicians*, vol. 3, 320.
31   *MT* 88 (1947), 24.
32   Elizabeth Roche, 'Early Music and the BBC', *MT* 120 (1979), 823.
33   See Eduard Gröninger and Alfred Krings, 'Erfahrungen mit alter Musik im Hörfunk', in

Kurt Blaukopf, Siegfried Goslich and Wilfried Scheib, eds., *50 Jahre Musik im Hörfunk* (Munich and Vienna, 1973). Concert programmes of the Cappella Coloniensis are given in *Zwanzig Jahre Musik im Westdeutschen Rundfunk* (Cologne, 1968).
34   See 'Alte Musik ist keine Mode' [interview with Franzjosef Maier], *Concerto* 2 (August 1985), 43–48.
35   *MT* 69 (1928), 350.
36   The films were 'The Lady of the Lake' (1929; soundtrack added 1931) and 'Colonel Blood' (1934).
37   John Huntley, *British Film Music* (London, 1947), 62. For a discussion of early music in recent films, see Hans-Christian Schmidt, 'Alte Musik in neuen Medien', *NZ* 147 (February 1986), 14–19.
38   George C. Schoolfield, *The Figure of the Musician in German Literature* (Chapel Hill, N.C., 1956), 95.
39   Victor Hugo, *Oeuvres poétiques*, vol. 1 (Paris, 1964), 1098–1104.
40   Gabriele d'Annunzio, *Il Fuoco* (Milan, 1900); English trans. *The Flame of Life* (New York, 1900), 114–15.
41   Romain Rolland, *Jean Christophe* (Paris, 1905); trans. Gilbert Cannan (New York, 1938), 57. For Rolland's favourable opinion of d'Indy and the Schola Cantorum, see *Musicians of Today*, trans. Mary Blaiklock (London, 1915), 112–38 and 283–98.
42   Hermann Hesse, *Das Glasperlenspiel* (Zurich, 1943); translated by Mervyn Savill as *Magister Ludi* (London, 1949), 27.
43   'Old Music', in *My Belief*, trans. Denver Lindley (New York, 1974).
44   Thomas Mann, *The Story of a Novel*, trans. Richard and Clara Winston (New York, 1961), 73f.
45   Alex Aronson, *Music and the Novel* (Totowa, N.J., 1980), 161f.
46   Thomas Mann, *Doktor Faustus* (Stockholm, 1947); trans. H. T. Lowe-Porter (New York, 1948), 276. The viola di bordone (or 'bardone') was another name for the baryton.
47   Ibid., 177. Details of the concert are given in *Alte und Neue Musik II: 50 Jahre Basler Kammerorchester* (Zurich, 1977), 17f.
48   Christine Weston, *The Dark Wood* (New York, 1946), 166–68. The latest of James Gollin's mysteries is *The Verona Passamezzo* (New York, 1985); earlier novels in the series are *Eliza's Galiardo* and *The Philomel Foundation*.
49   For Pound's activities in Rapallo, see

R. Murray Schafer, ed., *Ezra Pound and Music* (New York, 1977), 321ff.

50 Robert Craft, 'Evviva Vivaldi!', in *Present Perspectives* (New York, 1984), 125–41.

51 Fred Hamel, 'A History of Music Recorded for Educational Purposes', in *Music in Education* [report of 1953 UNESCO conference in Brussels] (UNESCO, 1955), 260–63. See also Nicholas Anderson, 'Archiv at Forty', *Gramophone* 65 (1987), 538.

52 Jeremy Noble, 'Sixteenth-Century Music on Records. II: Sacred Music', *Music and Letters* 39 (1958), 154–59. Gilbert Reaney, 'Medieval Music on the Gramophone', ibid. 38 (1957), 180–90.

53 James Coover and Richard Colvig, *Medieval and Renaissance Music on Long-Playing Records*; 1962–71 supplement (Detroit, 1973), 8. Howard Mayer Brown, 'Performing Early Music on Record – 2: Continental Sacred Music of the 16th Century', *EM* 3 (1975), 373–77. Elizabeth Roche, 'Early Music on Records in the Last 25 Years', *MT* 120 (1979), 34.

54 *Revue internationale de musique* 2 (1938), 279.

55 Otto Gombosi, 'Reviews of Records', *MQ* 38 (1952), 659.

56 Armen Carapetyan, 'Some Remarks on the Current Performance of Early Music', *Musica Disciplina* 25 (1971), 6.

57 See, for example, Ralph Kirkpatrick, 'The Challenge of the Harpsichord', *Modern Music* 23 (1946), 273–76.

58 Denise Restout, ed., *Landowska on Music* (New York, 1964), 159.

CHAPTER 7
STAGING A COMEBACK

1 Robert Wangermée gives the complete programme in *François-Joseph Fétis: Musicologue et compositeur* (Brussels, 1951), 303–04.

2 Adolphe Jullien, *Musique: Mélanges d'histoire et de critique musicale et dramatique* (Paris, 1896), 333–47. See also the review in the *Allgemeine musikalische Zeitung* 15 (1880), 441–46.

3 *Revue et gazette musicale* 42 (7 March 1875), 77–78.

4 See Alberto de Angelis, *Domenico Mustafà* (Bologna, 1926), 160ff.

5 The performance of *L'Euridice* is listed in H. Earle Johnson, ed., *First Performances in America to 1900* (Detroit, 1979). On the Hamburg Handel production, see the report in the *Signale für die musikalische Welt* 36 (January 1878), 25;

and Friedrich Chrysander, 'Die Feier des zweihundertjährigen Bestandes der Oper in Hamburg', *Allgemeine musikalische Zeitung* 13 (1878), 145–48.

6 *NZ* 40 (1879), 288.

7 Andreas Hoffmann, 'V'adoro pupille: Händels Opern und ihre Renaissance', *Concerto* 3 (1985), 33.

8 *MT* 36 (1895), 811.

9 'The Purcell Commemoration', *The Times*, 21 November 1958, 8.

10 Ibid., 21 May 1900, 6.

11 *King Arthur* was revived in Birmingham on 6 October 1897, *The Fairy Queen* at St George's Hall, London, on 15 June 1901. A report of the Boston production of *Comus* appeared in the *Zeitschrift der internationalen Musikgesellschaft* 2 (1900–01), 351–52.

12 *Revue de musicologie* 1 (1917–19), 118–19. Another notable staging of *Robin et Marion* took place in 1907 at the Antique Theatre in St Petersburg. Directed by N. N. Evreinov, the production featured some medieval music played on period instruments; see Spencer Golub, *Evreinov: The Theatre of Paradox and Transformation* (Ann Arbor, Mich., 1984), 118–21.

13 *Le Ménestrel* 67 (10 February 1901), 46. The reviewer was mistakenly referring to the Paris Opéra's production of *Platée*; the premiere had taken place at Versailles in 1745.

14 According to a review in the *Journal de Genève* of 28 March 1903, members of the Société de Chant du Conservatoire sang the solo roles, accompanied by double string quartet and piano. Jaques-Dalcroze's experiments with combining Baroque music and movement are discussed in F. Martin et al., *Emile Jaques-Dalcroze: L'Homme, le compositeur, le créateur de la rhythmique* (Neuchâtel, 1965), 99f. and 447f.

15 *RM*(1) 3 (1903), 307–09.

16 *RM*(1) 4 (1904), 146.

17 Monteverdi, *Orfeo*, ed. Vincent d'Indy (Paris, 1904).

18 *RM*(1) 5 (1905), 174. Like *Orfeo*, the performance was sung in French.

19 Charles Bordes, *De l'opportunité de créer en France un théâtre d'application pour la reconstitution des anciens opéras français des XVIIe et XVIIIe siècles* (Paris, 1906).

20 'Les Fêtes musicales de Montpellier,' *Tribune de St Gervais* 11 (1905), 231. The group, known as the Jongleurs de St Genès, comprised the best students from the declamation class at the Schola Cantorum. The extent of its activities is unclear. See note 66 below.

21 Eduard Perrin, 'Castor et Pollux à Montpellier', Bulletin français de la S.I.M., 15 February 1908, 229–32.

22 Georges Imbart de la Tour, 'La Mise en Scène d'Hippolyte et Aricie', Bulletin français de la S.I.M., 15 March 1908, 247–71.

23 Ibid., 15 June 1908, 679.

24 RM(1) 8 (1908), 319–25.

25 Bulletin français de la S.I.M., 15 June 1908, 678–79.

26 Paul Dukas, for example, called for the 'reconstitution' of Rameau's orchestra as early as 1894; see Les Ecrits de Paul Dukas sur la musique (Paris, 1948), 192.

27 Henri Büsser, in an article in the Paris Opéra programme book on the 1952 revival of Les Indes galantes, reports that André Messager asked Gustave Lyon to design a more powerful harpsichord for the 1908 Hippolyte et Aricie. The combination of harpsichord and extra strings in the recitatives produced 'a sensation of devastating monotony', Büsser says.

28 Carlo Censi in Musica (Rome), 5 December 1909. Another Italian critic praised the decision not to stage Orfeo; after briefly discussing the stage conventions of Monteverdi's day, Gaetano Cesari concluded: 'With such scenic elements I believe that a historically faithful production of L'Orfeo might well have impeded the understanding of the music, which would have been compromised and receded into the background'. See the Rivista Musicale Italiana 17 (1910), 136.

29 See Nigel Fortune, 'The Rediscovery of "Orfeo"', in John Whenham, ed., Claudio Monteverdi: Orfeo (Cambridge, 1986), 86.

30 The New York Times, 15 April 1912, 9.

31 Max Schneider, 'Monteverdi's Orfeo in Breslau', Zeitschrift der internationalen Musikgesellschaft 14 (1912–13), 327–29. Erich Freund, 'Claudio Monteverdi's "Orfeo"', Die Musik 12/4 (1912–13), 26–27. Ernst Neufeldt, 'L'Orféo de Monteverde à Breslau', Revue musicale S.I.M., July–August 1913, 60.

32 Emile Vuillermoz, 'Le Couronnement de Poppée', Revue musicale S.I.M., 15 February 1913, 45.

33 The Galuppi opera was conducted by Ermanno Wolf-Ferrari, whose own operas of the period – notably Il Segreto di Susanna and I Quatro Rusteghi – were strongly indebted to Baroque models.

34 Die Musik 40/3 (1911), 55.

35 Oskar Hagen, 'Die Bearbeitung der Händelschen Rodelinde und ihre Uraufführung am 26.

36 See Rudolf Steglich, 'Die neue Händel-Opern-Bewegung', Händel-Jahrbuch 1 (1928), 83ff.

37 Hagen, op. cit., 727.

38 Edward J. Dent, 'Handel on the Stage', Music and Letters 16 (1935), 176.

39 Steglich, op. cit., 'Übersicht über die szenische Händel-Aufführungen von Sommer 1920 bis Sommer 1927' [foldout table inserted at page 158].

40 Steglich, 'Händels Oper Rodelinde und ihre neue Göttinger Bühnenfassung', Zeitschrift für Musikwissenschaft 3 (1920–21), 518–34.

41 Hermann Roth, 'Händel's Ballettoper Ariodante am Stuttgarter Landestheater,' NZ 88 (1927), 270–72.

42 Heinz Fuhrmann, 'Händelopern-Renaissance im alten, neueröffneten Celler Schlosstheater', ibid. 94 (1935), 642–43. Dent, op. cit., 178.

43 Hellmuth Christian Wolff, Die Händel-Oper auf der modernen Bühne (Leipzig, 1957), 38.

44 On modern stagings of Handel's oratorios, see Winton Dean, Handel's Dramatic Oratorios and Masques (London, 1959), 122ff. and 622ff.; and 'How Should Handel's Oratorios Be Staged?', The Musical Newsletter 4/1 (1971), 11–15.

45 MT 66 (1925), 137.

46 Hugh Carey, Duet for Two Voices (Cambridge, 1979), 119. Percy Scholes, '"Semele" at Cambridge', MT 66 (1925), 252.

47 Carey, op. cit., 119.

48 Dent, 'Handel on the Stage', Music and Letters 16 (1935), 184. Dent suggested that singers perform the A section of the aria to the cadence at the end of the 'exposition', then proceed straight into the B section, adjusting the harmonies as necessary. At the end of the B section, they were to pick up where they had left off in the A section and finish with the 'recapitulation'.

49 Scholes, op. cit., 252.

50 MT 66 (1925), 137.

51 Dent, op. cit., 180. For an expression of similar views fifty years later, see J. Merrill Knapp, 'Problems with Handel Opera', Händel-Jahrbuch 29 (1983), 33–38.

52 Carey, op. cit., 107.

53 MT 61 (1920), 338. See also Michael Hurd, 'The Glastonbury Festivals', ibid. 126 (1985), 435–37.

54 See Eric Walter White, 'A Note on Opera at Oxford', in F. W. Sternfeld, Nigel Fortune and

Edward Olleson, eds., *Essays on Opera and English Music* (Oxford, 1975).
55 Frank Howes, 'Monteverde's "Orfeo" at Oxford', *MT* 67 (1926), 61.
56 *The Times*, 7 December 1927, 12.
57 Ibid., 1 January 1930, 10.
58 Ibid., 4 January 1930, 8.
59 Oscar Thompson, 'Opera Afield, from Schönberg Back to Handel', *The Sackbut* 10 (1929–30), 68–72.
60 All quotations in this section are taken from *Baroque Opera at Smith College 1926–31* (New York, 1966). See also Philip Keppler, 'Baroque Beachhead', *Opera News*, 1 December 1958, 30–33.
61 David Hall, *The Record Book* (New York, 1940), 435.
62 Olin Downes, 'A Modern Version of Poppea', *The New York Times*, 7 November 1937, sect. IX, 7.
63 Ibid., 10 November 1937, 28.
64 Andreas Liess, *Carl Orff*, trans. Adelheid and Herbert Parkin (London, 1966), 77–78.
65 Elsa Respighi, *Ottorino Respighi*, trans. Gwyn Morris (London, 1962), 152.
66 André Tessier, 'Le Retour d'Ulysse de Monteverde (à la Petite Scène)', *RM*(2), 1 June 1925, 252–54. An offshoot of the Schola Cantorum, the Petite Scène belatedly realized Bordes's dream of a company devoted to early opera. See note 20 above and Chapter 3, note 16.
67 Henry Prunières, '*Le Triomphe de l'Amour* [Lully], à l'Opéra', *RM*(2), 1 February 1925, 168–70.
68 H. Prunières, 'Le Triomphe de l'Amour', ibid., January 1933, 44–45.
69 Ibid., April 1935, 285.
70 Hellmuth Christian Wolff, *Die Händel-Oper auf der modernen Bühne* (Leipzig, 1957), 22.
71 Oliver Daniel, *Stokowski: A Counterpoint of View* (New York, 1982), 441.
72 Nigel Fortune, 'The Rediscovery of "Orfeo"', in John Whenham, ed., *Claudio Monteverdi: Orfeo* (Cambridge, 1986), 105.
73 *Purcell's 'The Fairy Queen' as presented by the Sadler's Wells Ballet and the Covent Garden Opera* (London, 1948), 32.
74 Janet Flanner, *Paris Journal 1944–65* (New York, 1977), 176.
75 Henry Quittard, '"Hippolyte et Aricie" à l'Opéra', *RM*(1), 1 June 1908, 319–25.
76 Henry Prunières, '*Le Triomphe de l'Amour* [Lully], à l'Opéra', *RM*(2), 1 February 1925, 170.
77 Meredith Little, 'Recent Research in European Dance, 1400–1800', *EM* 14 (1986), 4–14.

78 This and the following quotations are taken from Walther Siegmund-Schultze, 'Report from Halle; the Handel Opera Renaissance', *Current Musicology* 7 (1968), 68–74.
79 *The Times*, 7 January 1930, 12.
80 Michael and Mollie Hardwick, *Alfred Deller: A Singularity of Voice* (London, 1968; repr. London and New York, 1980), 141.
81 Ibid., 75.
82 Raymond Leppard, 'Cavalli's Operas', *Proceedings of the Royal Musical Association* 93 (1966), 67–76.
83 Robert Donington, *The Interpretation of Early Music*, rev. ed. (London, 1977), 58.
84 *MT* 125 (1984), 454.
85 *The New Yorker*, 15 March 1976, 137.
86 Ibid., 18 October 1978, 148.
87 Will Crutchfield, 'Handel opera: a tercentenary report', *EM* 14 (1986), 147.
88 Andrew Porter, 'Opera Seria Today: A Credo', in Michael Collins and Elise K. Kirk, eds., *Opera and Vivaldi* (Austin, 1984), 364.
89 Ernst Neufeldt, 'L'Orféo de Monteverde à Breslau', *Revue musicale S.I.M.*, July–August 1913, 60.

CHAPTER 8
THE EARLY MUSIC SUBCULTURE

1 Allen Percival obituary in *MT* 112 (1971), 478–79. A discography of Dart's recordings is in Ian Bent, ed., *Source Materials and the Interpretation of Music* (London, 1981), 438–41.
2 Charles van den Borren, 'La pureté du style et l'interprétation de la musique du Moyen âge', *Revue internationale de musique* 2 (1938), 279.
3 Noah Greenberg letter to Edward Lowinsky, 30 July 1961 (New York Pro Musica Archives, New York Public Library, JOB 82–5). I am grateful to Ros Morley Storr for calling this to my attention.
4 Paul Collaer, 'Notes musicologiques: Le IXe festival de musique de chambre d'Haslemere et le retour à la musique ancienne', *RM*(2), September–October 1933, 220. Collaer, a noted conductor as well as musicologist, founded the Concerts anciens et modernes in Brussels in 1933 to present both pre-Classical and contemporary music.
5 Michael and Mollie Hardwick, *Alfred Deller: A Singularity of Voice* (London, 1968; repr. London and New York, 1980), 176.
6 Robert Donington, *The Interpretation of Early*

Music, rev. ed. (London, 1977), 55.

7 John M. Thomson in *EM* 1 (1973), 1.

8 David Munrow, *Instruments of the Middle Ages and Renaissance* (London, 1976), in album of same title featuring the Early Music Consort of London (EMI SAN 391-2).

9 Anthony Lewis in *EM* 4 (1976), 376.

10 Jacques Lonchampt, 'The Private World of Gustav Leonhardt', *The Manchester Guardian Weekly*, 21 July 1985. See also Arnd Richter, 'Ich fordere nichts vom Publikum [interview with Leonhardt]', *NZ* 147 (September 1986), 34-30.

11 Joel Cohen and Herb Snitzer, *Reprise: The Extraordinary Revival of Early Music* (Boston and Toronto, 1985), 44.

12 See J. M. Thomson, *Recorder Profiles* (London, 1972), and Edgar Hunt, *The Recorder and Its Music*, rev. ed. (London, 1977), 136ff.

13 See Ichiro Tada, 'The Recorder in Japan', *EM* 10 (1982), 38-40; and Yuske Arimura, 'Japan', ibid. 12 (1984), 159.

14 See János Malina, 'Old Styles, New Trends', *The New Hungarian Quarterly* 26 (1985), 210-13; Peter Phillips, 'A Recent View of Croatia', *Early Music Gazette*, July 1980, 9; and Igor Pomyalko, 'Architecture and Music in Zadar, Yugoslavia', *EM* 4 (1976), 89-91.

15 Judith Davidoff, 'The New York Pro Musica and the Soviet Union', *Journal of the Viola da Gamba Society of America* 2 (1965), 30-33. See also Noah Greenberg, 'A Soft Sound in the USSR,' *High Fidelity* 15 (May 1965), 41-43; F. Jonas, 'New York Pro Musica in Russia', *American Choral Review* 7/4 (1965), 1ff.; and the references to Volkonsky in Boris Schwarz, *Music and Musical Life in Soviet Russia*, rev. ed. (Bloomington, Ind., 1983).

16 For a survey of Telemann performances in East Germany, see *Telemann-Pflege in der DDR* (Magdeburg, 1981).

17 For information on the early music revival in these countries, see, *inter alia*, Robert Wangermée and Philippe Mercier, *La Musique en Wallonie et à Bruxelles* (Brussels, 1982); Ian Parker, 'Spotlight on Holland', *Early Music Gazette*, July 1979, 4-5; Fiona McAlpine, 'Paris: A Survey', *EM* 4 (1976), 91-95; and Adrienne Simpson, 'Early Music in New Zealand', *Dolmetsch Foundation Bulletin*, June 1986.

18 Mauricio Kagel, sleeve note to Deutsche Grammophon 104993. See also Harry W. Gay, 'Kagel's Musik für Renaissance-Instrumente', *Journal of the Viola da Gamba Society of America* 9 (1972), 59.

19 Humphrey Searle and Robert Layton, *Twentieth Century Composers: Britain, Scandinavia and the Netherlands* (New York, 1972), 120.

20 'Ancient and Modern – 3' [interview with Peter Maxwell Davies], *Early Music Gazette*, October 1980, 3-5.

21 Paul Griffiths, *Peter Maxwell Davies* (London, 1982), 146-47.

22 Conrad Cummings, 'Notes on the Music of "Eros and Psyche"', Oberlin Opera Theater programme book, 1983.

23 Paul Hillier quoted by Timothy Robson in 'Conference Report: The Second Symposium on Early Vocal Practices. Case Western Reserve Univ., 29-31 October, 1982', *Journal of Musicology* 2 (1983), 98-102.

24 Laurence Dreyfus, 'Early Music Defended Against Its Devotees', *MQ* 69 (1983), 311.

CHAPTER 9
PLAYING BACH 'HIS WAY'

1 Marie Leonhardt, 'The Present State of Early Music in Northern Europe, in Particular the Netherlands', *EM* 4 (1976), 51.

2 Joseph Kerman, *Contemplating Music: Challenges to Musicology* (Cambridge, Mass., 1985); *Musicology* (London, 1985), 192.

3 Denis Stevens, 'Some Observations on Performance Practice', *Current Musicology* 14 (1972), 161.

4 Cited in Frederick Dorian, *The History of Music in Performance* (New York, 1942), 313.

5 Jules Ecorcheville, 'La Schola Cantorum et le Style de Bach', *Le Mercure musicale et bulletin français de la S.I.M.*, 15 April 1907, 399-406.

6 Arnold Dolmetsch, *The Interpretation of the Music of the XVIIth and XVIIIth Centuries* (London, 1915; repr. Seattle, 1969), vii.

7 Denise Restout, ed., *Landowska on Music* (New York, 1964), 407.

8 Cited in Olin Downes, 'On Interpretation', *The New York Times*, 19 October 1930, sect. IX, 8.

9 Bernard Gagnepain, 'Safford Cape et le "Miracle" Pro Musica Antiqua', *Revue Belge de musicologie* 34-35 (1980-81), 217.

10 Helen S. Slosberg, Mary V. Ullman and Isabel K. Whiting, eds., *Erwin Bodky: A Memorial Tribute* (Waltham, Mass., 1965), 141.

11 Theodor Adorno, 'Bach Defended Against His Devotees,' in *Prisms*, trans. Samuel and Shierry Weber (London, 1967), 133-46.

12 Paul Hindemith, *A Composer's World* (Cambridge, Mass., 1952), 167-68 and 170-71.

13 Adorno, op. cit., 144.

14 Paul Collaer, 'Renaissance de la musique ancienne', *Atti del terzo congresso internazionale di musica* (Florence, 1940), 157.
15 Hans Redlich, *Claudio Monteverdi: Life and Works*, trans. Kathleen Dale (London, 1952), 196. Redlich had first used the phrase *musealer Klangmaterialismus* in 1936.
16 Adrian Cedric Boult and Walter Emery, *The St Matthew Passion, Its Preparation and Performance* (London, 1949), 1.
17 For Gould's views on the harpsichord, see Geoffrey Payzant, *Glenn Gould: Music and Mind* (Toronto, 1978), 101–08.
18 Robert Marshall, 'Bach's "Choruses" Reconstituted', *High Fidelity/Musical America* 32 (October 1982), 64ff. Marshall was responding to arguments advanced by Rifkin in 'Bach's "Choruses" – Less Than They Seem?', ibid. (September 1982), 42–44. See also Rifkin's 'Bach's "Choruses": The Record Cleared', ibid. (December 1982), 58–59.
19 Robert Marshall, review of Telefunken Bach cantata recordings, *MQ* 59 (1973), 148.
20 Daniel Waitzman, 'Historical Versus Musical Authenticity', *The American Recorder* 21 (1980), 11–13.
21 Arnold Dolmetsch, introduction to Gerald R. Hayes, *Musical Instruments and Their Music*, vol. 2 (London, 1930), ix.
22 Manfred Bukofzer, 'On the Performance of Renaissance Music,' *Proceedings of the Music Teachers National Association* (1941), 225–35.
23 Redlich, op. cit., 196.
24 Robert Donington, *Baroque Music: Style and Performance* (London, 1981), 166–67.
25 John M. Thomson, 'Musica Reservata', *EM* 4 (1976), 517.
26 Richard Taruskin's contribution to the symposium 'The Limits of Authenticity: A Discussion', *EM* 12 (1984), 5.
27 Joseph Kerman, *Musicology* (London, 1985), 182–217.
28 Waitzman, op. cit., 11.
29 Donald J. Grout, 'Historical Authenticity in the Performance of Old Music', in *Essays on Music in Honor of Archibald Thompson Davison* (Cambridge, Mass., 1957), 341.
30 Howard Mayer Brown, 'Performing practice', *The New Grove Dictionary of Music and Musicians*, vol. 14, 390.
31 Hans Keller, 'Arrangement for or against?' *MT* 110 (1969), 23. Keller returned to the attack in 'Whose Authenticity?' *EM* 12 (1984), 517–19.
32 Peter Hill, '"Authenticity" in Contemporary Music', *Tempo* 159 (December 1986), 7.
33 Richard Taruskin, 'On Letting the Music Speak for Itself', *Journal of Musicology* 1 (1982), 338–49.
34 Kerman, op. cit., 203.
35 Denise Restout, ed., *Landowska on Music* (New York, 1964), 407.
36 Paul Henry Lang, 'Performance Practice and Musicology', in Martin Bente, ed., *Musik, Edition, Interpretation: Gedenkschrift Günter Henle* (Munich, 1980), 315.
37 Will Crutchfield, 'A Report from the Musical Battlefield', *The New York Times*, 28 July 1985, sect. II, 8.
38 Michael Morrow, 'Musical Performance and Authenticity', *EM* 6 (1978), 243.
39 See Randall R. Dipert, 'The Composer's Intentions: An Examination of Their Relevance for Performance', *MQ* 66 (1980), 205–18.
40 Zuzana Růžičková, 'The Manner of Interpretation', *EM* 8 (1980), 172.
41 Kerman, op. cit., 193.
42 Putnam Aldrich, 'The "Authentic" Performance of Baroque Music', in *Essays on Music in Honor of Archibald Thompson Davison* (Cambridge, Mass., 1957), 166.
43 Laurence Dreyfus, 'Early Music Defended Against Its Devotees', *MQ* 69 (1983), 313.

CHAPTER 10
BEETHOVEN, BRAHMS AND BEYOND?

1 Joseph Kerman, *Contemplating Music: Challenges to Musicology* (Cambridge, Mass., 1985); *Musicology* (London, 1985), 209.
2 See Alfred Heuss's report from Leipzig in the *Zeitschrift der internationalen Musikgesellschaft* 8 (1906–07), 138–39.
3 Hugo Daffner in *NZ* 68 (1907), 536.
4 Eva and Paul Badura-Skoda, *Mozart-Interpretation* (Vienna and Stuttgart, 1957); translated by Leo Black as *Interpreting Mozart on the Keyboard* (London, 1962), 7.
5 Ralph Kirkpatrick, *Early Years* (New York, 1985), 127.
6 Malcolm Bilson, 'The Viennese Fortepiano of the Late 18th Century', *EM* 8 (1980), 158–62.
7 Will Crutchfield, 'A Report from the Musical Battlefield', *The New York Times*, 28 July 1985, sect. II, 1.
8 Robert Winter, 'Performing Nineteenth-Century Music on Nineteenth-Century Instruments', *19th Century Music* 1 (1977), 163–75. See also Winter's 'The Emperor's New Clothes:

19th-Century Instruments Revisited', ibid. 7 (1984), 251–65.

9   Sergiu Luca, 'Looking Beyond Music's Missing Link', *Symphony News* 27 (October 1976), 14–16.

10   John Rockwell, 'The Symphony Orchestra Looks Back to the Future', *The New York Times*, 22 February 1987, sect. II, 1.

11   In 1907, the music publishers Breitkopf & Härtel called for the establishment of a central office to promote revivals of early music. Among other things, the office was to assist conductors in locating scores by German composers; see the *Zeitschrift der internationalen Musikgesellschaft* 9 (1907–08), 80–81.

12   Interview with author, 21 October 1984.

13   See Jean W. Seiler, 'Degree Programs in Early Music in the United States and Canada', *The American Recorder* 24 (January 1983), 15–19.

14   Allan Kozinn, 'Christopher Hogwood Takes on the Modern Orchestra', *Symphony* 35 (December 1984), 80. Rockwell, op. cit., sect. II, 26.

15   Kerman, op. cit., 214–15.

16   Winter, op. cit., 173.

17   Paul Henry Lang, 'Rigor Antiquarii: The Great "Performance Practice" Muddle', *High Fidelity/Musical America* 29 (July 1979), 126.

18   Martin Dreyer, 'York Early Music', *MT* 127 (1986), 495–96.

ACKNOWLEDGMENTS

American Society of Ancient Instruments, Pa. 19; Erica Anderson 13; Valda Aveling 15; British Broadcasting Corporation 1973 34; The Bach Choir of Bethlehem, Pa. 18; Thomas Binkley, Early Music Institute, Ind. 33; Bibliothèque Royale Albert Ier, Brussels fig. 1 (p. 12); By permission of the Provost and Scholars of King's College, Cambridge 16; Nellie Carson 5; Peggy Deller 31; Silva Devos 7; DGP-Archive 30; Dr Carl Dolmetsch 4; Photo Herb Weitman. Washington University, St. Louis, Mo. 25; Guy Gravett, Glyndebourne Festival Opera 27; Hamburger Theatersammlung 24, Kurpfälzisches Museum der Stadt Heidelberg 2; Hiroshi Kurosawa 35; The Landowska Center, Ct. 10, fig. 3 (p. 104); Jean van Lingen & Phillips Classics 38; Bo Lutoslawski 29; Magenta Music, photo Max Milikan 39; Moeck Verlag, Celle fig. 5 (p. 171); Andres Mustonen 40; Davitt Moroney 32; Münchner Stadtmuseum 14; Deutsches Theatermuseum, Munich 23; National Film Archive, London 36; New York Public Library 21; The Bodleian Library, Oxford (MS. M. Deneke Mendelssohn c. 68, p. 240) 1; Bibliothèque Nationale, Paris 6, 8, 11, 22; Radio Times fig. 4 (p. 148); Alexandra Roosevelt 37; Schola Cantorum Basiliensis fig. 2 (p. 63); Eric Stahlberg/Smith College Archives 26; Emil Telmányi 12; Collection Viollet 9; By permission of the Dean and Canons of Windsor 17; Yale University Archives, Yale University 20; Photo Susan Schimert-Ramme, Opernhaus Zürich 28.

BIBLIOGRAPHY

CHAPTER 1
'THE MUSICAL POMPEII'

Few musical performances have been as exhaustively documented as Mendelssohn's revival of the St Matthew Passion. Martin Geck's exemplary monograph Die Wiederentdeckung der Matthäuspassion im 19. Jahrhundert (Regensburg, 1967) is a convenient point of embarkation for a study of the nineteenth-century Bach revival. Geck quotes extensively from Eduard Devrient's (not wholly reliable) first-hand account of the performance in Meine Erinnerungen an Felix Mendelssohn-Bartholdy und seine Briefe an mich (Leipzig, 1869), translated by Natalia Macfarren as My Recollections of Felix Mendelssohn-Bartholdy (London, 1869). Friedrich Blume's Two Centuries of Bach, translated by Stanley Godman (London and New York, 1950), contains much valuable background information.

The historical resurgence of which the Bach movement was part is examined in Walter Wiora, ed., Die Ausbreitung des Historismus über die Musik (Regensburg, 1969); Herfrid Kier's essay 'Musikalischer Historismus in vormärzlichen Wien' and Monika Lichtenfeld's 'Zur Geschichte, Idee und Ästhetik des historischen Konzerts' are of particular interest. Kier goes into greater detail in Raphael Georg Kiesewetter (Regensburg, 1968) and 'Kiesewetters historische Hauskonzerte', Kirchenmusikalisches Jahrbuch 52 (1968), 95–119. Frederick Niecks's articles on historical concerts in the Monthly Musical Record 12 (1882), 217–22 and 242–45, survey this distinctively nineteenth-century phenomenon. Thomas Day examines the origins of the British early music revival in 'Old Music in England, 1790–1820', Revue Belge de musicologie 26–27 (1972–73), 25–37.

A lively and highly partisan account of Choron's life is L. E. Gauthier's Eloge d'Alexandre Choron (Paris and Caen, 1845). It should be read in conjunction with Gabriel Vauthier's articles on Choron in the Revue musicale 8 (1908), 376–89, 436–42, 613–24 and 664–70; and 9 (1909), 54–58. Willi Kahl offers

a rather more dispassionate assessment in 'Zur musikalischen Renaissancebewegung in Frankreich während der ersten Hälfte des 19. Jahrhunderts', in Dagmar Weise, ed., Festschrift Joseph Schmidt-Görg zum 60. Geburtstag (Bonn, 1957). On the Société de la Moskova and the Niedermeyer school, see H. Kling's 'Le Centenaire d'un compositeur suisse célèbre: Louis Niedermeyer' in Rivista Musicale Italiana 9 (1902), 830–59. Pierre Combe documents the work of Guéranger, Pothier and Mocquereau in great detail in Histoire de la restauration du chant grégorien d'après des documents inédits (Solesmes, 1969).

The standard biography of Fétis is Robert Wangermée's François-Joseph Fétis: Musicologue et compositeur (Brussels, 1951). Wangermée discusses the historical concerts at length and reproduces the programmes in an appendix. Virginia Hancock has made a special study of Brahms's role in the early music revival. 'Brahms's Performances of Early Choral Music' in 19th Century Music 8 (1984), 125–41, complements her illuminating discussion of musical influences in Brahms's Choral Compositions and His Library of Early Music (Ann Arbor, Mich., 1983). Two articles in The New Grove Dictionary of Music and Musicians – 'Cecilian movement' by Karl Gustav Fellerer and 'Chorus' by James G. Smith and Percy Young – are concise introductions to the nineteenth-century choral revival.

CHAPTER 2
'THE APOSTLE OF
RETROGRESSION'

Arnold Dolmetsch and Richard Terry, the great pioneers of England's early music revival, have been well served by their biographers. Margaret Campbell's Dolmetsch: The Man and His Work (London and Seattle, 1975) is a mine of factual information and stimulating leads, superseding the vivid but naturally one-sided picture that Mabel Dolmetsch painted in her Personal Recollections of Arnold Dolmetsch (London, 1958). Westminster Retrospect by Terry's pupil Hilda Andrews (London, 1948) describes his work at Westminster Cathedral with commendable clarity and insight.

Dolmetsch's The Interpretation of the Music of the XVIIth and XVIIIth Centuries (London, 1915; repr. Seattle, 1969) is essential for an understanding of his musical philosophy. Good sources for general historical background are Peter Hardwick's unpublished dissertation 'The Revival of Interest in Old English Music in Victorian England, and the Impact of This Revival on Music Composed into the Twentieth Century' (U. of Washington, 1973), and Percy A. Scholes's The Mirror of Music 1844–1944 (London, 1947), an anthology drawn from the pages of the Musical Times. George Bernard Shaw's reviews of Dolmetsch and his contemporaries are gathered in Music in London 1890–94 (London, 1932); unfortunately, John Runciman's equally stimulating articles in the Saturday Review have not been reprinted. Two perceptive appreciations are Ernest Newman's 'Arnold Dolmetsch' in the Sunday Times of 17 March 1940, and Thurston Dart's 'The Achievement of Arnold Dolmetsch' in The Listener 59 (1958), 400–02.

Of the many memoirs written by Dolmetsch's friends, students and contemporaries, J. A. Fuller Maitland's A Door-Keeper of Music (London, 1929) and Edmund H. Fellowes's Memoirs of an Amateur Musician (London, 1946) are particularly worthwhile. Also informative are Stanley Godman's 'Francis William Galpin: Music Maker' in the Galpin Society Journal 12 (1959), 8–16, and Steuart Wilson's 'The English Singers' in Recorded Sound 20 (1965), 375–81. Anselm Hughes recounts the early history of the Plainsong and Mediaeval Music Society in Septuagesima (London, 1959).

CHAPTER 3
FROM SCHOLA TO SCHOLA

René de Castéra offers an insider's account of the Chanteurs de St Gervais and the founding of the Schola Cantorum in Dix années d'action musicale religieuse (Paris, 1902). Philip M. Dowd gives a better balanced appraisal in his unpublished dissertation 'Charles Bordes and the Schola Cantorum of Paris: Their Influence on the Liturgical Music of the Late 19th and Early 20th Centuries' (Catholic U. of America, 1969). Vincent d'Indy et al., La Schola Cantorum en 1925 (Paris, 1927) fills in the Schola's later history. A sampling of sympathetic critical reaction to the Schola may be found in Les Ecrits de Paul Dukas sur la musique (Paris, 1948) and in Debussy on Music, edited by François Lesure and translated by Richard Langham Smith (London and New York, 1977). Ursula Eckhart-Bäcker deals with the turn-of-the-century early music movement in France in Frankreichs Musik zwischen Romantik und Moderne (Regensburg, 1965), 228–33.

Régina Patorni-Casadesus's Ma famille Casadesus: Souvenirs d'une claveciniste (Paris, 1962), though self-serving and factually capricious, is the best source of information about the Casadesus family's Société des Instruments Anciens. The definitive biography of Wanda Landowska remains to be written; Howard Schott's 'Wanda Landowska, A Centenary Appraisal' in Early Music 7 (1979), 467–72, sheds light on the magnitude and richness of her achievement. Denise Restout, ed., Landowska on Music (New York, 1964), contains a biographical essay as well as a generous selection of excerpts from her writings. Landowska's Musique ancienne (Paris, 1909) was translated into English by William Aspenwall Bradley as Music of the Past (New York, 1924). Schott offers an excellent historical overview in 'The Harpsichord Revival', Early Music 2 (1974), 85–95.

From 1899 to 1914 the Zeitschrift der internationalen Musikgesellschaft published regular listings of early music performances around the world; students of the revival will find them a useful guide to who was doing what during that period. Christian Döbereiner's Zur Renaissance alter Musik (Tutzing, 1950) and 50 Jahre alte Musik in München (Munich, 1955), and Paul Grümmer's Begegnungen (Munich, 1963), portray the revival in Germany through the eyes of two of its protagonists. H. H. Eggebrecht's Die Orgelbewegung (Stuttgart, 1967) is a concise and thorough study of the Organ Revival; Peter Williams covers some of the same ground in A New History of the Organ (Bloomington, Ind., 1980). Hilmar Höckner's Die Musik in der deutschen Jugendbewegung (Wolfenbüttel, 1927) and Karl Vötterle's Haus unterm Stern (Kassel, 1969) provide much insight into the Youth Movement. Hermann Moeck's 'The Twentieth-Century Renaissance of the Recorder in Germany' in The American Recorder 23 (May 1982), 61–67, and Edgar Hunt's The Recorder and Its

Music, rev. ed. (London, 1977) offer complementary perspectives on the recorder movement.

Bernard Gagnepain's 'Safford Cape et le "Miracle" Pro Musica Antiqua', in the *Revue Belge de musicologie* 34–35 (1980–81), 204–19, is a thorough if somewhat uncritical portrait. On the Société de Musique d'Autrefois, see Jean Jenkins's 'Geneviève Thibault, Madame H. de Chambure: An Appreciation' in *Early Music* 4 (1976), 39–41, and Thibault's own 'A la Société de Musique d'Autrefois', in Denise Mayer and Pierre Souvtchinsky, eds., *Roger Desormière et son temps* (Monaco, 1966). The history of the Schola Cantorum Basiliensis is ably chronicled by its former director, Wulf Arlt, in 'Zur Idee und zur Geschichte eines "Lehr- und Forschungsinstituts für alte Musik" in den Jahren 1933 bis 1970', in Peter Reidemeister and Veronika Gutman, eds., *Alte Musik: Praxis und Reflexion* (Winterthur, 1983).

CHAPTER 4 'BACK TO BACH'

The early music revival's impact on composition in the nineteenth and twentieth centuries is a large topic. I know of no comprehensive treatment, but many specialized studies exist. To the aforementioned works by Virginia Hancock, Peter Hardwick and Philip M. Dowd may be added Siegfried Borris's 'Historische Symptome in den Kompositionsverfahren des 20. Jahrhunderts', in Heinrich Poos, ed., *Festschrift Ernst Pepping* (Berlin, 1971); and Adam Adrio's 'Renewal and Rejuvenation', in Friedrich Blume et al., *Protestant Church Music* (New York, 1974; London, 1975).

The literature on Neoclassicism, on the other hand, is comparatively plentiful. Among the books I found helpful were Ferruccio Busoni's *The Essence of Music*, translated by Rosamund Ley (London, 1957); Alfredo Casella's *Music in My Time*, translated by Spencer Norton (Norman, Okla., 1955); Karen Forsythe's *Ariadne auf Naxos by Hugo van Hofmannsthal and Richard Strauss* (London, 1982) [especially Chapter 1: 'Divertissement, Molière, and Historical Authenticity in the 1912 *Ariadne*']; Paul Hindemith's *A Composer's World* (Cambridge, Mass., 1952); Constant Lambert's *Music Ho!* (London, 1934; repr. New York, 1967); and Ernst Krenek's *Music Here and Now*, translated by Barthold Fles (New York, 1939). Stravinsky's pronouncements on Neoclassicism are scattered throughout his

books of conversations with Robert Craft, notably *Memories and Commentaries* (London and Garden City, N.J., 1960), *Expositions and Developments* (London and New York, 1962) and *Retrospectives and Conclusions* (New York, 1969). Alan Lessem provides a good overview in 'Schoenberg, Stravinsky, and Neo-Classicism: The Issues Reexamined' in the *Musical Quarterly* 68 (1982), 527–42.

The fascinating subject of musical forgeries merits fuller examination than it has received. Despite the diligent musicological sleuthing that has uncovered scores of misattributions in recent years, no account has superseded the compilation that Charles L. Cudworth made in his famous article 'Ye Olde Spuriosity Shoppe or, Put it in the *Anhang*' in *Notes* 12 (1954–55), 25–40 and 533–53. Among the many surveys of modern music written for early instruments are Hans-Martin Linde's 'Neue Musik für alte Instrumente', in Peter Reidemeister and Veronika Gutman, eds., *Alte Musik: Praxis und Reflexion* (Winterthur, 1983); Robin de Smet's *Published Music for the Viola da Gamba and Other Viols* (Detroit, 1971); Michael Civiello's 'A Case for Contemporary Music' in *The Harpsichord* 2/1 (1969), 8–9; Donald Nitz's 'More New Music for Harpsichord', ibid. 2/3 (1969), 15–16; Michael Steinberg's 'Some Observations on the Harpsichord in Twentieth Century Music' in *Perspectives of New Music* 1 (1963), 189–94; Niall O'Loughlin's 'The Recorder in 20th-Century Music' in *Early Music* 10 (1982), 36–37; Peter H. Bloom's, 'New Music for Old Flutes' in *Flute Talk* (forthcoming); Harry Danks's *The Viola d'Amore* (Paris, 1976); Karl Stumpf's 'Der Viola d'Amore in der neuen Musik' in *Musikerziehung* 21 (1968), 230–31; and Michael Thomas's 'Modern Music for the Clavichord' in *The Consort* 18 (1961), 96–101.

CHAPTER 5
OLD MUSIC IN THE NEW WORLD

Paul C. Echols gives an excellent survey of America's early music movement in his article 'Early-music revival' in *The New Grove Dictionary of American Music* (New York and London, 1986), vol. 2, 2–6. The only significant omissions in his account are Sam Franko's 'Concerts of Old Music', the Baroque opera revivals at Smith College in the 1920s and 1930s, and Walter Damrosch's pioneering Musical Art Society. The latter's programmes from 1894 to 1920 can be consulted at the Library of Congress. In *Chords and Discords* (New York, 1938), Franko recounts his attempts to promote pre-Classical instrumental music in the early years of the century.

The *History of the Handel and Haydn Society of Boston, Massachusetts* by C. C. Perkins, J. S. Dwight, W. F. Bradbury and C. Guild (Boston and Cambridge, Mass., 1883–1934) is exhaustive and ponderous, as befits such a venerable institution; H. Earle Johnson treats the subject in a livelier fashion in *Hallelujah, Amen!* (Boston, 1965). Raymond Walters's *The Bethlehem Bach Choir* (Boston and New York, 1918) contains illuminating extracts from contemporary reviews. Morris Steinert tells his own story in Jane Maslin, ed., *Reminiscences of Morris Steinert* (New York and London, 1900), an autobiographical sequel to his *The M. Steinert Collection of Keyed and Stringed Instruments* (New York, 1893).

Rose Fay Thomas quotes liberally from her father's diaries and other writings in *Memoirs of Theodore Thomas* (New York, 1911). Charles Edward Russell amplifies her account in *The American Orchestra and Theodore Thomas* (New York and Garden City, N.J., 1927). Dolmetsch's activities in the United States are covered by Margaret Campbell and Mabel Dolmetsch in the books cited under Chapter 2. The histories of two prominent early music organizations are briefly chronicled in *The American Society of Ancient Instruments* (Philadelphia, 1983) and Henry S. and Sophie H. Drinker's *Accademia dei Dilettanti di Musica 1930–1960* (Merion, Pa., 1960).

Ralph Kirkpatrick's *Early Years* (New York, 1985), despite its frequently snide and self-righteous tone, yields a good deal of information about the revival from the late 1920s onwards. Frank Hubbard tells about his career in 'Reconstructing the Harpsichord', in Howard Schott, ed., *The Historical Harpsichord*, vol. 1 (New York, 1984). Also useful, though erratically edited, are the interviews with builders and players in *The Harpsichord*, especially the portraits of Hubbard, 5/1 (1972), 5–15; John Challis, 2/3 (1969), 14–23; and Claude Jean Chiasson, 5/3 (1972), 4–9ff. Peter Williams devotes a section of his article 'Organ' in *The New Grove* (vol. 13, 774–75) to the Organ Revival in the United States.

A comprehensive history of the American Recorder Society is promised. Meanwhile, much pertinent material can be found in Suzanne Bloch's 'Saga of a Twentieth-Century Lute Pioneer' in the *Journal of the Lute Society of America* 2

(1969), 37–43, and in the short essays by various contributors to 'Reflections on the Early Music Scene' in *The American Recorder* 26 (1985), 4–11. Edward J. Kottick sketches the growth of the American collegium movement in *The Collegium: A Handbook* (Stonington, Conn., 1977). Prime sources for the Yale Collegium Musicum are Eckhart Richter's 'Paul Hindemith as Director of the Yale Collegium Musicum' in *College Music Symposium* 18 (1978), 20–44; and 'Hindemith's Performances of Old Music' by Howard Boatwright in the *Hindemith-Jahrbuch* 3 (1973), 39–62. The complete programmes of the Cambridge Society for Early Music are reproduced in Helen S. Slosberg, Mary V. Ullman and Isabel K. Whiting, eds., *Erwin Bodky: A Memorial Tribute* (Waltham, Mass., 1965).

A comprehensive, thoroughly documented account of the New York Pro Musica is urgently needed. Noah Greenberg's papers and much other material relevant to such a study are in the Pro Musica Archives at the New York Public Library. S. J. Gaskill's unpublished thesis 'The Artist as Manager: Noah Greenberg and the New York Pro Musica' (American U., 1984) concentrates on one aspect of his multi-faceted career. Other useful accounts are Richard Murphy's 'Giving New Life to Old Music' in *Horizon*, November 1960, 88–95; and Susan T. Sommer's 'Vale atque Ave: The Late Pro Musica and the State of Early Music in America Today' in *The Musical Newsletter* 5/3 (1975), 15–17.

Joel Cohen profiles Greenberg and other American early musicians in *Reprise: The Extraordinary Revival of Early Music* (Boston and Toronto, 1985). More information can be found in Elaine Brody's 'The Performance of Early Music in the United States Today', in the colloquium *Musica Antiqua: Acta Scientifica* [Festival of Old Music of Central and Eastern Europe] (Bydgoszca, 1978); Alejandro Planchart's 'The Performance of Early Music in America' in the *Journal of Musicology* 1 (1982), 19–28; and Jean W. Seiler's survey of 'Degree Programs in Early Music in the United States and Canada' in *The American Recorder* 24 (1983), 15–19.

CHAPTER 6
'TO OPEN WIDE THE WINDOWS'

Two indispensable aids to discographic research on early music are Trevor Croucher's *Early Music Discography* (London, 1981) and James

Coover's and Richard Colvig's *Medieval and Renaissance Music on Long-Playing Records* (Detroit, 1964), with its supplement for 1962–71 (Detroit, 1973). Both contain excellent composer and performer indices, though the lack of information on recording dates (a common problem with discographies) limits their usefulness to the historian. Derrick Henry covers much the same territory as Coover and Colvig in *The Listener's Guide to Medieval and Renaissance Music* (New York and Poole, 1983), augmenting his selective list of recordings with commentary on the music and performances.

For pre-LP recordings, the basic references are R. D. Darrell's *The Gramophone Shop Encyclopedia of Recorded Music* (New York, 1936) and later editions under successive editors; and Francis F. Clough's and G. J. Cuming's *The World's Encyclopedia of Recorded Music* (London, 1952), with supplements up to 1955. The latter contains detailed listings of the various historical anthologies. The publication on microform of the monumental *Rigler and Deutsch Record Index* (Syracuse, N.Y., 1985) has been a godsend for discographic researchers. A complete catalogue of 78-rpm recordings in several major American sound archives, it is vastly more comprehensive and easy of access than any previous compilation. Excellent performer and composer indices, as well as photographs of the record labels themselves, make it an invaluable resource. Roberto Bauer's *The New Catalogue of Historical Records 1898–1908/09* (London, 1947) lists vocal and a handful of instrumental recordings. Another useful discography is Fritz Zobeley's 'Ältere Musik auf Schallplatten' in the *Zeitschrift für Musikwissenschaft* 14 (1931–32), 117–27, which covers mainly German releases.

In *The Record Book* (New York, 1940) and *Records: 1950 Edition* (New York, 1950), David Hall has much to say about the small, independent record companies that played a crucial role in the early music revival. Roland Gelatt touches on this and other relevant topics in *The Fabulous Phonograph 1877–1977*, 2nd ed. (New York, 1977). On the *Anthologie Sonore* and Deutsche Grammophon's *Archiv* series, see René Dumesnil's *Dix siècles de musique: l'Anthologie Sonore* (Paris, 1943) and Fred Hamel's 'A History of Music Recorded for Educational Purposes' in *Music in Education* (UNESCO, 1955), 260–63. Three articles in *Concerto* 2 (1984), 42–62, give an excellent historical overview of early music recordings: Martin Elste's 'Propagierung und Verrat der Alten Musik', Helmut Schmitz's 'Der

ferne Klang' and Stephan Schmid's 'Leonhardt, Harnoncourt und Andere'. Elizabeth Roche presents some telling statistics in 'Early Music on Records in the Last 25 Years' in the *Musical Times* 120 (1979), 34–36 and 215–17.

Discographies of specific composers and performers are found in Michael Gray's and Gerald D. Gibson's *Bibliography of Discographies*, vol. 1: *Classical Music, 1925–1975* (New York and London, 1977). To their listings should be added the discographies in Michael and Mollie Hardwick's *Alfred Deller: A Singularity of Voice* (London, 1968; repr. London and New York, 1980), 193–97; Denise Restout, ed., *Landowska on Music* (New York, 1964), 411–23; Bernard Gagnepain's 'Safford Cape et le "Miracle" Pro Musica Antiqua', *Revue Belge de musicologie* 34–35 (1980–81), 214; and Nanie Bridgeman's 'On the Discography of Josquin and the Interpretation of His Music on Recordings', in Edward Lowinsky, ed., *Josquin des Prez* (London, 1976), 633–41.

Roche offers a penetrating analysis of the BBC's Third Programme and its legacy in 'Early Music and the BBC', *Musical Times* 120 (1979), 821–32 and 912–14. In the 1920s and 1930s, especially, the major music journals gave extensive coverage to radio and, to a lesser extent, film. Periodic reviews, reports and listings of early music broadcasts and film scores can be found in the *Musical Times*, the *Neue Zeitschrift für Musik*, the *Revue musicale*, *Musical America* and elsewhere. Record magazines such as *Gramophone* in England, *Fanfare* and *High Fidelity* in the United States, *Disques* in France, *HiFi Stereophonie* in Germany and *Musica e Dischi* in Italy are founts of information about recordings and broadcasts, though much of it is rather difficult to track down.

CHAPTER 7
STAGING A COMEBACK

Alfred Loewenberg's *Annals of Opera 1597–1940*, 3rd ed. (London, 1978; revised edition by the late Harold Rosenthal in preparation) is an indispensable tool for the operatic historian. It gives the dates and locations of most of the major Baroque opera revivals in modern times. The standard book on the Handel revival is Hellmuth Christian Wolff's *Die Händel-Oper auf der modernen Bühne* (Leipzig, 1957). Wolff describes many of the early German productions, supplementing his brief but extremely informative text with dozens of historic photographs. One of Wolff's prime sources, still worth consulting, is Rudolf Steglich's 'Die neue Händel-Opern-Bewegung' in the *Händel-Jahrbuch* 1 (1928), 71–158.

Winton Dean writes from a somewhat broader perspective in 'The Recovery of Handel's Operas', in Christopher Hogwood and Richard Luckett, eds., *Music in Eighteenth-Century England: Essays in Memory of Charles Cudworth* (Cambridge, 1983). In an appendix to *Handel's Operas 1704–1726* (Oxford, 1987), Dean and John Merrill Knapp list modern stagings of Handel's first seventeen operas up to 1984. Among Dean's many other books and articles on Handel, two should be singled out in this context: 'Twenty Years of Handel Opera' in *Opera* 26 (1975), 924–30; and 'How Should Handel's Oratorios Be Staged?' in the *Musical Newsletter* 4/1 (1975), 11–15. Edward J. Dent's 'Handel on the Stage' in *Music and Letters* 16 (1935), 173–87, reflects the thinking of a distinguished Handelian of an earlier generation. For a Marxist approach to Handel's operas, see Walther Siegmund-Schultze's 'Report from Halle: the Handel Opera Renaissance' in *Current Musicology* 7 (1968), 68–74; and Siegmund-Schultze, ed., *Fragen der Aufführungspraxis und Interpretation Händelscher Werke in Vergangenheit und Gegenwart* (Halle, 1980). Walter Meyerhoff, ed., *50 Jahre Göttinger Händel-Festspiele* (Kassel, 1970) contains annals of the Göttingen Festival performances from 1920 to 1970, as well as an essay tracing the spread of the Handel opera revival to other countries.

Inevitably, Handel has all but monopolized the attention of historians of the Baroque opera revival. Much spadework remains to be done on the French and Italian repertoires. Nigel Fortune's 'The Rediscovery of "Orfeo"', in John Whenham, ed., *Claudio Monteverdi: Orfeo* (Cambridge, 1986), is an auspicious start. One hopes this model of scholarly and critical acumen will inspire more such particularized studies in operatic performance history. Another welcome addition to the literature is Michael Collins and Elise K. Kirk, eds., *Opera and Vivaldi* (Austin, 1984), which contains stimulating essays on Baroque opera production by Andrew Porter, Alan Curtis and Shirley Wynne.

A great deal of information about Baroque opera revivals is tucked away in books, pamphlets and articles about individual opera companies and other producing organizations. *Baroque Opera at Smith College 1926–1931* (New York, 1966) commemorates Werner Josten's pioneering work in America. It consists of programmes, reviews and production photographs, presumably compiled as a scrapbook by a contemporary archivist. The flavour and ambience of England's early Monteverdi revivals are captured in Eric Walter White's 'A Note on Opera at Oxford', in F. W. Sternfeld, Nigel Fortune and Edward Olleson, eds., *Essays on Opera and English Music* (Oxford, 1975); and in Robert Ponsonby's and Richard Kent's *The Oxford University Opera Club: A Short History (1925–1950)* (Oxford, 1950).

CHAPTER 8
THE EARLY MUSIC SUBCULTURE

The most wide-ranging portrait of the post-war early music revival is Joel Cohen's and Herb Snitzer's aforementioned *Reprise: The Extraordinary Revival of Early Music* (Boston and Toronto, 1985). Cohen (the director of the Boston Camerata) writes as a participant in the revival, not as a historian, but his breezy essays are enjoyable and often provocative. The rather odd assortment of early musicians' photographs by Snitzer adds little to the text. The best portrait of Thurston Dart is Allen Percival's biographical essay in Ian Bent, ed., *Source Materials and the Interpretation of Music* (London, 1981). David Scott's judicious article on David Munrow in *The New Grove* should be read in conjunction with the tributes published shortly after his death in *Early Music* 4 (1976), 376–80. Gustav Leonhardt has been interviewed many times; Arnd Richter's 'Ich fordere nichts vom Publikum' in the *Neue Zeitschrift für Musik* 147/9 (1986), 34–38, is especially enlightening. Also worth noting is Manfred Wagner's conversation with Nikolaus Harnoncourt, 'Ich bin kein Spezialist', in the *Österreichische Musik Zeitschrift* 40 (1985), 352–63.

The many specialized magazines – *Early Music* in England, *Concerto* in Germany, *Continuo* in Canada, *Flûte à bec & instruments anciens* in France, *Tijdschrift voor oude muziek* in Holland, *The American Recorder* in the United States, and so forth – contain a wealth of news, reviews and prognostications. Regrettably, few surveys of early music activity in individual countries have been published. Some helpful sources are Paul C. Echols's aforementioned article in the *New Grove Dictionary of American Music*; Yuske Arimura's 'Japan' in *Early Music* 12 (1984), 159; János

Malina's 'Old Styles, New Trends' in the *New Hungarian Quarterly* 26 (1985), 210–13; John Solum's and Igor Kipnis's 'Old Music in Current Russia' in *High Fidelity/Musical America* 34 (January 1984), 38–39; Robert Wangermée's and Philippe Mercier's *La Musique en Wallonie et à Bruxelles* (Brussels, 1982); Ian Parker's 'Spotlight on Holland' in the *Early Music Gazette*, July 1979, 4–5; Fiona McAlpine's 'Paris: A Survey' in *Early Music* 4 (1976), 91–95; Adrienne Simpson's 'Early Music in New Zealand' in the June 1986 *Dolmetsch Foundation Bulletin*; and the article 'Instruments: medieval, renaissance, baroque' in Helmut Kallmann, Gilles Potvin and Kenneth Winter, eds., *Encyclopedia of Music in Canada* (Toronto, 1981).

Edgar Hunt surveys the post-war recorder movement around the world in *The Recorder and Its Music*, rev. ed. (London, 1977). John M. Thomson's *Recorder Profiles* (London, 1972) contains chapters on Brüggen, Clemencic, Krainis, Munrow, Scheck and other leading players. Much has been written about contemporary music for the recorder. The following can be recommended in addition to the books and articles cited under Chapter 4: Michael Vetter's *Il Flauto dolce e acerbo* (Celle, 1969) and 'New Recorder Music from Holland' in *Sonorum Speculum* 31 (1967), 19–25; Gerhard Braun's *Neue Klangwelt auf der Blockflöte* (Wilhelmshaven, 1978); and Kees Boeke's 'Recorder Now' in *Early Music* 10 (1982), 7–9. Ule Traxler and Markus Kutter, eds., *Antoinette Vischer: Dokumente zu einem Leben für das Cembalo* (Basle, 1976) documents the Swiss harpsichordist's remarkable commitment to commissioning new music.

CHAPTER 9
PLAYING BACH 'HIS WAY'

So much ink has been spilled on the subject of authenticity that a reasonably comprehensive bibliography would run to hundreds of citations. An excellent introduction is the forthcoming symposium *Authenticity and Early Music*, edited by Nicholas Kenyon. It contains important essays by Richard Taruskin, Howard Mayer Brown, Robert P. Morgan and Philip Brett. Brown's cogent survey of the historical performance movement is especially pertinent in the context of the present study.

Joseph Kerman devotes a perceptive and stimulating chapter of his book *Contemplating Music: Challenges to Musicology* (Cambridge, Mass., 1985) – published in England under the title *Musicology* – to the historical performance movement. Nikolaus Harnoncourt discusses the phenomenon from a performer's vantage point in *Musik als Klangrede* (Salzburg and Vienna, 1982), an anthology of miscellaneous essays written at various times in his career. Two influential articles by performing musicologists provide further food for thought: Taruskin's 'On Letting the Music Speak for Itself' in the *Journal of Musicology* 1 (1982), 338–49, and Laurence Dreyfus's 'Early Music Defended Against Its Devotees' in the *Musical Quarterly* 69 (1983), 297–322.

Much discussion of the authenticity issue reposes in conference reports and journalistic symposia. 'The Limits of Authenticity: A Discussion' in *Early Music* 12 (1984), 3–25, contains valuable articles by Taruskin, Daniel Leech-Wilkinson, Nicholas Temperley and Robert Winter. The ripostes by Barbara Thornton and Nigel Rogers in the same volume, 523–25, should not be overlooked. The relationship between musicology and performance is explored in 'The Spheres of Music: Harmony and Discord', a symposium edited by Léonie Rosenstiel in *Current Musicology* 14 (1972), 81–172. A similar approach, focusing on Bach's music, is taken in Reinhold Brinkmann, ed., *Bachforschung und Bachinterpretation heute: Wissenschaftler und Praktiker im Dialog* (Kassel, 1981); see especially pp. 185–206. Several performers and musicologists contributed to another symposium on historical performance in the *Neue Zeitschrift für Musik* 140/2 (1979), 113–49. For a somewhat different perspective, see the *Atti del terzo congresso internazionale di musica* (Florence, 1940), which was devoted to a discussion of 'modern taste and the music of the past'.

Frederick Dorian's *The History of Music in Performance* (New York, 1942), though dated in its scholarship, provides a useful historical context. The many books on performance practice by Dolmetsch, Dart, Donington and others yield invaluable insights into changing concepts of authenticity; helpful bibliographies are given in Howard Mayer Brown's article 'Performing practice' in *The New Grove*; in the corresponding entry in Don Michael Randel, ed., *The New Harvard Dictionary of Music* (Cambridge, Mass., and London, 1986); and in Mary Vinquist and Neal Zaslaw, eds., *Performance Practice: A Bibliography* (New York, 1971).

CHAPTER 10
BEETHOVEN, BRAHMS AND BEYOND?

The incursion of the historical performance movement into the late-eighteenth- and nine-teenth-century repertoires has added appreciably to the already considerable body of literature dealing with vocal and instrumental performance practice in the Classical era. The journal *19th Century Music*, founded in 1977 by Robert Winter and Joseph Kerman, among others, consistently devotes space to topics of interest to performers. Like *Early Music*, it bridges the worlds of musicology and performance, making it a reliable source of up-to-date information in this rapidly growing field.

Neal Zaslaw set the ball rolling with his paper 'Toward the Revival of the Classical Orchestra' in *Proceedings of the Royal Musical Association* 103 (1976–77), 158–87. Christopher Hogwood puts the case for performing the Beethoven symphonies on original instruments in 'Hogwood's Beethoven', *Gramophone* 63 (1985–86), 1136. Standley Howell passes well-considered scholarly judgment on the performances of Hogwood and other conductors in '"Authentic" Beethoven Symphonies on Record', *The Journal of Musicological Research* 7/1 (1986), 98 123. For a contrasting view, see Richard Taruskin, 'Beethoven Symphonies: The New Antiquity', *Opus* 3/6 (1987), 31ff. Ann P. Basart's *The Sound of the Fortepiano: A Discography of Recordings of Early Pianos* (Berkeley, Cal., 1985) lists nearly a thousand recordings released from the 1930s to 1984.

Further manifestations of the growing scholarly interest in nineteenth-century performance problems include A. Peter Brown's *Performing Haydn's 'The Creation': Reconstructing the Earliest Renditions* (Bloomington, Ind., 1986), part of the series 'Music: Scholarship and Performance' under the general editorship of the early music specialist Thomas Binkley; Daniel J. Koury's *Orchestral Performance Practices in the Nineteenth Century* (Ann Arbor, Mich., 1986); Rollin Smith's *Toward an Authentic Interpretation of the Organ Works of César Franck* (New York, 1983); Jon W. Finson's 'Performing Practice in the Late Nineteenth Century, with Special Reference to the Music of Brahms' in *Musical Quarterly* 70 (1984), 457–75; Will Crutchfield's 'Brahms, by Those Who Knew Him', *Opus* 2/5 (1986), 12ff.; Robert Philip's 'The Recordings of Edward Elgar (1857–1934): Authenticity and Performing Practice' in *Early Music* 12 (1984), 481–89; and Manuel Gervink's 'Das typisch "Russische": Sergej Rachmaninow als Klavierkomponist' in *Concerto* 3 (July 1986), 29–34.

INDEX

Principal references are shown in **bold** type and references to illustrations in *italics*.

INDEX

INDEX

INDEX

A CATALOG OF SELECTED
DOVER BOOKS
IN ALL FIELDS OF INTEREST

A CATALOG OF SELECTED DOVER
BOOKS IN ALL FIELDS OF INTEREST

CONCERNING THE SPIRITUAL IN ART, Wassily Kandinsky. Pioneering work by father of abstract art. Thoughts on color theory, nature of art. Analysis of earlier masters. 12 illustrations. 80pp. of text. 5⅜ × 8½.　　　23411-8 Pa. $3.95

ANIMALS: 1,419 Copyright-Free Illustrations of Mammals, Birds, Fish, Insects, etc., Jim Harter (ed.). Clear wood engravings present, in extremely lifelike poses, over 1,000 species of animals. One of the most extensive pictorial sourcebooks of its kind. Captions. Index. 284pp. 9 × 12.　　　23766-4 Pa. $12.95

CELTIC ART: The Methods of Construction, George Bain. Simple geometric techniques for making Celtic interlacements, spirals, Kells-type initials, animals, humans, etc. Over 500 illustrations. 160pp. 9 × 12. (USO)　　　22923-8 Pa. $9.95

AN ATLAS OF ANATOMY FOR ARTISTS, Fritz Schider. Most thorough reference work on art anatomy in the world. Hundreds of illustrations, including selections from works by Vesalius, Leonardo, Goya, Ingres, Michelangelo, others. 593 illustrations. 192pp. 7⅛ × 10¼.　　　20241-0 Pa. $9.95

CELTIC HAND STROKE-BY-STROKE (Irish Half-Uncial from "The Book of Kells"): An Arthur Baker Calligraphy Manual, Arthur Baker. Complete guide to creating each letter of the alphabet in distinctive Celtic manner. Covers hand position, strokes, pens, inks, paper, more. Illustrated. 48pp. 8¼ × 11.
24336-2 Pa. $3.95

EASY ORIGAMI, John Montroll. Charming collection of 32 projects (hat, cup, pelican, piano, swan, many more) specially designed for the novice origami hobbyist. Clearly illustrated easy-to-follow instructions insure that even beginning papercrafters will achieve successful results. 48pp. 8¼ × 11.　　　27298-2 Pa. $2.95

THE COMPLETE BOOK OF BIRDHOUSE CONSTRUCTION FOR WOOD-WORKERS, Scott D. Campbell. Detailed instructions, illustrations, tables. Also data on bird habitat and instinct patterns. Bibliography. 3 tables. 63 illustrations in 15 figures. 48pp. 5¼ × 8½.　　　24407-5 Pa. $1.95

BLOOMINGDALE'S ILLUSTRATED 1886 CATALOG: Fashions, Dry Goods and Housewares, Bloomingdale Brothers. Famed merchants' extremely rare catalog depicting about 1,700 products: clothing, housewares, firearms, dry goods, jewelry, more. Invaluable for dating, identifying vintage items. Also, copyright-free graphics for artists, designers. Co-published with Henry Ford Museum & Green-field Village. 160pp. 8¼ × 11.　　　25780-0 Pa. $9.95

HISTORIC COSTUME IN PICTURES, Braun & Schneider. Over 1,450 costumed figures in clearly detailed engravings—from dawn of civilization to end of 19th century. Captions. Many folk costumes. 256pp. 8⅜ × 11¾.　　　23150-X Pa. $11.95

MY BONDAGE AND MY FREEDOM, Frederick Douglass. Born a slave, Douglass became outspoken force in antislavery movement. The best of Douglass' autobiographies. Graphic description of slave life. 464pp. 5⅜ × 8½. 22457-0 Pa. $8.95

FOLLOWING THE EQUATOR: A Journey Around the World, Mark Twain. Fascinating humorous account of 1897 voyage to Hawaii, Australia, India, New Zealand, etc. Ironic, bemused reports on peoples, customs, climate, flora and fauna, politics, much more. 197 illustrations. 720pp. 5⅜ × 8½. 26113-1 Pa. $15.95

THE PEOPLE CALLED SHAKERS, Edward D. Andrews. Definitive study of Shakers: origins, beliefs, practices, dances, social organization, furniture and crafts, etc. 33 illustrations. 351pp. 5⅜ × 8½. 21081-2 Pa. $8.95

THE MYTHS OF GREECE AND ROME, H. A. Guerber. A classic of mythology, generously illustrated, long prized for its simple, graphic, accurate retelling of the principal myths of Greece and Rome, and for its commentary on their origins and significance. With 64 illustrations by Michelangelo, Raphael, Titian, Rubens, Canova, Bernini and others. 480pp. 5⅜ × 8½. 27584-1 Pa. $9.95

PSYCHOLOGY OF MUSIC, Carl E. Seashore. Classic work discusses music as a medium from psychological viewpoint. Clear treatment of physical acoustics, auditory apparatus, sound perception, development of musical skills, nature of musical feeling, host of other topics. 88 figures. 408pp. 5⅜ × 8½. 21851-1 Pa. $9.95

THE PHILOSOPHY OF HISTORY, Georg W. Hegel. Great classic of Western thought develops concept that history is not chance but rational process, the evolution of freedom. 457pp. 5⅜ × 8½. 20112-0 Pa. $9.95

THE BOOK OF TEA, Kakuzo Okakura. Minor classic of the Orient: entertaining, charming explanation, interpretation of traditional Japanese culture in terms of tea ceremony. 94pp. 5⅜ × 8½. 20070-1 Pa. $3.95

LIFE IN ANCIENT EGYPT, Adolf Erman. Fullest, most thorough, detailed older account with much not in more recent books, domestic life, religion, magic, medicine, commerce, much more. Many illustrations reproduce tomb paintings, carvings, hieroglyphs, etc. 597pp. 5⅜ × 8½. 22632-8 Pa. $10.95

SUNDIALS, Their Theory and Construction, Albert Waugh. Far and away the best, most thorough coverage of ideas, mathematics concerned, types, construction, adjusting anywhere. Simple, nontechnical treatment allows even children to build several of these dials. Over 100 illustrations. 230pp. 5⅜ × 8½. 22947-5 Pa. $7.95

DYNAMICS OF FLUIDS IN POROUS MEDIA, Jacob Bear. For advanced students of ground water hydrology, soil mechanics and physics, drainage and irrigation engineering, and more. 335 illustrations. Exercises, with answers. 784pp. 6⅛ × 9¼. 65675-6 Pa. $19.95

SONGS OF EXPERIENCE: Facsimile Reproduction with 26 Plates in Full Color, William Blake. 26 full-color plates from a rare 1826 edition. Includes "The Tyger," "London," "Holy Thursday," and other poems. Printed text of poems. 48pp. 5¼ × 7. 24636-1 Pa. $4.95

OLD-TIME VIGNETTES IN FULL COLOR, Carol Belanger Grafton (ed.). Over 390 charming, often sentimental illustrations, selected from archives of Victorian graphics—pretty women posing, children playing, food, flowers, kittens and puppies, smiling cherubs, birds and butterflies, much more. All copyright-free. 48pp. 9¼ × 12¼. 27269-9 Pa. $5.95

PERSPECTIVE FOR ARTISTS, Rex Vicat Cole. Depth, perspective of sky and sea, shadows, much more, not usually covered. 391 diagrams, 81 reproductions of drawings and paintings. 279pp. 5⅜ × 8½. 22487-2 Pa. $6.95

DRAWING THE LIVING FIGURE, Joseph Sheppard. Innovative approach to artistic anatomy focuses on specifics of surface anatomy, rather than muscles and bones. Over 170 drawings of live models in front, back and side views, and in widely varying poses. Accompanying diagrams. 177 illustrations. Introduction. Index. 144pp. 8⅜ × 11¼. 26723-7 Pa. $8.95

GOTHIC AND OLD ENGLISH ALPHABETS: 100 Complete Fonts, Dan X. Solo. Add power, elegance to posters, signs, other graphics with 100 stunning copyright-free alphabets: Blackstone, Dolbey, Germania, 97 more—including many lower-case, numerals, punctuation marks. 104pp. 8⅛ × 11. 24695-7 Pa. $8.95

HOW TO DO BEADWORK, Mary White. Fundamental book on craft from simple projects to five-bead chains and woven works. 106 illustrations. 142pp. 5⅜ × 8. 20697-1 Pa. $4.95

THE BOOK OF WOOD CARVING, Charles Marshall Sayers. Finest book for beginners discusses fundamentals and offers 34 designs. "Absolutely first rate . . . well thought out and well executed."—E. J. Tangerman. 118pp. 7¾ × 10⅝. 23654-4 Pa. $5.95

ILLUSTRATED CATALOG OF CIVIL WAR MILITARY GOODS: Union Army Weapons, Insignia, Uniform Accessories, and Other Equipment, Schuyler, Hartley, and Graham. Rare, profusely illustrated 1846 catalog includes Union Army uniform and dress regulations, arms and ammunition, coats, insignia, flags, swords, rifles, etc. 226 illustrations. 160pp. 9 × 12. 24939-5 Pa. $10.95

WOMEN'S FASHIONS OF THE EARLY 1900s: An Unabridged Republication of "New York Fashions, 1909," National Cloak & Suit Co. Rare catalog of mail-order fashions documents women's and children's clothing styles shortly after the turn of the century. Captions offer full descriptions, prices. Invaluable resource for fashion, costume historians. Approximately 725 illustrations. 128pp. 8⅜ × 11¼. 27276-1 Pa. $11.95

THE 1912 AND 1915 GUSTAV STICKLEY FURNITURE CATALOGS, Gustav Stickley. With over 200 detailed illustrations and descriptions, these two catalogs are essential reading and reference materials and identification guides for Stickley furniture. Captions cite materials, dimensions and prices. 112pp. 6½ × 9¼. 26676-1 Pa. $9.95

EARLY AMERICAN LOCOMOTIVES, John H. White, Jr. Finest locomotive engravings from early 19th century: historical (1804–74), main-line (after 1870), special, foreign, etc. 147 plates. 142pp. 11⅜ × 8¼. 22772-3 Pa. $10.95

THE TALL SHIPS OF TODAY IN PHOTOGRAPHS, Frank O. Braynard. Lavishly illustrated tribute to nearly 100 majestic contemporary sailing vessels: Amerigo Vespucci, Clearwater, Constitution, Eagle, Mayflower, Sea Cloud, Victory, many more. Authoritative captions provide statistics, background on each ship. 190 black-and-white photographs and illustrations. Introduction. 128pp. 8⅞ × 11¾. 27163-3 Pa. $13.95

EARLY NINETEENTH-CENTURY CRAFTS AND TRADES, Peter Stockham (ed.). Extremely rare 1807 volume describes to youngsters the crafts and trades of the day: brickmaker, weaver, dressmaker, bookbinder, ropemaker, saddler, many more. Quaint prose, charming illustrations for each craft. 20 black-and-white line illustrations. 192pp. 4⅝ × 6. 27293-1 Pa. $4.95

VICTORIAN FASHIONS AND COSTUMES FROM HARPER'S BAZAR, 1867–1898, Stella Blum (ed.). Day costumes, evening wear, sports clothes, shoes, hats, other accessories in over 1,000 detailed engravings. 320pp. 9⅜ × 12¼. 22990-4 Pa. $13.95

GUSTAV STICKLEY, THE CRAFTSMAN, Mary Ann Smith. Superb study surveys broad scope of Stickley's achievement, especially in architecture. Design philosophy, rise and fall of the Craftsman empire, descriptions and floor plans for many Craftsman houses, more. 86 black-and-white halftones. 31 line illustrations. Introduction. 208pp. 6½ × 9¼. 27210-9 Pa. $9.95

THE LONG ISLAND RAIL ROAD IN EARLY PHOTOGRAPHS, Ron Ziel. Over 220 rare photos, informative text document origin (1844) and development of rail service on Long Island. Vintage views of early trains, locomotives, stations, passengers, crews, much more. Captions. 8⅞ × 11¾. 26301-0 Pa. $13.95

THE BOOK OF OLD SHIPS: From Egyptian Galleys to Clipper Ships, Henry B. Culver. Superb, authoritative history of sailing vessels, with 80 magnificent line illustrations. Galley, bark, caravel, longship, whaler, many more. Detailed, informative text on each vessel by noted naval historian. Introduction. 256pp. 5⅜ × 8½. 27332-6 Pa. $6.95

TEN BOOKS ON ARCHITECTURE, Vitruvius. The most important book ever written on architecture. Early Roman aesthetics, technology, classical orders, site selection, all other aspects. Morgan translation. 331pp. 5⅜ × 8½. 20645-9 Pa. $8.95

THE HUMAN FIGURE IN MOTION, Eadweard Muybridge. More than 4,500 stopped-action photos, in action series, showing undraped men, women, children jumping, lying down, throwing, sitting, wrestling, carrying, etc. 390pp. 7⅞ × 10⅝. 20204-6 Clothbd. $24.95

TREES OF THE EASTERN AND CENTRAL UNITED STATES AND CANADA, William M. Harlow. Best one-volume guide to 140 trees. Full descriptions, woodlore, range, etc. Over 600 illustrations. Handy size. 288pp. 4½ × 6⅜. 20395-6 Pa. $5.95

SONGS OF WESTERN BIRDS, Dr. Donald J. Borror. Complete song and call repertoire of 60 western species, including flycatchers, juncoes, cactus wrens, many more—includes fully illustrated booklet. Cassette and manual 99913-0 $8.95

GROWING AND USING HERBS AND SPICES, Milo Miloradovich. Versatile handbook provides all the information needed for cultivation and use of all the herbs and spices available in North America. 4 illustrations. Index. Glossary. 236pp. 5⅜ × 8½. 25058-X Pa. $6.95

BIG BOOK OF MAZES AND LABYRINTHS, Walter Shepherd. 50 mazes and labyrinths in all—classical, solid, ripple, and more—in one great volume. Perfect inexpensive puzzler for clever youngsters. Full solutions. 112pp. 8⅛ × 11. 22951-3 Pa. $4.95

AUTOBIOGRAPHY: The Story of My Experiments with Truth, Mohandas K. Gandhi. Boyhood, legal studies, purification, the growth of the Satyagraha (nonviolent protest) movement. Critical, inspiring work of the man responsible for the freedom of India. 480pp. 5⅜ × 8½. (USO) 24593-4 Pa. $8.95

CELTIC MYTHS AND LEGENDS, T. W. Rolleston. Masterful retelling of Irish and Welsh stories and tales. Cuchulain, King Arthur, Deirdre, the Grail, many more. First paperback edition. 58 full-page illustrations. 512pp. 5⅜ × 8½. 26507-2 Pa. $9.95

THE PRINCIPLES OF PSYCHOLOGY, William James. Famous long course complete, unabridged. Stream of thought, time perception, memory, experimental methods; great work decades ahead of its time. 94 figures. 1,391pp. 5⅜ × 8½. 2-vol. set.
Vol. I: 20381-6 Pa. $12.95
Vol. II: 20382-4 Pa. $12.95

THE WORLD AS WILL AND REPRESENTATION, Arthur Schopenhauer. Definitive English translation of Schopenhauer's life work, correcting more than 1,000 errors, omissions in earlier translations. Translated by E. F. J. Payne. Total of 1,269pp. 5⅜ × 8½. 2-vol. set.
Vol. 1: 21761-2 Pa. $11.95
Vol. 2: 21762-0 Pa. $11.95

MAGIC AND MYSTERY IN TIBET, Madame Alexandra David-Neel. Experiences among lamas, magicians, sages, sorcerers, Bonpa wizards. A true psychic discovery. 32 illustrations. 321pp. 5⅜ × 8½. (USO) 22682-4 Pa. $8.95

THE EGYPTIAN BOOK OF THE DEAD, E. A. Wallis Budge. Complete reproduction of Ani's papyrus, finest ever found. Full hieroglyphic text, interlinear transliteration, word-for-word translation, smooth translation. 533pp. 6½ × 9¼. 21866-X Pa. $9.95

MATHEMATICS FOR THE NONMATHEMATICIAN, Morris Kline. Detailed, college-level treatment of mathematics in cultural and historical context, with numerous exercises. Recommended Reading Lists. Tables. Numerous figures. 641pp. 5⅜ × 8½. 24823-2 Pa. $11.95

THEORY OF WING SECTIONS: Including a Summary of Airfoil Data, Ira H. Abbott and A. E. von Doenhoff. Concise compilation of subsonic aerodynamic characteristics of NACA wing sections, plus description of theory. 350pp. of tables. 693pp. 5⅜ × 8½. 60586-8 Pa. $14.95

THE RIME OF THE ANCIENT MARINER, Gustave Doré, S. T. Coleridge. Doré's finest work; 34 plates capture moods, subtleties of poem. Flawless full-size reproductions printed on facing pages with authoritative text of poem. "Beautiful. Simply beautiful."—*Publisher's Weekly*. 77pp. 9¼ × 12. 22305-1 Pa. $6.95

NORTH AMERICAN INDIAN DESIGNS FOR ARTISTS AND CRAFTSPEOPLE, Eva Wilson. Over 360 authentic copyright-free designs adapted from Navajo blankets, Hopi pottery, Sioux buffalo hides, more. Geometrics, symbolic figures, plant and animal motifs, etc. 128pp. 8⅜ × 11. (EUK) 25341-4 Pa. $7.95

SCULPTURE: Principles and Practice, Louis Slobodkin. Step-by-step approach to clay, plaster, metals, stone; classical and modern. 253 drawings, photos. 255pp. 8⅛ × 11. 22960-2 Pa. $10.95

CATALOG OF DOVER BOOKS

THE INFLUENCE OF SEA POWER UPON HISTORY, 1660–1783, A. T. Mahan. Influential classic of naval history and tactics still used as text in war colleges. First paperback edition. 4 maps. 24 battle plans. 640pp. 5⅜ × 8½.
25509-3 Pa. $12.95

THE STORY OF THE TITANIC AS TOLD BY ITS SURVIVORS, Jack Winocour (ed.). What it was really like. Panic, despair, shocking inefficiency, and a little heroism. More thrilling than any fictional account. 26 illustrations. 320pp. 5⅜ × 8½. 20610-6 Pa. $8.95

FAIRY AND FOLK TALES OF THE IRISH PEASANTRY, William Butler Yeats (ed.). Treasury of 64 tales from the twilight world of Celtic myth and legend: "The Soul Cages," "The Kildare Pooka," "King O'Toole and his Goose," many more. Introduction and Notes by W. B. Yeats. 352pp. 5⅜ × 8½. 26941-8 Pa. $8.95

BUDDHIST MAHAYANA TEXTS, E. B. Cowell and Others (eds.). Superb, accurate translations of basic documents in Mahayana Buddhism, highly important in history of religions. The Buddha-karita of Asvaghosha, Larger Sukhavativyuha, more. 448pp. 5⅜ × 8½. 25552-2 Pa. $9.95

ONE TWO THREE . . . INFINITY: Facts and Speculations of Science, George Gamow. Great physicist's fascinating, readable overview of contemporary science: number theory, relativity, fourth dimension, entropy, genes, atomic structure, much more. 128 illustrations. Index. 352pp. 5⅜ × 8½. 25664-2 Pa. $8.95

ENGINEERING IN HISTORY, Richard Shelton Kirby, et al. Broad, nontechnical survey of history's major technological advances: birth of Greek science, industrial revolution, electricity and applied science, 20th-century automation, much more. 181 illustrations. ". . . excellent . . ."—Isis. Bibliography. vii + 530pp. 5⅜ × 8¼.
26412-2 Pa. $14.95

Prices subject to change without notice.

Available at your book dealer or write for free catalog to Dept. GI, Dover Publications, Inc., 31 East 2nd St., Mineola, N.Y. 11501. Dover publishes more than 500 books each year on science, elementary and advanced mathematics, biology, music, art, literary history, social sciences and other areas.